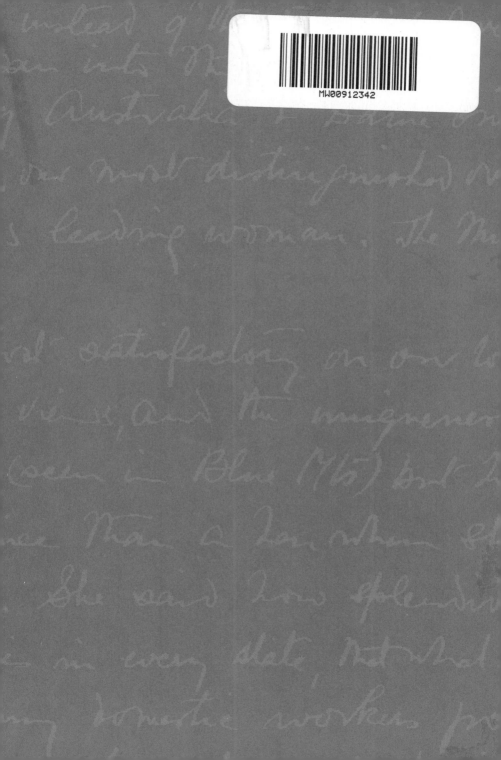

The Diaries of
MILES FRANKLIN

The Diaries of
MILES FRANKLIN

Edited by Paul Brunton

ALLEN&UNWIN

in association with

State Library of
New South Wales

Allen & Unwin
83 Alexander Street
Crows Nest NSW 2065
Australia
Phone: (61 2) 8425 0100
Fax: (61 2) 9906 2218
Email: info@allenandunwin.com
Web: www.allenandunwin.com

National Library of Australia
Cataloguing-in-Publication entry:

The diaries of Miles Franklin.

Includes index.
ISBN 1 74114 296 2.

1. Franklin, Miles, 1879-1954 - Diaries. 2. Authors,
Australian - Diaries. I. Brunton, Paul, 1950- .

A823.2

Set in 12.5/15 pt Spectrum MT by Bookhouse, Sydney
Printed by Ligare Pty Ltd, Sydney

10 9 8 7 6 5 4 3 2 1

CONTENTS

ACKNOWLEDGEMENTS

My first acknowledgement is to Miles Franklin. No one who has had the privilege of working among the literary papers of this indomitable and brave Australian writer could fail to love and admire her. To publish her diaries is an honour and I only hope I have done them and her justice. She will undoubtedly let me know if I have not.

I am grateful to Dagmar Schmidmaier, State Librarian and Chief Executive of the State Library of New South Wales, for her support and encouragement; to Elizabeth Ellis, Mitchell Librarian, for her invaluable advice and counsel and unflagging interest in the midst of many other pressing duties; to Hilary McPhee for her expertise and enthusiasm; and to those at Allen & Unwin who edited this book with such professionalism: Annette Barlow, Colette Vella and Jo Jarrah. Photographers Scott Wajon and Kate Pollard from the State Library prepared the illustrations to their usual high standards. All those who venture into Franklin studies are in the debt of Dr Jill Roe for her scholarship over the last two decades.

Paul Brunton
December 2003

INTRODUCTION

Miles Franklin never spoke of her private life. 'I won't tell you now. You'll find it all later in my diaries.'[1] These diaries she bequeathed to the Mitchell Library on her death in 1954, deliberately ensuring their preservation and making it likely that one day they would be published.

Success had come early to Franklin. At the age of 21 she published *My Brilliant Career* (1901) which would imprint her name firmly in the annals of Australian literature and make her famous for a time. But it did not ease the way to the publication of further works. That would be the problem which would bedevil her her whole life, for she wanted passionately to be a writer and she wanted the success and recognition which would come from this.

Stella Maria Sarah Miles Franklin was born on 14 October 1879, the eldest of seven, at Talbingo, near Tumut, New South Wales, at the home of her grandmother, Sarah Lampe. 'Miles' was in deference to Edward Miles, an illiterate maternal ancestor who had arrived on the First Fleet in 1788 as a convict.

Her mother, Susannah Franklin, aged 28, had ridden side-saddle for 110 kilometres along treacherous mountain tracks from her home at Brindabella station, in a beautiful valley on the western

---

1 Quoted in Beatrice Davis 'An enigmatic woman', *Overland* 91, 1983.

edge of present-day Canberra, in order to have the support and assistance of her own mother at the birth of her first child.

Her father, John Franklin, nearly three years older than his wife, had a poetic temperament whereas Susannah was 'sane and practical, without eccentricity'.[2] Both parents were readers and Susannah painted and had a great love of music which was inherited by Miles. Susannah had managed to transport a piano into Brindabella valley on her marriage in November 1878. Miles was always conscious of how her mother's abilities had been wasted as a bush wife and mother with the unremitting hard physical work and lack of outlets for intellectual pursuits. A woman's life was circumscribed by domesticity and Miles pulled against this fate.

For Miles Franklin the years spent at Talbingo and Brindabella would always be the golden years. Nothing ever surpassed them in her view and she never really came to terms with the world outside these two beautiful, isolated and enchanted places. It was an exceedingly happy childhood among a large extended family where the expression of individual opinion, even from a child, was encouraged. She was taught, along with other family members, by a private tutor, Charles Blyth, one of those well-bred and erudite but perhaps damaged individuals who ended up in the isolated regions of the colonies for reasons unexplained. Blyth thought highly of Miles' intellectual abilities and wrote: 'You had not only the ability to succeed but the desire to do so and the energy to persevere'.[3]

In 1889 the family moved from Brindabella to a property near Thornford, 20 kilometres south-west of Goulburn. The first sight of it filled Miles with desolation:

---

2   Miles Franklin *Childhood at Brindabella*, Sydney, Angus & Robertson, 1974 (first published 1963), p58.
3   Miles Franklin papers, Mitchell Library, ML MSS 364/6, p70.

The trees were not so majestic. The ranges were low and ragged without gorges and mighty rocks like castles and cascading streams draped with tree-ferns and maidenhair and flowering shrubberies along their banks. No lyrebirds gambolled across the track to flute in eucalyptus aisles across a big singing creek. Oh, Ajinby [Miles' fictional name for Talbingo station], with its river, its creeks, large and small, full of fish, its wealth of orchards and ornamental trees, its flower gardens with pomegranates and magnolias! Here there were no rocks or ferns at all. There were no permanently running creeks, only weedy waterholes. Mother named the place Stillwater.[4]

Here at Thornford Public School, which had only just been established, Miles was educated to intermediate level. She had been 'afflicted with scribbling at 13' and her first published writing was a report on her school picnic which appeared in the *Goulburn Evening Penny Post* when she was sixteen. Miles stood out as a child and adolescent:

I had a reputation as an amusing chatterbox, and I would set off with anyone I liked anywhere, agog for travel. At night I did not collapse into sobs and fret for my mother. To undress and go to bed with a new set of elders with a slightly different routine was adventure. I had no fear of elders, no matter how fierce their beards or loud their voices, so long as people did not wake in me swift instinctive dislike. This could be embarrassing with a child so plaguily articulate. An old sea captain once asked me for a kiss. I refused.[5]

---

4   Miles Franklin *Childhood at Brindabella*, op. cit., pp95–6.
5   ibid., p33.

She loved the company of adults and often felt like an exile among children of her own age.

In 1897, Miles started her working life as a tutor, instructing her cousins, the children of George and Margaret Franklin, at Oakvale, near Yass. She began *My Brilliant Career* on 20 September 1898, just a few weeks short of her nineteenth birthday. The novel purports to be the autobiography of Sybylla Melvyn, aged 16, daughter of poor dairy farmers at Possum Gully. Sybylla escapes briefly into the more cultured world of her grandmother at Caddagat Station and there meets wealthy Harold Beecham, whose proposal of marriage she rejects though she is clearly attracted to him. 'He offered me everything—but control.' For a time, she is sent by her mother to work as a tutor in the home of the feral McSwats, a further descent into insensitivity and vulgarity from Possum Gully. Sybylla's story is a sensitive, intelligent bush girl's cri de coeur against the fate of becoming a dependent wife.

When submitting the manuscript to the publishers, Angus & Robertson, on 30 March 1899, she signed her accompanying letter 'S.M.S. Miles Franklin' to obscure her sex in the hope of increasing the chances of publication. 'Nothing great has been attempted', she wrote, 'merely a few pictures of Australian life with a little of that mythical commodity love, thrown in for the benefit of young readers (always keeping in mind should there be readers of any age). There will be no mistakes in geography, scenery or climate as I write from fact not fancy. The heroine, who tells the story, is a study from life and illustrates the misery of being born out of one's sphere.'[6] She titled the book 'My Brilliant (?) Career'.

---

6 Jill Roe (ed) *My Congenials: Miles Franklin and Friends in Letters*, volume 1, Sydney, State Library of New South Wales in association with Angus & Robertson, 1993, p8.

Angus & Robertson rejected the novel and in November—
following another unsuccessful approach, this time to J.F. Archibald,
editor of the *Bulletin*—Miles approached Henry Lawson, whom she
only knew from his poetry, asking whether he would give an opinion
on the manuscript. Lawson agreed and replied enthusiastically the
same day he received it, in January 1900, asking whether he could
keep it to show to his publisher. 'I believe that you have done a big
thing. I've been through the life you write of.'[7]

In January 1900 Miles started nursing at Sydney Hospital. This only
lasted three weeks, Miles returning home in February following the
death from typhoid of her brother, Mervyn, who was 16 years old.

In April 1900 Lawson sent the manuscript to George Robertson,
who had just returned from overseas and had therefore not been
involved when his firm rejected it the previous year. Lawson
wrote:

> The truth and vividness of the work was startling even to me . . .
> In my opinion it is the Australian *African Farm* and immeasurably
> ahead of *Jane Eyre* . . . Altogether—with the exception, perhaps,
> of some too emotional passages in middle of novel—and as a
> vivid yet humorous description of selection and farming life in
> Australia, I think the work goes deeper, is more vividly realistic
> and more perfect than my own.[8]

The comparison with Olive Schreiner's *The Story of an African Farm*,
first published in 1883, would be made by others. It was in fact one
of Miles' favourite books.

---

7   ibid., p10.
8   Colin Roderick (ed) *Henry Lawson: Letters, 1890–1922*, Sydney, Angus & Robertson,
    1970, p122.

The manuscript was not taken up by Angus & Robertson. Robertson seems to have been too busy to read it himself, and it was forwarded in May 1900 to Henry Lawson, who had left for Britain and had been given permission by Franklin to place the book with a British publisher. It was accepted by the Scottish firm William Blackwood and Sons in January 1901, and was printed by April, the author receiving her copies at Stillwater in September. The book had a preface by Lawson in which he blew her cover of a male identity.

It was extensively reviewed in both Britain and Australia. The reviews were positive though Havelock Ellis' 1903 review dismissing the literary qualities of the book apparently hurt Miles deeply. He wrote:

> It is a vivid and sincere book, certainly the true reflection of a passionate young nature, impatient of the inevitable limitations of the life around her . . . but something more than emotion is needed to make fine literature; and here we miss any genuine instinct of art or any mature power of thought, and are left at the end only with a painful sense of crudity. Miles Franklin is ardently devoted to Australia, but to a remote ideal Australia, and in the eagerness of her own embittered and egoistic mood she tramples under foot the things that really make Australia.[9]

The story has arisen that so many people were offended by perceived portraits in the book that Miles was forced in the end to leave the country and suppress the book. It does not appear that Miles' immediate family was upset. Her father, who was certainly

---

9 Havelock Ellis 'Fiction in the Australian Bush', *Weekly Critical Review*, Paris, 17 September 1903. Reproduced in Geoffrey Dutton (ed) *Kanga Creek: Havelock Ellis in Australia*, Sydney, Picador, 1989, pp231–5.

not the pathetic drunk that Sybylla Melvyn's father was, seemed untroubled, in fact was rather proud of his daughter. Miles' sister Linda wrote to say that their grandmother 'nearly killed herself laughing at parts of it, I can't get her nose out of it'[10] and reported that old Sarah Lampe would not give too much of the story away because this might diminish sales. Linda herself was looking forward to the next novel. Even George Franklin at Oakvale, whose children Miles had tutored and who might have been offended by the portrait of the McSwats, was not, though his wife, Margaret, was.

The book was not withdrawn by Miles, at least not immediately. It was in fact reprinted five times with the sixth impression appearing in 1904. And Miles complained in 1902 to Blackwood that not enough copies had been sent out to Australia. It appears that it was not until 1910 that Miles asked that no further copies be printed, for reasons which are not clear, and even then she was quite happy for remaining copies to be distributed in Australia. It would appear that the reception of the book had no bearing on her leaving Australia in 1906.

Her publishing success in fact opened doors. A.B. ('Banjo') Paterson, himself made famous by *The Man from Snowy River* a few years earlier, offered her a literary collaboration and there are suggestions of a romance, perhaps even an offer of marriage. In Sydney, Rose Scott, rich and prominent in social reform, took her under her wing. Vida Goldstein, feminist activist in Melbourne, provided introductions. The Governor-General, Lord Tennyson, son of the poet, wrote in his own hand saying that he had read the book 'with much pleasure'.

In search of further literary material, Miles worked in domestic service in Sydney and Melbourne in 1903–4. While in Melbourne she met Joseph Furphy, whose classic book, *Such Is Life*, had just been

---

10   Jill Roe, op. cit., p14.

published. Furphy and his book would be an inspiration to Miles all her life.

Although *My Brilliant Career* had brought her fame and an entree into sections of society, it had brought little money. Her first royalty cheque was received in July 1902 and was only £16/5/6. Copies sold in Australia were the 'colonial edition' and attracted a much reduced royalty. Nor did it lead to the publication of further books. She attempted without success to enter journalism.

As many writers before and since have done, she decided to leave the country. Under the influence of Vida Goldstein she opted for America, where Goldstein had been for a time. It seemed the land of hope, and perhaps also of some literary glory. With introductions to a number of feminists, provided by Goldstein, and also a number of completed, and rejected, manuscripts, she sailed on SS *Ventura* on 7 April 1906, crossing the Pacific to another country and another culture. Lovelorn Edwin Bridle, her cousin who had proposed marriage in 1905, followed, if only by letters, and insistent letters, but to no avail, and he quickly married another, as often happens in such cases. Her younger sister Linda, 24, wrote lamenting for the suitors Miles had left behind. 'You bad girl to leave such a lot of broken hearts behind. To be hoped you won't break so many in America, if so stay with *one* of them & console the poor thing.'[11]

Miles arrived in San Francisco a few days after the famous earthquake had devastated that city on 18 April and wrote a graphic account of the situation which appeared in the *Sydney Morning Herald* on 23 June:

It is impossible to overdraw the razing of the city. Viewed closely, it not only resembled a vast rubbish tip, but a burned rubbish

---

11 ibid., p47, undated letter of about mid 1906.

tip, with nothing left that fire could consume . . . Tram lines were twisted and disrupted, smooth pavements cracked and broken, and large hollows to be found where once had been level spaces . . . At every turn horrible odours meet the nostrils from great cracks in the earth, and through the bursting and mingling of the sewerage and water mains an epidemic of typhoid is feared . . . Over all there is a comparative stillness. One misses the buzz of machinery and the hum and rattle of street cars, and the patter arising from foot and wheel traffic . . . Of course the caterer for the picture post card fashion is 'right there', he would be at a funeral or amputation in these times, and droves of him are along the streetways offering photographed represent-ations of every conceivable turn of the wreck.[12]

By late 1906 she had arrived in Chicago. Chicago was second only to New York in population and wealth. It was the city in which and for which the phrase 'conspicuous consumption' had been invented. It was a magnet for immigrants from around the world, who were often exploited, and it teemed with life and social problems. It was the raw face of American capitalism which a number of organisations were attempting to tame. One of these was Hull House, presided over by Jane Addams, who had pioneered social work in the United States. Miles had a letter of introduction to Addams and at Hull House met a fellow Australian, Alice Henry. Here she also met a circle of talented women engaged in social reform, especially the wealthy Margaret Dreier Robins, president of the nascent National Women's Trade Union League, which met at Hull House. Robins offered her a part-time position as personal secretary, paid for from

---

12   *Sydney Morning Herald*, 23 June 1906, p11. Reproduced in Jill Roe & Margaret Bettison (eds) *A Gregarious Culture: Topical Writings of Miles Franklin*, St Lucia, University of Queensland Press, 2001, pp25–30.

Robins' own income, which she began in January 1908. This was the first of a number of positions which Miles would hold with the League over the next eight years.

The month in which this position was offered, October 1907, was the month that Miles received news of the death from pneumonia on 24 August of her sister Linda, aged 25. It precipitated a nervous collapse which she survived with the help of her Hull House friends.

Work with the League was pioneering, exciting and exhausting. 'I love my work very much as it brings me in to close friendship with everyone in the world who is making thought and history',[13] she wrote to Annie Franklin at Brindabella in 1913. She was the League's press officer for the legendary 22-week Garment Workers' strike in 1910–11 which resulted in the loss of millions of dollars by both sides and the death of five people. Her publicity skills achieved favourable press coverage for the workers. Simultaneously, she became assistant editor (with Alice Henry, editor) of the League's journal, *Life and Labor*, the first issue of which appeared in January 1911. At this time she was also involved with the organisational work for the League's third biennial convention which took place in Boston in July 1911 and at which she was elected national secretary.

She was, in the midst of all this activity, still writing, though in secret. None of her colleagues knew of her other life as an author. Short stories, plays and novels were offered to publishers who either promptly or tardily rejected them. She could publish nothing in America, though in 1909 Blackwood in Edinburgh, who had published *My Brilliant Career*, published *Some Everyday Folk and Dawn*. This, however, had been written before she left Australia.

The novel is based in Penrith, New South Wales, to where her family had moved in 1903, a further descent in worldly terms

---

13   ibid., p83.

from Stillwater, which was itself a descent from the beloved Brindabella. The novel is a romance and centres around the first election in New South Wales at which women could vote, that of August 1904. By the time the book was published, female suffrage was an area in which the bush girl from Australia could hold her head high, for while Australian women had the vote federally and in all states their American sisters were still fighting for it. The book did not sell well and it would be the last under her own name until 1931.

In November 1911, Blackwood rejected *The End of My Career*, the sequel to *My Brilliant Career*. It had now been rejected in Australia, in Britain and probably in America. But Miles would never give up; she had caught the scribbling disease early and, as she would write in one of her last letters, it is 'worse than TB for TB can be cured'.[14]

In addition, the Chicago years were years of frantic social activity. Singing lessons, piano lessons, French lessons, lunches, dinners, dancing, the theatre, concerts, learning to drive, the opera. There were summer camps and summer schools. She was sought after as a companion, as she would be all her life, for her vibrant personality, her wit, charm and keen intellect. There were a number of eligible and ineligible young men. There was Guido Mariotti, there was Fred Pischel, there was William Bross Lloyd, who was married but who squired Miles around town with the full knowledge and approval of his wife. There was his brother, Demarest Lloyd, Harvard educated, pillar of the establishment, handsome, wealthy, sophisticated, very keen on Miles, and available. She was flirtatious by nature and would always be, even in old age. 'Why do you encourage them

---

14   Jill Roe (ed) *My Congenials: Miles Franklin and Friends in Letters*, volume 2, State Library of New South Wales in association with Angus & Robertson, 1993, p352. Letter to Pixie O'Harris, 3 September 1954.

if you do not intend to continue?' Grandmother Lampe had reproved her, many years previously.

Beneath the surface, though, it was a different story. On the last day of 1909, Miles wrote in her diary 'hoping the coming one [year] will be more eventful, less futile and very lucrative'; on 22 November 1911 she 'went to bed feeling as if Life had become a deadly cul-de-sac and I wished it was all over'; summing up 1913 she lamented that 'the futility of my existence, my weakness in effort, my failure in accomplishment fill me with a creeping melancholy that grows more impenetrable. I will fight against it, once more by hard work, and if in two years the results are no better than in the past I shall die of my own volition'. She was still writing of her 'hitherto unsatisfactory life' a year later.[15] The companionable, intelligent, witty person whom men and women sought out was in private deeply unsettled.

Added to this mental anguish during the Chicago years are regular bouts of painful ill health. Days are spent in bed. Doctors, many doctors, are consulted. An alarming but unrevealed— unrevealed by Miles, that is—diagnosis is given. She later refers to 'the old familiar death sentence'. In 1912 her health broke down completely and she went to a sanatorium for a period. She did have a painful spinal problem but it is difficult not to draw the conclusion that at least some of this ill health was psychosomatic. Perhaps she had diagnosed herself when she wrote to Angus & Robertson in 1899 that the story of her heroine Sybylla Melvyn 'illustrates the misery of being born out of one's sphere'.

By 1915 there were financial problems at the League and personality clashes. America had not yet entered the European war and in

---

15 Miles Franklin papers, op. cit., ML MSS 364/2/1; ML MSS 364/2/31; ML MSS 364/2/6; ML MSS 364/2/7.

Chicago, particularly with its large contingent of German-Americans, sympathies were by no means with the British. Miles felt like an alien. She had visited Britain and France briefly on holiday in 1911 and when she returned wrote to Isabella Goldstein (Vida's mother) in Melbourne that 'after my sojourn in another country it [going to Britain] was absolutely like going home. I fell into everything like an old habit and it somehow must have eased up the tightness and homesickness that I have endured so long'.[16] The war settled her against the idea of motherhood—breeding future heroes for destruction—so she cut loose from the League, cut loose from America, and cut loose from her suitors. She went to the heart of her Empire, as she put it. She took three months leave and, sailing across an enemy patrolled Atlantic, reached England on 7 November 1915. She resigned from her position with the League from the emotional security of London.

The year 1915 also saw the publication in London of another novel, one written in Chicago. *The Net of Circumstance* was not published under her own name—maybe she did not want to risk possible humiliation after the reception of *Some Everyday Folk and Dawn*. She used the pseudonym Mr and Mrs Ogniblat L'Artsau, Austral Talbingo reversed. As with all her pseudonyms, there is always a hint of her real identity. The novel deals with the dilemma for women of maintaining independence within the confines of marriage and motherhood. The protagonist, while deciding whether to marry, suffers a series of illnesses which are reminiscent of Miles' own illnesses during her Chicago years.

In London Miles worked as a cook, earned some money from journalism and hawked her manuscripts around the publishing trade, to no avail. In March 1917 she applied for war work with the

16   Jill Roe, volume 1, op. cit., p69.

Scottish Women's Hospitals for Foreign Service and was accepted in June. She served with the Serbs as a cook in a tent hospital near Lake Ostrovo, Macedonia. 'In evening patients were entertained at simple games. How very simple the male of the species is. With him running the planet, little wonder it is being run off its axis.'[17] She contracted malaria and was back in London by February 1918.

From 1919 to 1926 she worked as secretary with the National Housing and Town Planning Council in Russell Square. She was busy at work, though frustrated at the muddling ways of the English in general and of Henry Richard Aldridge, her employer, in particular. 'All up till a ghastly hour with the muddle. No hope of doing anything against Mr A's megalomaniac conceit. He is like a hen scratching in a haystack. A genius setting out to be disorderly on purpose couldn't exceed his mad hatterness.'[18] In 1924 she was general secretary of a women's international housing convention. She continued to write, especially for the theatre, with no success, and enjoyed the cultural offerings of the great Imperial city in its last golden years. In May 1934 she would write to Mary Fullerton: 'Times do eat into us but we had those lovely days of inspiration and association and the feasts of culture provided by old London and they cannot be taken from us'.[19]

However, as in Chicago, discontent was never far below the surface. She found the living conditions in England primitive after America; she found her literary work spurned; she was living on a very small budget. 'I had supper in room of potatoes to make ends meet, and buy a new pair of shoes as there has been a hole in my only street pair ever since this time last year.'[20] As early as May 1920, she wrote to Margaret Dreier Robins in Chicago: 'I too wish

17 Miles Franklin papers, op. cit., ML MSS 364/2/10. Diary, 11 August 1917.
18 Miles Franklin papers, op. cit., ML MSS 364/2/13. Diary 2 June 1920.
19 Jill Roe, op. cit., p300.
20 Miles Franklin papers, op. cit., ML MSS 364/2/17. Diary, 9 December 1924.

I were back in the United States but cannot make up my mind what I want to do'.[21]

From December 1923 to March 1924 she visited Australia and was refreshed and inspired by this renewed encounter. She wrote to the publisher George Robertson: 'I'm on a flying pilgrimage to see my parents and all "old hands" and to see if my own, my unbelievable country is as I have been dreaming it. It is.'[22] But all had not been well at an emotional level. After she left, her mother wrote to her, in April 1924: 'Whilst here I did all in my power to make you feel somewhat happy but often had a feeling that you were miserably disappointed with the whole thing, & wished you had never come, & I would often have loved to have taken you in my arms & kissed you, but you seemed averse to any affection & I do hope you did not think me wanting in feeling it often gave me much pain & I do hope you will get along so that you can soon see your way to coming back . . .'[23]

Just prior to her visit she had the idea for a series of novels based on her own family's pioneering history in the Monaro and she worked on this while in Australia and subsequently back in England. She seems to have been inspired by the *Forsyte Saga*, the various volumes of which had appeared in a collected edition in 1922 which her aunt, Sara Lampe, had given her as a Christmas present that year. This would be the series of novels she would publish under the pen-name Brent of Bin Bin. Again, she gives a hint of her identity in the name as Bin Bin was a run adjoining Brindabella that her father leased. The six Brent novels were completed by 1933.

Miles saw the creation of this pseudonym as very much a publicity device. 'My faithful second sight in hiding under a pen-name at the last will be more fruitful of publicity than any amount of the

21 Jill Roe, op. cit., p149.
22 ibid., p166.
23 ibid., pp171–2.

conventional paragraphs about a man's braces or how he trims his whiskers', she wrote in January 1929.[24] The mystery would compound, she thought, until on publication of the final novel in the series her authorship would be revealed to an astonished literary world. In this she was defeated because she was not able to organise publication of all the books in her lifetime.

Miles enjoyed the speculation on Brent's identity. In 1941, with a straight face, she even chaired a meeting of the Fellowship of Australian Writers which discussed this very subject. She had no scruples about praising Brent's books publicly as though she had had nothing to do with them, as she does in her diaries. She even praised them in her Commonwealth Literary Fund lectures in 1950 which does show, in a phrase which Miles would have relished, more front than Mark Foy's.

The first Brent book, *Prelude to Waking*, was completed in December 1925 though not published until 1950. *Up the Country* was the first to appear, in late 1928, by which time Miles was back in Australia again, having arrived in August 1927. This time she would stay until January 1931, living with her parents in the Sydney suburb of Carlton, in a weatherboard cottage which had been their retirement home since 1914.

But there were irritations here as well, as her diary entries recorded: 'God, if I can't get respite I'll die. Mother is killing me by inches' (7 September 1928); 'So mentally tired that writing is like walking in heavy mud, but must press on to finish' (21 August 1929); 'Feeling utterly defeated. No gifts. Nothing to live on. Dull. Tired. What to do? Go on blindly like an ox' (19 March 1930); 'Poked about. Wish I had one friend near. These spiteful ingrate souls are cruel.

---

24 William Blackwood and Sons—publishing file for Brent of Bin Bin novels, Mitchell Library, ML MSS 6329.

They kill my soul' (2 January 1931).[25] Even as early as December 1927, she had written to fellow Australian Alice Henry in Chicago: 'Australia is a wilderness of arrested mental development in all its arrangements . . .'[26] and by the following August she was telling Miss Henry that 'I consider life here incarceration of the dreariest possible kind'.[27] She rented a room in Hurstville for privacy while writing. The second Brent book, *Ten Creeks Run*, appeared in 1930.

The times were bad financially but Miles longed to see old friends, especially in America. It was madness to use up all her savings in this way, she said, but she must get away from Australia. She wrote to Margaret Dreier Robins in November 1930: 'I have enough for a return ticket steerage, I have all the clothes I had six years ago (the change in the length of skirts will gravel me a bit—bust it!) and my friends who are ashamed of the look of me can see me behind closed doors; I can buy a loaf and some butter to eat en route—one eats too much at home . . .'[28]

Miles sailed for England via New York in January 1931. Negotiations with American publishers came to nothing. 'Resolve on my part never to shake hands with a publisher again. One may travel among coolies and go on one meal a week . . . but one need not have hypocritical routine of friendliness. Svelte young ladies in latest clothes and bobs (and painted nails). Can't afford to have my hair bobbed, never had paid shampoo or manicure in my life.'[29]

Back in England, 1931 saw the publication of the third Brent novel, *Back to Bool Bool* (which actually appeared while Miles was

---

25 Miles Franklin papers, op. cit., ML MSS 364/2/21, ML MSS 364/2/22, ML MSS 364/2/23, ML MSS 364/2/24.

26 Jill Roe, op. cit, p191.

27 ibid., pp197–8.

28 ibid., p241.

29 Miles Franklin papers, op. cit., ML MSS 364/4/7. Diary, 5 March 1931.

en route from Australia) and the publication of *Old Blastus of Bandicoot*, the first work published under Miles' own name since 1909. But the year ended with tragedy when, in early November, she received a cable saying her father had died. 'Just flat as if the light had gone out. I never remember my Dad saying an unkind word to me— such a blank I cannot bear.'[30] Even Yehudi Menuhin at the Albert Hall at the end of the month could not lift her spirits.

It was a hard slog financially. 'My heart too heavy for life. Forced ever to work',[31] she told her diary in February 1932. A visit to Henry Handel Richardson in comfortable Regents Park Road later that month was a painful contrast in the lives of two expatriate Australian writers: 'with exactly 2s 6d to do me for everything after my board was paid for two weeks, I looked around the luxurious, quiet withdrawn room with a piano (my God, my hunger for a piano—atrophied now) and five books in twenty years and I had produced seven (four of them published) in four years during interruptions, tragedies of what was practically a twenty-four-hours-on-duty-per-day regime and so distressed by noises that forbade sleep—well—I was not a hero-worshipper in that direction'.[32] Miles' mother, who had suffered a heart attack following her husband's death, sent money but Australian currency had such a reduced value in London that Miles asked her to desist. Susannah Franklin was now 81 years of age, lonely, and wanting her eldest child, and only surviving daughter, home.

On 8 September 1932, Miles Franklin boarded the *Olympic* for New York. She travelled across America via Chicago to San Francisco, where she boarded the *Monowai*, arriving in Sydney, via Rarotonga and Wellington, on 27 November. She was buoyed by the hope offered

30   ibid., ML MSS 364/2/24. Diary, 2 November 1931.
31   ibid., ML MSS 364/2/25. Diary, 21 February 1932.
32   ibid., ML MSS 364/5/14. Diary, 26 February 1932.

by P.R. Stephensen's recently established Australian publishing company and by the fact that in her view Australia was the coming fashion in fiction.

She was now 53 years old, the unmarried daughter of an elderly widowed mother. There was really no choice: Miles must return to the family home and care for Susannah Franklin.

Her mother's death in June 1938 brought the inevitable guilt and sense of real loss. She wrote later in her diary (5 December 1943): 'anguish drowned me in the realisation that never again would I do anything for you; never, never again would you do anything for me. The one constant anchorage of my life was gone. I cannot write— the tears blind me'.

It did not really change her domestic situation as her nephew Jack was now living with her, and her widowed brother Norman moved in in April 1939. The duty was accepted but resented, Miles acting as unpaid housekeeper. Her financial situation did not improve. From her mother's estate she received an income of £3 per week which reduced to £2 in the war years. Norman's death in January 1942 added to her desolation, a word which appears now again and again in her diaries, and she was increasingly troubled by Jack's errant behaviour and eventual descent into alcoholism.

The war was another blow. She had been through the Great War, the war to end all wars, and here it was all over again. Much later she would write to Jean Devanny: 'I still am an independent in politics and am against war—*all* wars. I shd be against even a war to emancipate women, because war never can be won. To contemplate war is to be defeated . . .'[33]

On 26 September 1940 she wrote to Mary Fullerton: 'I have nothing to tell you personally except that I can just stay alive and that is all. I wish I had the pluck to lie down and die and be done

---

33 Jill Roe, volume 2, op. cit., p293. Letter dated 21 April 1952.

with it'.[34] In July 1940 in a letter to Angus & Robertson she was referring to 'real poisoned dingo depression'.[35]

And to Eleanor Dark she wrote on 8 October 1941: 'The buckram has gone out of me. I sometimes think I am dead but still walk around. I am paralysed by desolation'.[36] With her immediate family dead, by 25 February 1946 she was writing to Mary Fullerton: 'no one left to do things for or to whom I meant anything, if ever I did mean anything to anyone'.[37] And to David Martin on 23 August 1949: 'I am weary of writing letters to contact a world outside of an isolation that is practically solitary confinement'.[38]

She tended her archive for posterity, the most comprehensive archive of a writer ever assembled in Australia at that time. Thousands of letters, hundreds of manuscripts, diaries, photographs, financial papers and family papers, dating from 1841. 'A select archive of the paradoxes of Australian history and culture, of which she was a proud and challenging, but elusive, expression,' as Jill Roe wrote in the *Australian Dictionary of Biography*. This archive would be left to the nation, so Miles would have the last word, but not before it had been carefully vetted.

She wrote to Dymphna Cusack on 13 October 1943:

I recently went into a great trunk and destroyed scores of letters. One dear old friend went around telling everyone how I had refused him. I used to argue that he had never really proposed. Had entirely forgotten; but there among the letters were his

---

34   ibid., p41.
35   Angus & Robertson records, Mitchell Library, ML MSS 3269/274.
36   Jill Roe, op. cit., p61.
37   ibid., p157.
38   ibid., p230.

very definite proposals; not only from him but from others I had similarly forgotten. A Senator from another state called me up some months ago and asked me had I forgotten his proposal to me on board the ship when I first left Australia. I'm sure he never proposed, but he swore he had done so. So I said flippantly, 'Are you proposing again now?' He said, 'Yes, if you are the same radiant creature that I knew.' 'Don't be an ass,' I replied; 'how radiant would you be after thirty years?' I'm sure this man never proposed to me, but I think he imagines he did. I think that when a girl is the rage lots of men who have never said a love word to her imagine they have had great sentimental sessions . . .'[39]

She had written to Ambrose Pratt on 2 May 1936: 'I have no companions: I can't talk to myself, so instead of putting things into my forgettery I jap them roughly into exercise books . . .'[40] But her exercise books and pocket diaries tell another story. Throughout the 1930s and 1940s, she is, if not out every night of the week, making a good fist of it. There are literary functions, lunches, dinners, the movies, broadcasting, committees, speeches. And they were full days. She would leave Carlton by train, having done the necessary domestic chores, and meet up with one or two for lunch, perhaps writers or publishers, journalists or social activists; then to the Mitchell Library to read and have discussions with some of the librarians such as Ida Leeson or Kathleen Monypenny; tea in the Botanic Gardens with one or two others; then a social drink (always non-alcoholic for Miles) before a meeting or committee or the theatre; then supper and more talk and then the train home, arriving

39 ibid., p101
40 Jill Roe, volume 1, op. cit., p333.

at twelve-thirty or one in the morning, having walked for ten minutes from Carlton railway station.

She was a much sought after companion who exhibited in her public persona no trace of her inner unhappiness. Even in the last year of her life when she was physically fragile and undoubtedly mentally and emotionally very tired, Katharine Susannah Prichard could write following a visit to Carlton: 'I do love the wit & play of your so original mind. Nobody makes me laugh so much. And I've had Dodie & Ric chortling over some of your bits & pieces— so delightfully Miles, gay, intrepid & unique! . . . Love to you—my dear, incomparable Miles—and thank you again for so much stimulus—and the happiness of being with you.'[41] Prichard's comment is typical of the comments made about Miles again and again and again throughout her entire life. The personal testimony is unequivocal. She was a life enhancer.

She received the King George V Silver Jubilee Medal in 1935 and she refused the OBE in 1937. Rivalry with Dame Mary Gilmore, who had received her higher accolade earlier that year, seems to have influenced the rejection. From 1938 she appeared in *Who's Who* without a date of birth except for one edition, 1947, when she allowed her birth date to be given as 1883, thereby appearing four years younger than was in fact the case. As if writing *My Brilliant Career* at the age of 19 was not good enough! Miles had to appear even younger.

She continued to write and the years of her homecoming were years of regular publication. Just before she arrived home, Lothian in Melbourne published an Australian edition of *Old Blastus of Bandicoot* and, later, P.R. Stephensen published an edition in Sydney. The Australian Pocket Library reissued the book in 1945.

---

41 Jill Roe, volume 2, op. cit., pp338–9. Letter of 2 December 1953.

In 1933 *Bring the Monkey* was published by Endeavour Press, a subsidiary of the *Bulletin*. It was a thriller set in an English country house with a female detective, but it failed to attract interest.

In 1936 *All That Swagger* won the S.H. Prior Memorial Prize sponsored by the *Bulletin*, in which it was serialised before publication in book form the same year. Based on her own family's pioneering history in the Monaro, it re-established her literary reputation in Australia.

She satirised the Sesquicentenary celebrations—'too many over-loadings with overlords', as she wrote in her diary for 4 February 1938, in *Pioneers on Parade*, written in collaboration with Dymphna Cusack and published in 1939. Nineteen forty-four saw the publication of *Joseph Furphy: The Legend of a Man and His Book*, written in association with Kate Baker; Miles had done the writing, with Baker supplying the raw materials. The manuscript had won a second Prior award for Miles in 1939, Baker having spent the first part of that year at Carlton working on it with her.

In 1946 *My Career Goes Bung*, the sequel to *My Brilliant Career*, finally appeared. The next year saw the publication of her children's book, *Sydney Royal*, and the *Newcastle Morning Herald* published 'The Thorny Rose' as a serial.

The fourth Brent of Bin Bin novel to be published, *Prelude to Waking*, appeared in 1950 and the fifth, *Cockatoos*, just a few weeks before her death in 1954. The latter was dedicated to 'Sybylla Melvyn, the legendary and temerarious'; another hint of the identity of the author, though by this stage many had already guessed.

In July 1950 Miles delivered the Commonwealth Literary Fund lectures, on the novel in Australia, at the University of Western Australia. They were published after her death as *Laughter, Not for a Cage* (1956).

The last Brent of Bin Bin novel, *Gentlemen at Gyang Gyang*, appeared posthumously in 1956.

In 1963 Angus & Robertson published *Childhood at Brindabella*, Miles' reminiscences of her first ten years.

Miles had been found unconscious at her home in Carlton in July 1954 and was taken to her cousin Thelma Perryman, née Lampe, at Beecroft. She occupied the old four-poster bed which had been that of her beloved grandmother at Talbingo, more than half a century before. Holding a pencil in a shaky hand she wrote to Dymphna Cusack on 18 August: 'Ah! If we could once again sit on the rim of the lily-pond at Government House [where in February 1938 they hatched the idea of *Pioneers on Parade*]. Why is life so absorbing, so cruel and so fleeting? I have to leave the game nearly a full generation ahead of you, and then silence.'[42]

Miles Franklin died of a coronary occlusion on 19 September 1954 at the Seacombe Private Hospital, Drummoyne, where she had been taken a few days previously. She was cremated and her ashes scattered, as was her wish, in Jounama Creek, Talbingo, close to where she had been born almost 75 years before. Dymphna Cusack wrote: 'Impossible to believe all that vitality and courage quenched' and later spoke of Miles' indomitable courage, vigorous thought and scintillating wit.[43] Katharine Susannah Prichard wrote: 'I'd have given anything for her to have had more appreciation and recognition in her lifetime. She has such wonderful qualities. Such grit and wit, and such a capacity for love, loyal and generous friendship.'[44]

Her will brought a surprise. She had left her estate to fund a prize for Australian writing. It appears that the intention to establish the award was not known to her contemporaries. It is not mentioned in her diaries or correspondence. No reference to it was made in her

---

42   Marilla North (ed) *Yarn Spinners: A Story in Letters. Dymphna Cusack, Florence James, Miles Franklin*, St Lucia, University of Queensland Press, 2001, p367.

43   ibid., pp368, 370.

44   ibid., p369.

obituary in the *Sydney Morning Herald*. Only after probate on her estate had been finalised did this benefaction from a woman of modest means emerge.

It is not known when the idea occurred to her, although the will which established it had been drawn up in 1948, six years before her death. The annual Miles Franklin Award remains the most prestigious literary award in Australia and was first won by Patrick White for *Voss* in 1957.

NOTE ON THE SOURCES

The Miles Franklin papers are in the Mitchell Library, State Library of New South Wales (Ref: ML MSS 364), having been bequeathed by the author.

Miles kept a number of sequences of diaries and notebooks. Her pocket diaries cover the period from 1909 to 1 January 1954. A numbered sequence of notebooks dealing with literary subjects extend from 1934 to approximately 1948. Four volumes termed 'reminiscence' have entries covering the years 1935 to 1944. Two numbered diaries cover the period 1944 to 1953. In addition there are various other miscellaneous volumes and loose pages of notes, diary entries and jottings.

None of these sources, with the exception of the pocket diaries, is strictly chronological. Miles revised and added material. Where Miles has not dated an entry it has been dated as accurately as possible from internal evidence.

Selections have been made from all these sources and placed in one chronological sequence. A listing at the back of this book gives precise citations within the Franklin papers for each extract.

Ellipses within each extract indicate that text has been omitted. Ellipses have not been used at the beginning or end of an extract unless it begins or ends mid-sentence.

Punctuation has been slightly altered on occasions to aid comprehension. Spelling has been corrected unless it captures one of Miles' word plays.

Some pocket diaries, from 1926 to 1935, are written in shorthand. I am grateful to the late Mrs Dorothy A. Hayes of Sydney who, with great determination and skill, deciphered this shorthand between 1979 and 1984, eventually identifying it as Clark's and providing a full transcript of those diaries where it is employed.

I am also grateful to the Permanent Trustee Company Ltd (now Trust), the executors of Miles Franklin's estate, for the financial support which made possible Mrs Hayes' work as well as this edition of the diaries.

The Diaries of
MILES FRANKLIN

Miles Franklin left England in September 1932 to return to Australia via America. Apart from a visit home of a few months over the summer of 1923–24 and a longer visit from August 1927 to January 1931, she had been away from her native land since April 1906. Her father had died in October 1931, aged 83, while she was overseas, and her mother would celebrate her 82nd birthday a week after her arrival. Miles Franklin was now 53. Of her six siblings, only her widowed brother Norman, aged 46, was alive. She would take up the dutiful, unmarried daughter role of caring for her mother at the family home at 26 Grey Street, in the Sydney suburb of Carlton, soon to become one of the most famous literary addresses in Australia.

18 November 1932   Arrived in harbour after lunch. Warships in evidence. Reporters came on after me but I hid in First Class. They got me in Customs. I refused interview. Rotters will never publish anything I write. How am I to live? Mother, Lena [Lampe], Mrs Morgan and Mrs McCarthy met me. Was met with death of little Mary. Ghastly homecoming. Gibsons and May [Fogden] and girls came in evening. Norman [Franklin] came up from Wollongong.

*24 November 1932*____ Very tired. Pottered. In evening Harry came to tea and took me to Church Hall to hear Douglas Credit System explained but speaker was a fiasco.[1] Named Wilson.

*21 December 1932*____ Went to town in afternoon and did errands. Went to see Muriel Swain on behalf of Miss Henry [Alice Henry] and then to Art Gallery to see Gruner Exhibition.[2] Home with Dr and Miss Booth.[3] Home across Bridge for first time.[4]

*30 December 1932*____ Watered garden. Pottered. Mother has me in constant stew of disharmony. Nice thunder shower in evening.

*1 January 1933*____ Was at Springwood with Lindsay family all four, Stephensen family plus dog. [Talked] all day, very hot in morning. Cool and mist turning to rain at night.[5]

---

1 The Douglas Social Credit Movement proposed views held by the Englishman Major C.H. Douglas, which maintained that the liabilities of a national economy could be offset by the value of its assets. It was proposed as a solution to the Great Depression. When Douglas himself toured Australia in 1934 there were hundreds of branches of the Movement in the country. Franklin voted for the social credit candidate in the 1934 State election.
2 Elioth Gruner, 1882–1939, one of the most successful and popular painters at this time.
3 Presumably sister of Dr Mary Booth.
4 The Sydney Harbour Bridge was opened on 19 March 1932.
5 Stephensen, reporting on this occasion in a letter to Nettie Palmer dated 3 January 1933, said that Franklin was 'the most gifted woman writer in the world' and 'Images fall from her like ripe fruit even when she is talking'. Palmer papers, National Library of Australia, MSS 1174, 1/4182.

2 January 1933 Lovely grey wet day. Talked again. Left about 5. Do not agree with Lindsay's sex obsession but he is a dear, nevertheless. Home at 8.

31 January 1933 Went to Shoalhaven Lookout on my Daddy's birthday. Heard the bellbirds—heavenly. Passed through Tallong and Glenrock.

10 February 1933 Pottered. No peace in house. No money, hope receding.

11 March 1933 Went to O'Sullivan's for tea and after tea 'Collit's Inn' at Mosman Town Hall.[6] Got home at midnight and found Norman.

12 March 1933 Pottered. In evening went to Revivalist meeting at Allawah. Oh hell.

16 March 1933 Mother her most fiendish. She is the most infernal devil I know with her tongue. Nothing will stop her.

19 March 1933 Went to Griffins [Walter and Marion Mahony Griffin]. Mother walked the one and a half miles each way and

---

6 *Collit's Inn*: a musical play, libretto by Thomas Stuart Gurr, lyrics and music by Varney Monk. First staged in Melbourne in 1933 followed by the Sydney season.

would not go to bed.[7] As her mind was, she got disagreeable and more trying. God help me, but He never does.

5 May 1933 _____ Another wasted day. To be with Mother is purgatory. Terrible old woman.

12 June 1933 _____ Threatening day. Wrote some of 'All That Swagger'. Feeling very depressed. Wish I had some friend near to take and extend a little affection. Jean [Hamilton] for choice.

28 June 1933 _____ Mother went out after torturing me. I got out T.C. [Tom Collins] letters. Very like benediction.

30 August 1933 _____ Garden very dry. Warm weather. At 3 went to hear Adela Pankhurst at School of Arts. Am convinced she is a moron—she babbles—without coherence.

28 October 1933 _____ Cool day. Very exhausted. In afternoon went to Mascot to see Ulm, Taylor and Allen land from 'Faith in Australia'.[8] Took Jack [Franklin] for 15 minute flight in 'The Southern Cross'.[9] Home at 6. Norman came.

---

7   This perhaps refers to the distance from the bus stop to the Griffin home on the Castlecrag peninsula.
8   In 1933 in *Faith in Australia* Charles Ulm and Patrick Gordon Taylor established a new record for the Europe–Australia flight of six days, 17 hours and 56 minutes.
9   In 1928 Charles Ulm and Charles Kingsford Smith completed the first trans-Pacific flight from the US to Australia in *Southern Cross*. In 1928, they made the first trans-Tasman flight. In 1929, en route to London, *Southern Cross* was lost for 13 days when the aeroplane was forced to land near the north-west Australian coast but the flight was resumed and Ulm and Smith arrived safely in London.

23 November 1933   Went to town. Called on Inky [Stephensen] and left black pansy.[10] Left note for K. Monypenny. Bought present for Mother's birthday and then to Town Hall to hear Clara Butt. Looked so ill but a goddess still.

21 December 1933   Mother cantankerous, Lena [Lampe] babbling, taps dripping.

The duty of caring for her ageing mother was not shirked by Miles Franklin but it was increasingly resented as Susannah's restless senility robbed her daughter of thinking time and writing time. In addition, Miles' financial situation was hardly robust. She had spent much of her savings on her recent voyage and royalties from her books were rather thin. This situation would continue. To wealthy Margaret Dreier Robins she would write on 16 December 1935: 'I feel quite dead spiritually and mentally. It is terrible to be robbed of life, really just for lack of a little means, and that in a world loaded with every good thing.'[11] She told both Henry Handel Richardson and Eleanor Dark in 1936 that she could not afford to buy books.

21 March 1934   Went to Authors Society meeting about censorship. Visited Lena [Lampe] first & went to Mitchell [Library] for a while. Also called on Inky [Stephensen] for moment but

---

10   In 1929 in London, P.R. Stephensen had allowed his name to be used as the ostensible publisher of D.H. Lawrence's unexpurgated book of poems, *Pansies*, thereby risking prosecution for obscenity.

11   Jill Roe (ed) *My Congenials: Miles Franklin and Friends in Letters*, volume 1, Sydney, State Library of New South Wales in association with Angus & Robertson, 1993, p325.

Mr and Mrs Lemont were there and I flew.[12] Inky lent me 'Capricornia' in MS.[13]

15 August 1934 Went to town alone. Saw 'Silence of Dean Maitland' and Mae West. Went to Mitchell Library. Tea with K. Monypenny. Austral and Amadio at night in Town Hall. Austral sang Mad Scene from 'Lucia'. Home at 11.30.

11 September 1934 Tried to work a little in spite of maddening conditions and ceaseless interruptions.

11 October 1934 Met Lena [Lampe] and Dr Booth and went to see Miss Pring's water colours and have tea at Sue's Parlor. Then to P.R. Stephensen and Vivian Crockett, talked till 8 in office and then to café till 10 and Vivian Crockett had another half hour talking to me at entry of St James Station. Home at 11.30.

In other continents there lies between the living present and the oblivion of lost aeons, a comforting, and sometimes depressing padding of recorded history, history in the making and beyond that the pagan myths from which to weave a glamorous past. In Australia the valiant struggling present has nothing between it

---

12   E.C. Lemont was an architect and his wife, Ruby, a writer. Her book, *Makala Farm: A South African Romance* was published by Stephensen in 1934. The Lemonts had financially assisted Stephensen in his publishing venture.

13   P.R. Stephensen assisted Xavier Herbert in the revision of *Capricornia*. It was rejected by several British publishers and twice by Angus & Robertson and eventually published on Australia Day 1938 by the Publicist Publishing Company with which Stephensen was associated.

and oblivion but phantoms. A land of phantoms—a phantom land, bewitched and bewitching.

Australians of the requisite spiritual and mental stature have all to themselves the material from which to weave additions to the world's literary stores; those lacking such stature fall back on rechauffes of old world creations.

To me one gallant attempt in the former domain is infinitely a greater adventure than half-a-dozen belletristic achievements in the latter.

In Australia the forces of progress, though unorganised, are massing against those who hold the passes with outworn ideas.

24 October 1934   Went to town . . . Called on J. and L. Drummond. Joan Hammond there. Took Inky [Stephensen] to California Café at Darlinghurst for meal and sat on Archibald Fountain discussing Brennan via R. Hughes and A.G. Stephens till it began to rain.[14]

20 November 1934   Made biscuits for Mother's birthday. Ivy [Abrahams] and Mother went to town. Edward very cranky. Bullied Maggie all day. Nasty selfish old Bridle bluster.[15]

29 November 1934   Went to read in [Mitchell] Library and Inky [Stephensen] came and fished me out for tea in Gardens

---

14 Randolph Hughes published *C.J Brennan: An Essay in Values* in 1934 and A.G. Stephens' *Chris. Brennan* appeared in 1933.

15 Sarah Bridle, Franklin's grandmother, had married Oltmann Lampe in February 1850. John Theodore Lampe, Franklin's maternal uncle, married Margaret Elizabeth Bridle in 1884.

and wandering in Domain and dinner at the Florentino and then to Players' presentation of one-acters at St James's Hall.

1934 'Prelude to Christopher', Eleanor Dark, Stephensen, Sydney, 1934.

Here we have a brilliant novel that is definitely & exclusively concerned with tragedy . . . The whole action of the novel takes place during these four days, but in a technical tour de force, by a series of flash-backs the author reveals the lives of her characters for twenty years, and in the case of the two principals right back to their childhood. It is the artistry with which the materials are handled that makes this such an arresting book. There is not a superfluous sentence in the supple, clear, adequate prose employed. On the other hand there is none of that stark bald aridity of some so-called 'powerful' writers. No cul-de-sacs are explored. The chart is clear & trimmed. The deft precision of the author's exposition of her theme and the delineation of her characters are unexampled in Australian fiction. This story of the interplay of characters is of such a high order that it rises to the universal genre and is independent of its date and its parish. It is unloaded with detail, but all essential details are there in just proportion and are true to the Australian scene chosen.

It is undiluted tragedy but the action—the intellectual action is too swift and scientific for tears. One feels like a responsible alienist privileged to observe a clinic of exceptional interest. The flash-backs employed fit like perfect joinery with no artistic jolting or mental meandering into by-paths or cul-de-sacs. The whole thing is too antiseptic for sentimentality or even sentiment. The balance is perfect, attained through exactitude in quantity, intelligence of choice, suppleness of arrangement.

There is economy of characters and deaths but one of Shake-speare's tragedies with most of the characters all justly or unjustly despatched at the end would be a comfortable family squabble by comparison. This leaps back to the relentless Greek plays sans chorus. The author credits her reader with intelligence to be her own chorus . . .

The technique and the thought are modern, the actions of the people are post-war, even that of the hen of a 'normal' girl with her sound body and limited mentality so sympatica to the mother-in-law. A book by its argument well in the tide of progressive thought and by its tragedy as old as man and as universal.

This writer is master of her creations. She has no favorites, she presents without an extraneous word . . .

As a work of art it is free from untidy strands or superfluous sentences: as an intellectual exercise it is free from fustiness or mawkish sentimentality. Though modern there is not one in-delicate or dull sentence from cover to cover, frank, yet triumphantly reticent, it has the decency of a first-class clinic where doctors & nurses are all gentlemen. So terribly beautiful is this work with hardly a word that could be improved & no slips that one is impatient for later work by Eleanor Dark.[16]

Too thrilling, too quick in its intellectual action to horrify or over-sadden the reader. No starkness: no lushness.

Miles Franklin had returned to Australia in late 1932 inspired by the plans of P. R. Stephensen for the publication of Australian books. Stephensen had returned from England to Sydney earlier that year and Norman Lindsay had convinced the Bulletin *to support financially the establishment of Endeavour Press with Stephensen in charge. At this time London publishers had a hold on the Australian market and*

16 *Prelude to Christopher* was Eleanor Dark's second published novel. It had been preceded by *Slow Dawning*, 1932.

it was difficult for serious local authors to have their books published in Australia. And as London was the glamorous literary capital, aspiring authors naturally wanted a London imprint. Angus & Robertson dominated the local publishing scene and published the popular authors of the 1930s: Ion Idriess; Frank Clune (for whom, ironically, Stephensen would become ghost-writer in order to pay the bills) and E.V. Timms. F.J. Thwaites was also very popular but he published his own books. Stephensen's Endeavour Press lasted only two years but managed to publish Norman Lindsay's Saturdee *(1933); A.B. Paterson's* The Animals Noah Forgot *(1933); Miles Franklin's* Bring the Monkey *(1933); Brian Penton's* Landtakers *(1934) and Kylie Tennant's* Tiburon *(1935).*

The Fellowship of Australian Writers, which had been founded in November 1928, presided over the Sydney literary scene into which Miles launched herself. A major event which it organised was the inaugural Australian Authors' Week from 8 to 13 April 1935, held in the Blaxland Galleries of Farmer's department store in Sydney. More than 1500 books published in Australia were exhibited for sale. This was a point of contention because it excluded books written by Australians but published overseas, as Franklin's Brent of Bin Bin books had been. Each day ended with a pageant depicting scenes from Australian literature. Talks were given each afternoon by authors or critics and these talks were broadcast simultaneously on the ABC. The week concluded with an Authors' Ball under the patronage of the Governor. P.R. Stephensen, with powdered hair and white beard, went as Brent of Bin Bin.

Leslie Rees later recorded his impressions of Franklin at FAW meetings:

> *. . . a diminutive, rather quaint, unobtrusive figure sheltering under a large mushroom hat. She seldom said anything at meetings. But she was a pillar of the Australian idea. When she did speak,*

it was to make it clear that Australian literature should be well and truly Australian—in colour, settings, general character, everything. She was said to be writing down her candid impressions of every meeting and every person there, to be released to the world long after her death.[17]

There were some literary awards but no continuing award of any substance would exist until Franklin herself established the award which bears her name following her death in 1954. From 1928 the Australian Literature Society awarded a gold medal, but no money, to the year's best novel, though from 1937 other literary genres were included. The S.H. Prior Memorial Prize of £100 began in 1935. In 1934 there was a one-off Victorian Centenary Prize to celebrate the centenary of that State.

The Commonwealth Literary Fund, which had been established in 1908 by the second Prime Minister, Alfred Deakin, was now virtually moribund and would not be revived until 1939.

January 1935   'Capricornia' by Xavier Herbert. In galley, four last chapters in typescript.

I read this story about two thirds through . . . in typescript. Read it again now as above (Jan 1935). I'll say without reserve that this is an absorbingly interesting story. I skipped very little in the MSS even when pursuing the story: on a second reading I found it more interesting than a first, and skipped nothing. It is a big book, a book by one who loves Australia and is up in the Brent of Bin Bin Class, though it deals with the other end of Australia, and the different set of circumstances there. It is in the

---

17   Leslie Rees *Hold Fast to Dreams: Fifty Years in Theatre, Radio, Television and Books*, Sydney, Alternative Publishing Co-operative Ltd, 1982, p144.

Brent Class in its emotion, its wealth of characters, all clearly defined and alive. The author is ironically and satirically humorous, but smoulders & simmers rather than bursts out in hilarity. Of his considerable gifts there can be no doubt, and he courageously attacks the northern part of Australia, frankly setting out the miscegenation, the hypocrisy of the white man's prestige.

He may be a partisan for the [word indecipherable] but that does credit to his heart & sense of fair play—his humanity . . .

It is a long book & it could have been longer for I felt that it was rushed at the last in rather synopsis style to finish up within reasonable limitations . . . Mr Herbert's emotion, his partisanship does him credit. Most of the giants whose stories remain with us were partisans.

It belongs to the Brent Class and it may be that Brent is the leader of a school of typically indigenous fiction. It shows a whole field—with the towns, stations, camps complete—and also all the people appertaining thereto. There is no one character isolated in the artificiality imposed by stars on stage or screen, but numerous people in due proportion, as in the democracy of real life, from which realism cannot wholesomely escape. You get the whole community in a most diverting way, as in Brent, and settle to this with keen enjoyment. To belabor the writer for discursiveness would be to misunderstand this new and Australian contribution to fiction in the English tongue, and to be incapable of discerning it or appraising it.

Note: When talking to the Author I was amused by his claim to have mastered English composition. I maintained that the English language is too amorphous to be mastered and that those who most nearly master it are not infrequently mere stylists— bores—dry as dust. Now X.H. writes well, has a fine flow, a good vocabulary, but even I could on every galley pick holes in his

English compositionally—not sufficient to put him out of court, nor sufficiently jarring to disturb the rhythm of his intention, but ample and overflowingly sufficient to prove my contention as to the likelihood of his not having mastered English.

c. February 1935   I don't know that our attempts at organized literary groups are successful. We need a good fighting trade society to watch & promote our interests such as the Authors' Society in London was when founded by Besant & carried on by Thring. I have no gout for wasting evenings while someone reads a paper about Kipling or Shakespeare. Such societies as we have are, in conspicuous instances, carried on by & for men who have no connection with literature and no standards or feeling regarding it except that of the huckster.

We are also in a backward state concerning competitions for the best novel—putting aside for the moment the contention that such affairs may or may not be in the best interests of the novel. At present they are a great godsend to the lucky winner, like the State Lotteries, and one of our foremost novelists told me quite casually & frankly that she had never had any money for her novels except the prizes. In other countries a prize (or advance on royalties) is usually offered to discover a new writer (and it would be interesting to compute what percentage of these continue to distinguish themselves with subsequent work) whereas in Australia the most distinguished's only hope of money to carry on is to continue to compete against all comers—tyros or those who have won some sort of recognition. There is also a contention & belief too firmly-seated and wide-spread to be ignored, that these prizes always go to a little inner ring of friends, either the [Australian Literature Society] gold medal or the money prizes, and that the judges lack courage and perspicacity regarding original work. The Bulletin's two competitions[18] called forth a wealth of attempts but unearthed no unknown genius and in one conspicuous instance failed to list the most distinguished entrant even among the extra score of 'also-rans'.[19] They understand Australia neither bigly nor bravely enough to be able to appraise the most authentic illuminating or distinguished indigene.

We are divided into those who are satisfied with the gum tree school of literature as it exists and those who imagine that they have got beyond it or are above it. They flee to environments realised by countless forerunners—englamored by time & distance, where there is romance in the daily sunset because it has been made evident by a cloud of balladists. They shirk the tenacity & strength of belief & purpose necessary to endow a sunset empty of association. The first are worthy but feeble folk and the others are ignorant, ungardened and in trying to skip fundamentals have missed the significance of those fundamentals and the fact that the art that is distilled from the Australian bush scene contains the only indigenous original culture yet nurtured in Australia.

Each time I hear an artist who complains that there is nothing in Australia but a gum tree & that one soon gets enough of painting that I recall the story of a great music teacher who when

---

18 The *Bulletin*'s editor, S.H. Prior, initiated a literary competition for the novel in 1928 and continued this in 1929. Five hundred and thirty-six novels were submitted in 1928 and two hundred and seventy-five in 1929. There were three joint winners the first year: M. Barnard Eldershaw's *A House Is Built*, Katharine Susannah Prichard's *Coonardoo* and Vance Palmer's *Men Are Human*. In 1929 the winner was Vance Palmer's *The Passage*.

19 One wonders whether Franklin is in fact here referring to herself in the guise of Brent of Bin Bin. *Up the Country* had been published in late 1928 and *Ten Creeks Run* would be published in 1930. Franklin may have entered *Ten Creeks Run* in the 1929 competition.

a prodigy was brought before him would exclaim, 'Play the scale.' 'Which scale?' would ask the aspirant. 'The scale of C.' To a pupil who was heady about doing something else he would say that an artist might play the scale of C all his life without exhausting all its possibilities. So with our eucalypts—the A.B.C. of their possibilities has not yet been discovered. See the oak & its leaves & acorns in English handicraft, the acanthus leaf in Greek & Roman architecture & then return O, Australian painters & liberate . . . the gum tree and what it stands for.

15 March 1935   Mother went to meet Lena at 11, thank God. A little blessed quiet. Had little rest and wrote a little. The only moments that are not torture are those when I have house to myself.

Authors' Week, 8–13 April 1935   Why should Authors have a week like the Blind, or the Crippled or Animals? (be kind to them). The author has lost his authority—it is to be seen. He comes forward as a seller of mere commercial wares who lacks customers.

Our authors' week also showed painfully our circumscription to the English Garrison. It was beaten into retreat a generation ago by such full-sized men as Archibald, Stephens and Lawson, Tom Collins. One more would have saved the city. Perhaps the war killed too much talent in embryo: or it may be that it merely hastened the confusion, the impasse sure to occur when an economic system no longer functions and transition to another is resisted by the privileged of the old order & their echoing minions. We are more enervatedly and mediocrely a mental Colony of England (& Hollywood) today than we were physically in the old garde-major days.

27 April 1935   Mother went out traipsing to May [Fogden] and Ruby. I attended meeting of Propeller Writers[20] and heard Ella McFadyen spout and spout. Called on Miss Gillespie and came home.

19 July 1935   At 8 o'clock went to Theo Lucas' meeting to form Censorship Abolition League.[21] Inky in Chair, Shalimar Café. Read 'Seven P. Men of Sydney' in interstices.[22]

20 July 1935   I smiled sardonically on reading this paragraph.[23] Henry Handel Richardson has a pushing press agent whom I once saw in action. Here she gets the second longest paragraph in the column & it reads as if there were only one Jubilee Medal & it an important literary award. My unmirthful amusement is to recall my 'King's Silver Jubilee Medal'. I was called to the telephone by P.R. Stephensen who congratulated me. I had to inquire what for. This was my first intimation that there was such a souvenir. Mother called out with characteristic peremptoriness to know who was ringing and what about. 'It appears that I am awarded the King's Jubilee Medal.' 'What is it?' 'I don't know.' 'Why did you get it?' 'For being an author.' 'Pooh! Something that they

---

20 The Propeller Young Writers' League was formed in 1930 under the auspices of *The Propeller*, the local newspaper of the St George district of Sydney which includes Carlton where Franklin lived. Franklin was at various times Vice-President and Patron.

21 Miss Theo Lucas was a prominent member of the Victorian Book Censorship Abolition League, formed in November 1934. In July 1935, an unsuccessful attempt was made to found a branch in Sydney.

22 *Seven Poor Men of Sydney* by Christina Stead was published in London in 1934.

23 In *John O'London*, 20 July 1935, announcing the award of the King's Jubilee Medal to Henry Handel Richardson.

give a silly old author.' That was the general attitude of that family. Metta [Lampe] was a shining exception. With her usual bluntness she wrote that I was the only member of the tribe that had got one anyhow. Aunt Eliza & Uncle Fred [Lampe] broadly contemptuous until they discovered that their Surgeon had received one. The Surgeon also had been contemptuous until he knew he had one himself. I have no idea who could have entered my name and am as astonished as uninformed that it should have been sent in.

31 August 1935   Mother particularly cross, & needing to be endured and humored. Went to door at 11 a.m. and there were Ed & Maggie [Bridle] come to spend day. Glad to see them especially Maggie—but there goes my day. And on Saturday afternoon after I have finished charing the house and polishing the floors I find myself stiff with fatigue. When I wash the dirt from me I lie down for an hour in the afternoon as then Mother seems appeased for a while by the sacrifice of me to charing— but here went my respite . . . Nor & Jack [Norman and Jack Franklin] went to movies and kept me awake till 12.05 a.m. By that time I was so nervous & weary I couldn't sleep at all and had to arise early to get Norman's breakfast.

1 September 1935   What a good thing it would be to be liberated from any filial complex or be an orphan. Those whose relatives are a help or are congenial are blessed.

9 September 1935   Attempting a rest after washing before ironing but in comes Mrs Gibson—very neurasthenic—hardly sane—raved about her troubles—no one else has any—impossible

to turn her thoughts. These dreadful old Australian women with no avocation but charing & gossip, when they get old have no more soul than a dog. It is like listening to the experiences of an animal—good heavens, is this life? Their ghastly ignorance fails me. Was glad of the ironing as a counter irritant.

30 October 1935   Went to town to Broadcast [on the radio] and had lunch with Eve [initials indecipherable] at Jones'.[24] Returned E.D.'s poems to Mr Quinn. In afternoon met Mrs Holman & Nan McKenzie & went to Hse of P. & heard [Premier B.S.B.] Stevens talking on unemployment. Also went during intervals to Mitchell [Library], saw book exhibition & read S. Roberts book on land settlement.[25]

2 November 1935   Rose up off floor (Sat. morning charing—polishing linoleum) to telephone. Baylebridge, bless him! to give me cheer about my broadcast on humor—said my voice carried very well and that the talk was interesting, but that he did not consider that I had defined humor. I said certainly not, that to define humor I'd need a lengthy treatise & would certainly enjoy discussing it with an alienist. He agreed, & said, yes, humor was one of the subtlest of all things to define . . .

14 November 1935   Met G.B. L[ancaster] at 2.15 & gave her tea at Metropole [Hotel]. Had lunch with Monypenny in Gardens.

---

24 Sydney department store, David Jones.
25 Stephen Roberts *History of Australian Land Settlement:1788–1920*, 1924. Franklin was undoubtedly researching background for *All That Swagger*.

Called in—E. O'Sullivan's C.W. Congress at Nock & Kirby's. Home & took Mother to Young Leagues plays at Masonic Hall, Hurstville. Dreadful—amateurishness—dreadful.

24 November 1935   Celebrated mother's birthday—32 all told for afternoon tea and 25 stayed for full tea. Fine day not too hot.[26]

26 November 1935   Mother went out for afternoon, thank Heaven, and I had an hour or two to assemble 'All That Swagger', but oh, for time to myself without interruption and the disharmony. May Fogden called in evening and stayed till 10.30.

20 December 1935   We called on Miss G [Gillespie] on the way home. Washing up after tea Jack [Franklin] expressed his regret that I was unmarried. 'Oh, Auntie, such a pity you are wasted. You would make such a splendid wife. Look at the way you make cakes, and iron Dad's shirts, and the way you can shop and cook! Couldn't you get married now?'

'I'm too old.'

'That oughtn't to be against you. You could keep house so well, and write books in your spare time. I'd marry you, only you are my relation.'

'Consanguinity as well as age spoils my chances,' said I, smothering a grin. The dear youngster was the general as well as the particular Australian male. Write books in my <u>spare time</u>.

---

26 Susannah Franklin's birthday was 25 November which was a Monday in 1935 so presumably the party was on the preceding Sunday.

People 3 & 4 times his age have no more understanding of writing
& its demands upon the writer.

December 1935? I wonder did Mother ever say a soothing
assuaging thing: she never did to me. Samples:

The first time I broadcast Mother said, 'You nearly broke my
machine. Your voice sounded awful.'

2ⁿᵈ time: 'Why do you speak so rapidly? You talk like a man.'

3ʳᵈ time: 'Why did you speak so slowly? You sounded as if you
had a stutter.'

4ᵗʰ time: She forgot to listen in at all.

5ᵗʰ time: Mrs Somerville gushed and called upon Mother to
confirm: 'It wasn't too bad, but there were two women spoke
after you that were splendid. They were lovely speakers and so
interesting. I did enjoy them.'

6ᵗʰ time: 'Yes, I heard you. Harry says no one is interested in
the speakers at that time of day. They are put at that hour so no
one will hear them.'

'Why don't you bob your hair?'

'I'll never cut my hair, too much expense, too much trouble.
You cured me of wanting cut hair when I was very small. You
said I'd look a fright.'

'Well', said Mother promptly, 'I didn't want to make you any
worse'.

_1935_ 'Heritage' (Expeditionary Films), Charles Chauvel.

Well, this is an attempt, and a good illustration of what happens
when an opportunist, instead of a dreamer with a touch of genius,
attempts to bend art to get-rich-quick business. The whole

Australian field being at the disposal of film makers, Mr Chauvel has tried to cover that whole field in one slap. There is hurry and congestion, and yet withal sparsity, consequent upon the lack of depth and infatuation in conception. The conception is imperio-politico. The lovers even halt to intersperse their cooing with well-worn soap-box platitudes about pioneering and the great future of Australia. They spout about the heritage of Australia at dates when they were growling about the beastly rotten colony and the droughts and the damned office seekers and agitators and the unionists. When Mr Chauvel discussed his project with me and said he was going to make an Australian 'Cavalcade',[27] I thought, 'Ah, me boy—there will be no originality then, just an imitative hash'. But still I thought it would be better than this, but it takes quite a big ability to pick other people's brains . . . This film depends upon flapdoodle for its appeal—though the heroes don't actually bring the flag out of their tail pocket one feels all the time that it is there. The dialogue—there isn't any. It has been picked from proper political sentiments and it is therefore entirely right that the film should have received a prize from politicians who know nothing about art but are flattered with this their mouthpiece as an inferior schoolmaster is pleased with the pupil who can most slickly echo him.

It shows lack of scholarship in historical details. Waltzing to a three-four time reminiscent of the Blue Danube and Merry Widow is too early introduced, also a concertino which was a

---

27 Play by Noel Coward, first performed October 1931 and widely considered, though not by the author, a patriotic epic. It traced the first 30 years of the twentieth century through the life of one family. It had 22 scenes, lasted three hours, employed a huge cast, ran for more than a year and has never been revived. It is possible that Franklin saw it in London.

new instrument in Barnum-Jenny Lind decade. Also the tune Toorali-Oorali-Arady so popular in the 'nineties is featured away back in very early days. Is this correct—was the '90s outbreak a revival? One does not trust the scholarship.

It is good to observe the improvement in mechanical technique—the cloud effects are beautiful. There were not long teams of bullocks available in those days. In the '40s there were only two drays in the whole of the Southern District and four or six bullocks were a lot. I never saw a tilted dray such as those employed here and of course the bullocks sprint along like a rodeo. In real life the beasts would have been raving mad and dead under such treatment.

Every advance is welcome—the only way to do things is to <u>do</u> them, and Australian film makers are advancing in mechanics. The whole unique field still lies awaiting the master—the man of vision as well as technical knowledge. But he will have to study the subtleties of Australian life and scenery. Failure, or at best mediocrity, will continue to attend those who strive to jazz Australia up to U.S.A. rhythm or seek to present her in the image of any outside conception imposed by financial pressure or umbilical relationships or the whole rag-bag of expediency.

'The Swayne Family' by Vance Palmer (half prize winner in Mr James Dyer's Centenary Bonus 1934) (Angus & Robertson 1934 price 6/-).

It was such a foregone conclusion that V.P. would get the prize that several other novelists did not send anything in. This book is one that could be given a prize by professors of the tepid depressive breed of Cowling (it reads like a novel which would be a complete & satisfying thesis of his recent anaemic emulsion in 'Age' about what Australia could & should not do & should not expect in setting a timid limit to expectation) literature.[28] It is exactly like a book written to University order and written by one of the competing professors. No canons of good form, as laid down by University profs., have been violated. Australia does not vulgarly intrude its own special pungent tang; has been carefully excluded in the most gentlemanly manner. The workmanship is sound and careful. In the whole book are not more than half-a-dozen sentences or phrases that I would question, and then not from the point of view of grammatical composition. It could safely be put into the hands of pupils from the most mid-Victorian of mothers. From this point of view it might have been written by the Sydney Morning Herald itself, with Napier as the mid-wife. On the other hand, despite the careful and detailed observation of the scenery there is not one passage of arresting beauty—not one moment of passion, that touches, that makes one shut the eyes & look away inward from the text. Pedestrian, grey, flat . . .

'The Salzburg Tales' by Christina Stead (Peter Davies).[29]

There is a Teutonic massivity about this book. It is I believe by an Australian. It shows an immense talent, industry, scope,

---

28 G.H. Cowling's article appeared in the *Age* on 16 February 1935. It advanced the view that Australia was not old enough to produce great literature. 'In spite of what the native born say about gum trees, I cannot help feeling that our countryside is "thin" and lacking in tradition . . . there are no ancient churches, castles, ruins—the memorials of generations departed . . . From a literary point of view Australia lacks the richness of age and tradition . . . I think that a wholly Australian novel is a feat of skill and rare. Australian life is too lacking in tradition, and too confused, to make many first-class novels.'

29 *The Salzburg Tales* was first published in New York in 1934. The London edition, published by Peter Davies, appeared in 1935.

vocabulary. The writer is fecund in delightful images of nature
& life & people but doesn't escape a great dullness though some
of her tales as short stories are equal to the best—one in the
Russian manner for example. There is one nasty Australian tale—
the Victress's, placed in Terrigal & Tuggerah—a very nasty tale of
a girl cohabiting with her father and killing him out of jealousy
of another girl also murdered—by the father who had outraged
her presumably—and a complaisant mother—a really sickening
tale. Another fairy tale mentions Morpeth on the Hunter River.
If only Miss Stead had known Australia and let loose her combination of talents for sustained fiction in presenting it she might
have attained something absorbingly interesting & new. Now that
she has gained spurs abroad it would be interesting to see what
she could do with the much more difficult material of the
Australian milieu.

'Seven Poor Men of Sydney' by Christina Stead (London: Peter
Davies Ltd 1934). This was a publisher's proof copy bound by the
Roycroft Library so they parasitically paid nothing to Author or
Publisher.

In this book, as in 'The Salzburg Tales', there is Teutonic
massiveness and also therefore there is clumsiness and much
dullness, but no thinness nor lack of ability. Many attempts to
put our bush into novels have suffered from the dressing up in
too much bushranger, brutality, etc. in imitation of N. America,
where they were richer in rougher elements & actual Indian raids,
& the result was failure through lack of truth. Insincerity can
spoil any art medium. Now there seems to be a tendency to dress
up the thin banality of our cities with post-Freudianism—all
the licence of confessions of the [word indecipherable] of the
subconscious under the charter of psycho-analysis & in post-war
chaos, take the vomit from Bloomsbury & Washington Square &

belch it upon Sydney. This will be commended by overseas intelligentsia from Washington Square to Bloomsbury & Moscow who know nothing of its relation or the contrary to Australia, but who are pleased because they can understand their own idiom. Australia meanwhile still waits.

These seven poor men may be a case in point. These ne'er-do-wells, failures—one a cripple, another a suicide, another who shows inconsistent sagacity by surrendering herself to a lunatic asylum. The book shows exuberant ability but it lacks charm. It is free from laughter and tears. These people do not touch the heart, they merely depress the mind. There is venery and vagrancy, dark hints of drug taking, and a repellent suggestion of the perversion of incest—or incest through sheer perversion, because in a normal, respectable family free from slum cold & crowding. Michael is an adulterous child, but it is never explained how or why his conventional ordinary mother thus strayed.

The book is modern in its chaos. There has been no attempt made to organize the material. It has the post war form or formlessness of the novel resulting from the destruction of the Victorian & Edwardian patterns, a no man's land of rebellion, cynicism, licence and rush which has not yet found new patterns —undigested conglomerate. It is only saved by the vigorous talent of the author from being mere case observations of the unfit: & the investigation of perverts is only valuable insofar as it helps normality to supernormality in the upward trend of man. When perversion becomes of consequence on its own account & is respected or tolerated as sophistication it is the symptom of racial decadence. When it becomes better to be born abnormal in the sub way than born gifted in the super way disaster is overtaking the race.

If C. Stead's characters are true to Sydney then Sydney is fuller of canker than a young city built on a few generations of hard pioneering should be. These people may be Sydney types. I have been depressed by finding how far the city people are growing from any knowledge of Australia that waits beyond the Gib[30] or the Blue Mts . . .

Miss Stead's powers of description are tremendous—her imagery of great magnitude, but the essence of Sydney has escaped her. She evidently is not near to Sydney as one is near who is infatuated with a place, and her wondrous descriptions, one feels, would be just as prolific of any other city she had visited with the intention of using as a literary background.

Her characters do not talk in the Australian idiom or rhythm. They are windbags of the stuff one gets in this kind of novel abroad—in translations from the Russian & German. A new and powerful writer but not necessarily Australian.

1 January 1936   Warm day, but not hot. Mother and I went to Miss Gillespie for day . . . Got home about 7. God, I hope this year holds something more than this.

Florence Austral and Amadio in short radio concert in evening.

8 January 1936   [Mother] is unfailingly <u>cruel</u> to me, always has been since my earliest memory. But in her prime she had much else to adulterate the cruelty. It is frightening to see the excellent qualities, the ability, fading while the opposite & undesirable qualities seem to strengthen.

9 January 1936   God! how I craved this morning to sit in peace and write my thoughts on Anzac, evoked by the competition

---

30   A prominent rise near Bowral, New South Wales.

stories[31]—as the stupidest blunder in history—past now as the rusty armour of an ancient knight crusader in a silent musty museum. The 'Straits Impregnable' as told me by Claude.[32]

I remember a <u>diseuse</u> in New York in 1914 making a great and telling point against the invaders of Gallipoli 'in another man's country'. That is irrefutable. As the Germans can never explain away their rape of Belgium. They were demolishing another man's country, who had not attacked them. The pity, the damnable madness of so much gallantry wasted!

I recall the headlines of those days. 'Suntanned Giants From Overseas', 'Gods like the Mythical Men' and so on. After 9 years absence from my native land I went to see my countrymen, the remnants of Anzac in the first anniversary celebrations in Caxton Hall, London. (Old Sir Geo Reid in evidence.) They had the physique, the bearing, the features (sweated by the sun) of young gods, and 'God, they were young' as later I read burnt on a little wooden cross in a wayside cemetery where the ambulance had rested in the Balkans. 'Killed in Battle' ran the legends—lads of 18–19–20, and the recorder had burned that phrase.

I saw, long after, the gates at Woolloomooloo being dedicated. Met the ageing Anzacs at the Town Hall celebration. They have to be cared for, many of them simple men who gave all in that one supreme effort, however false & foolish, who are now really derelicts. Oh, what misdirection of human potentialities! But Anzac cannot be glorified nor excused; that is to betray those who were sacrificed, thrown to Moloch.

---

31 Organised by the Anzac Festival Committee, the chairman of which was Dr Mary Booth. Franklin judged the short stories.

32 Reference to Claude unclear. *The Straits Impregnable* was a novel about Gallipoli written by Frederick Loch, 1889–1954, under the pseudonym Sydney de Loghe and published in Melbourne in 1916.

12 January 1936   I rather pooh-hoo dreams. I was reared on Dr Watts: 'He told me his dreams, talked of eating and drinking, but scarce reads his bible and never loves thinking'. That has always seemed to fit pretty well many garrulous and woozy egoists who will insist upon detailing their dreams. Then too the extraordinarily oblique interpretation put upon dreams by Freud has further alienated my respect for dreams. This attitude is supported by my own comparative freedom from dreams. I dream only when I have offended my digestion, and my digestion is a long suffering apparatus. Pounds of fruit late at night, fatty matter, heavy pastries, excessive sugar, irregularity in meals, nothing upsets me. Only for the damage done by the unconscionable quantities of quinine I swallowed for malaria contracted in the Balkans, I think I could digest anything, so long as I relish it. But there are occasional weaknesses. Too big a slice of cheese eaten next before retiring induces dreams almost unfailingly & militates against my belief that they can have any psychic significance.

Last evening I devoured a large over-ripe mango which had the same effect as cheese.

I dreamt. It was a coherent <u>dream</u> and it remains with me some hours later.

I suddenly found myself the guest of station people far from Sydney. They were to spend the night at a dance at a distance and I did not want to go. The alternative was to return to the homestead and remain quite alone. 'Would I be frightened?' 'Not the least, if someone would only come back to the house with me and take me in.'

Jimmy volunteered to take me. He was small, slight, young and most lovable. He was in the uniform of the AIF khaki, but very grey, and his hat turned up at the side was bleached almost grey. He took me back to the house and we entered. The lounge was a vast apartment with walls of glass and no blinds. I have a great dislike of being in a lighted room where anyone can look in at me. Jimmy was kind about it. He took me to the centre of the big place where there was a little sunken square containing a desk & chair. Around this he drew heavy screens making in fact a tiny room within the room. 'No one will see you here,' he said. 'Besides, there's no one living within a hundred miles, and no one will hurt you.'

No sooner was he truly gone than I began to hear people moving and talking, not one but a number. I froze with fear—that sickening paralysis of terror which, thank God, I have never experienced save in nightmare.

I turned out my light for safety and sat in goosefleshed horror, while form after form entered the room. I could see them silhouetted against the starlight against the glass. In a minute or two all fear left me, I was comfortable and interested. Little Jimmy's kindly words came back, 'No one will hurt you.' These people did not know I was there. They were in another dimension. They were all Australians. There was complete harmony between them and me. They were ghosts.

That vast apartment was some mansion lent as a convalescent rest home. Its comfortable divans and chairs were occupied by men in all stages of mutilation. Some had an arm missing, some a leg, others an eye or ear. All were maimed, but all were in the high spirits of war time, telling yarns, laughing. And I heard all they said, but it will not come back to me, though the room itself is as clear as actuality.

20 January 1936   Mother had a good sleep during afternoon, Norman a snooze at 8.30, so they are all lively now at 10 pm. And oh, God, what I would not give to go to bed and sleep. I am fatigued right through but too nervous to sleep while they blunder about. They will all be snoring in the morning when I get up to make the breakfast. Not one grain of understanding or sympathy. 'You think you don't sleep, but you do.' 'If you want sleep, you'll sleep alright.' Why was I born into a family not a member of which has any shred of tastes or ideas in common with me? They utterly despise anything & everything that is vital to me. If I could make money of course—how I should be admired!

Norman mentioned some of the old places on return from recent holiday and I (very foolishly) remarked that I should like to put all that old life and location into a poem but that it would take 20 years and I had not the leisure. 'What's the good of a poem when it's made? It's no use to you or anyone else,' observed Norman with rough contempt.

26 January 1936   A grey morning clearing into a glorious day, hot, as becoming January, but with a cooling breeze. Mother had insisted that Norman should take us to Palm Beach. He was miserable with heavy cold or hay-fever—catarrh, but Mother did not waver. I could hear her early awake. Hoped to linger until 7.30, but no, that senile restlessness could not be stemmed, and I had to turn out to get ahead of it. We got away at 9.30 and took Lena on our way.

There is a sense of liberation in coming on to the Harbor Bridge, but the view is stupidly obstructed; and what is the logic in being so conceited of ourselves and the Bridge when a screen has to be erected to prevent suicides? Are we so hysterical, or tragically unhappy? Something wrong.

From the crest going down to the Spit, and up and onward the coast line is of inspiring beauty. The rocks and native foliage (where left) are distinctive. It is immeasurably superior to the ugly rubble hills bordering the coast road from Los Angeles to Santa Barbara, over which the Americans enthuse. It is the serrated coast line that is so dignified with its draping of rare shrubs and trees. The bold headlands fill the imagination as though a royal line of gigantic prehistoric prows had drawn up there and become rock at the beginning of time.

The blues of the ocean were divine—an intense day. After noon there were a few white clouds, not enough to filch from brilliance, merely enough to lend variety in the patches of deepening of the Pacific's iridescence. It is the green blue of the distance lending softness to Barrenjoey Lighthouse that gives me ecstasy in beholding. The misty blue of those great prow headlines as they burst upon the gaze is a key of loveliness which unlocks delight in me.

We pulled in to Dee Why, returning for a cup of tea. This is where dear little Dolly Wilson had her quaint cottage overlooking the ocean. My mind goes back half a century with affection and delight in remembering Dolly. When a small child I had evidently got out of order, was being treated by my grandma with a stiff dose of senna tea—with raisins in the bottom as a bribe. I was consigned to the old sofa in the dining room. Perhaps it was wet and I was kept inside against a chill.

How clearly I remember that hand-made old sofa. A long one with rails at each end, one of them turned in the Jacobean way by some energetic and gifted carpenter out of hard intractable wood, and probably with the most primitive tools, concluding with the versatile pocket knife. The sofa had hardwood bars—no deep, sympathetic upholstering for the old pioneers' hard-used bones—and a mattress of flock or wool, and was covered with some flowering material, and had the regulation round bolsters at either end.

To the sofa came Dolly Wilson and devoted the whole day to me. I have remembered that day, its essence will remain with me forever. Dolly must have been a true child lover—one of those unusually gifted with children. I wallowed in being a 'dear little girl' instead of a naughty wicked child that needed to be kept under and on a tight rein. Dolly perhaps was then a mere girl herself, but to my four years was entirely adult. She made me a person of importance, any tendency towards which, as an egotism or a reality, my relatives, on my mother's side particularly, have from that day to this implacably stamped upon.

She gave me a book, the first I ever remember to have received. It was *A Frog He Would A-Wooing Go*, illustrated and with music.[33] To me it was and remains the greatest of all juvenile books—so precious, so indelible are early impressions.

The next time I saw Dolly I was ten years of age. It was on the verandah of the old cottage in Capper St. where E & J Bridle now make their home. I trembled with excitement to think I should see her again. My grandma had indulged me with a pair of gloves—the first pair I recall. They were of thick dark blue silk, and I must needs put them on to honor so great a person. My hot paws got stuck halfway up the fingers and made me feel foolish & stupid as Grannie hailed me forward to greet the guest and to 'behave myself'. I remember sitting in the dusk, my hands imprisoned fatly in the new gloves. I don't remember saying a word and Dolly after a time probably gave me best and got on with her adult talk. I wonder what she thought of my glovedness. I think that meeting must have been a rank unsuccess on both sides, but presently it receded and the early precious memory remained unmarred.

The next meeting with Dolly was during my visit of 1923–24. She came to spend the day, bringing me a bouquet of flannel flowers, angophora (gum nuts), grasses etc., some of them

---

33 In about 1883, G. Routledge in London published *A Frog He Would A-Wooing Go* as part of a series, R. Caldecott's picture books.

protected, but these came from her private allotment. How I revelled in them and she in my pleasure in them. She had picked what pleased me as deeply as Froggie had done.

It was a very happy, successful meeting. I was not able to produce the Amorous Froggie. I had kept it as perfectly as new until my departure from Australia and put it away among my special treasures. These, dear old Mother preserved for me with characteristic competency under years of hardship, but one or two things were missing & they my best beloved. Mother never knew what meant most to any of us, had no sympathy in that way. If she did not appreciate a thing she could not see why it should mean anything to us; and she had kept fairy tales from us as foolish lies and fantasy. What could I see in that foolish book about a frog? It was cluttering up the place & she gave it away to some unknown child. She had kept others that I did not know or need. She knew that Froggie was a pet, but that would not save it—rather the reverse.

January 1936   Poor old Mother's stories are always depressing —not so much for their sordid or unhappy content as by her heavy telling, and the placing of the emphasis. Father had so much wit, so much insight that his lively contes were a riot, and his tragedies moving by illumination rather than by the grim facts.

January 1936   I wrote 'Up the Country'[34] in six weeks—the only time I ever had free. I had had to cancel my passage home owing to a disabling attack of influenza.[35] Doctor said my heart

---

34 Blackwood agreed to publish *Up the Country* in January 1927 and Franklin sent them the manuscript in May of that year.
35 Franklin eventually left London for Australia in June 1927.

was dangerous. I staggered up. I had enough money to last for a few months, living in my tiny shabby room on Brunswick Square doing on two meals a day—boiling a piece of bacon or potatoes surreptitiously on my afternoon tea ring—contriving to do my laundry the same way, and creeping out to the British Museum. Mother would not know for 6 weeks that I was not coming on that boat, another six weeks till her letters would come, torturing me, wringing hope out of me with their gloom.

Free, free I was! In such different circumstances from George Moore & Yeats, but free. No one to dictate to me or to be managed. It was as if a cork popped out and freed stored thoughts. I wrote standing in queues, waiting at theatres, in train waiting-rooms, between the acts in theatres. No one to interrupt me—irritation fled: I recovered from the wounds of 41 Russell Square[36]—Oh the bliss of those days: tales rushed from me like a mill race; but ah! it was short-lived and then Mother's corrosive power began & has never ceased.

January 1936   I talk to her [Mrs Gunter; presumably a neighbour] and consent to walk with her on the homeward way.

How hideous is that way: this common ugly street reflecting the stage of development of its denizens. There is not a thread of beauty anywhere except the glory of the stars, and I am not strong enough for them tonight—they are too distant, too immutable, too pitiless.

I must be failing or too poisoned by fatigue and exasperation now: after my return, facing the heartbreaking tragedy of my

36 Location of the office of the National Housing & Town Planning Council in London, where Franklin had worked from 1919 to 1926.

parents, I have often been sunken in despair, but to emerge and see and smell the red rose at the foot of the garden would restore me: or the perfume of the pittosporums would save me: I could work back from that one spot of beauty.

Another thing in this awful suburb that would lift me was the energy of the electric suburban trains racketing past—the lights of their windows and doors spaced like pictures hung in a line: long ones regularly interspersed by shorter—oblongs and squares. It is the oblongs of light that please me: they are the doors, wide open. The passengers are locked into the New York subway trains, the London Tube, but here the doors are open. People are required without babying to be sufficiently resourceful and self reliant not to fall out. Long may the trains remain thus open.

6 February 1936   Last evening saw Paul Robeson in 'Sanders of the River'. Magnificent. I did not expect him to be so delightful. His rumbling burrs is arresting but not so melodious or appealing as that of Roland Hayes the tenor. But he is one creature in all the world as Clara Butt was in her genre—super. He walked in the consciousness of his superb physique, his personality with great geniality—temperament illuminating his work. Is he all negro? If so a superb example for his race, or can the white man claim a strain in him?

11 February 1936   'Tiburon' by Kylie Tennant (The Bulletin, 1935).

This novel won the S.H. Prior Memorial Prize for 1935. The jacket design is by H.A. Hanke, another prize winner—very bare design, in the Lutyens cenotaph style, of a silo and the steam from an engine at a siding—quite effective.

I do not always agree with these awards, but I hardly think that the Bulletin could have discarded any better manuscripts than this story. I should give it first prize among all the awards including those gold medals bestowed by Melbourne.[37] The (Melb) centenary pair of novels disappear as debris before it. To find its betters one has to go outside awards to 'Such is Life' and Brent books. I wonder how my own hundred years' story[38] measures up beside it. X. Herbert's is bigger and more interesting, more genius and more sprawl, but this is compact— a very good piece of work on the prosaic level. It lacks the emotion and variety of Brent's & Herbert's work, but a writer who could write thus is a tremendous recruit to the real Australian bookshelf—a disciplined craftsman . . .

13 February 1936   Mother & I went to Prince Edward's[39] before going to call for her new spectacles. There was one of Zane Grey's pictures on, indistinguishable from the others. Cowboys swaggering in the stiff gait imposed by chaps. I despise their 40 lb. weight equipment—rocking chairs weighing down the horses. No wonder they call our saddles 'self-emptiers'. There was a stick of a girl on a beautiful piebald but she only sat there: she did not ride. There were galloping cowboys—good shot of cattle swimming a stream —gambling—shooting—as many murders as a cavalry engagement, a rancher jailed as a crook and coming out as a hero and marrying the ingenue—as usual. This is called good wholesome entertainment. I wonder why?

---

37 Awarded by the Australian Literature Society, founded in Melbourne in 1899.
38 *All That Swagger*, which would win the S.H. Prior Memorial Prize later in 1936.
39 A Sydney city cinema.

8 April 1936   Mother & I went to the Sydney Show—lunch in Wilkes' tent. Cold wind & clear. Home about 5.30.

Governor-General had a military escort of band & walkers & mounted lancers—sign of the sinister speeding up of Europe's far-flung war mania.

18 June 1936   Last night shipped in to the F.A.W. [Fellowship of Australian Writers] meeting in Education Bldg. to hear Stephensen, Batchelor and others blither about Australian Culture. Batchelor opened. He is tubby, gross and genial, and oh, Lord how I envy him his rollicking self assurance. He looks like a Eurasian, admits birth in Bombay and pretends to a Spanish grandmother. He has a splendid platform personality, is jovial and glib. He speaks brightly and au fait journalistically, and man-about-townily-picking-every-fellow's-brains-ily. His squat figure is like a Hinder gone fat. His bearing is not refined—his manners are too-too, he has a blatant Oxford bleat, but there is no denying that he can keep his head on his feet & speak colloquially, wittily & fluently. He has attributes for brilliant mediocre commercial success. Tom Inglis Moore, charming, handsome, always jumps into the discussion if only thereby, using 'nice' ideas that would decorate the S.M.H. [*Sydney Morning Herald*].

Batchelor was decidedly popular: Stephensen was valiant but not so assured. Eric Baume, a specious specimen—inaccurate and off the axis in his blither. In the jabber, the essential point of the Australianness of Australian culture was entirely missed. Australian culture must be culture per se, it must eschew any characteristic perfume or accent. Every other culture can have its own personality, but not so Australia's. As an offshoot of English culture, Australian culture must not be too up & coming or it would be offensively Australian. It must in short be neutral, and neutrality is near to mediocrity & mediocrity is good material for the standardisation which is waiting to engulf us, & out of which only giants in independence & originality & spiritual integrity can drag us.

28 June 1936   All this time has elapsed without affording me time and repose to write my letter to you [her father].[40] When I returned from Goulburn I had to catch up ends. Ivy Vernon left. Easter supervened with both Norman and Jack. I had Mother six weeks on my hands unaided again—and she is a handful—2 handfuls—no chink of harmony or repose possible near her. Lena was in St Luke's [Hospital] involving visits. She was here nearly 3 weeks convalescing and her neurasthenic restlessness working with Mother's was enough to make a phlegmatic mollusc into a nervous wreck. Jack also took a chill and involved telephoning and the usual combat with Mother's restlessness & desire to interfere. Eventually Norman & I . . . brought him here, and at the end of a week he was recovered and went to his father down the coast.

In the short harried interstices I never gave up the struggle to get my MSS[41] in final order. Six weeks ago tomorrow, Charlotte Hall arrived as Mother's companion. While she was new enough to hold Mother's attention I plunged to my own work. I have wrought like a fury nine & more hours per day & evening, while the comparative peace would last. It is years since I have had enough unbroken time to do the paging of so long a MS in one slap. I have had many evenings, but latterly had found myself

---

40   Although Franklin's father is dead, she used the epistolary form in order to commemorate him and comfort her mind.

41   The manuscripts of _All That Swagger_.

too exhausted, after the ceaseless interruptions and the constant friction of the day, to do anything but chores such as mending, or light reading, until mother was pleased to retire. The strain of holding out usually left me so overdone at bedtime that sleep was elusive—and so it went.

But after Hall's arrival I had stretches of hours with only small interruptions such as the front door & the telephone, and by feats of application got the MSS away to New York, &, in duplicate, to London. I feel that they are nothing but faults but I have no more strength or time at my disposal. I have finished them at any rate as a satisfaction to character & tenacity. It is like clearing up a building that has been lying around partly done. I then turned to the garden, to which I have given only odd hours. It is still on top of me, but 2 or 3 more onslaughts and I shall be on top of the garden where you tended your plants so tenderly & patiently.

I am free this morning to tell you of 'Stillwater'.[42] I miss you always and ever. A spirit exerts a stronger influence than all else, and you were never unkind. You could not conquer the world financially any better than I can, but you never lost courage as I do. On, on you went on the oil of indestructible hopefulness, and when only spirit was left you, you were richer with each year . . .

On the morning of February 29th (Saturday) Dolly [Wilson] and I rode up to see the old home site!

We went along the ridge to Paton's. The dam—so first-class in its day, so deep and clean of weeds—and the little log canoe in which Edith or Alex would take me for a row!—is now broken away and diminished. The old home has gone entirely, but I had a feast from the mulberry tree . . .

---

42 Miles' parents' property near Goulburn, New South Wales where the family lived from 1889 to 1903.

The quince trees you planted around the orchard fence as a wind-break were cut down a year ago and were in piles awaiting burning—last record of your hard labor with such delicate hands. How you toiled to plant that orchard higher on the slope after the other had been washed away in acre-wide holes after the big flood!

Then up the hill to the old house place. The six or seven (was it more?) messmate saplings from one root, which you had spared as a phenomenon, stand ring-barked and dry-dead and soon will be no more. Twelve years ago I was pleased to note that they still lived and had grown up since our day. We had our clothing line attached to one of them. It was outside the fence running to the corner of the flower garden. You may recall coming one day to my cry. I had looked down expecting to see Ning, my cat, but saw instead that the caress was from a big fat lead-colored snake. You dispatched it with a spade. You remarked that it seemed so friendly, showing no disposition to strike nor any attempt to escape, that it was a pity to kill it.

The vacant house site. I remember, as a child, coming to this house new. A grand large house you built for us, considering your circumstances and the times. Every ceiling was lined with beaded pine boards; soft white pine boards on the floors. It was as dainty as a band box. Even the verandah was similarly ceiled and boarded, & the half walls at each end were also thus lined. You had made of it a fine outdoor apartment where we had afternoon tea for visitors in summer. The posts were of hard wood. These were carefully cut in four sides with narrower facets at the four corners—larger at top & base. I remember the passion vine that clung around one and the half-moss rose that I grew at another. At one end I grew a volicus vine in a pot & trained it along on twine.

I remember my passion for trees, which has not abated. I struggled to grow many kinds and when I planted them out about the hill side you built around them strong, high, neat enclosures to save them from sheep, or other animals. Of the nice young kurrajongs, only one remains, a miserable specimen which was half ring-barked by some young savage with a tomahawk.

I used to propagate my seedlings in a large wooden case of mould from the wood-heap. It was set against the fence on the path at the eastern end of the verandah. One seedling pepper tree grew up in this position, and still survives; but the book-leaf pine which Mother set in the middle of the round flower bed, & which was alive 12 years earlier, has now gone.

The mulberry tree, which you set behind the kitchen in the shelter of the angle formed by the wall of the large projecting fire-place, still lingers. Twelve years ago it carried large splendid fruit. It was a good variety and you had set it with characteristic thoroughness in a deep roomy hole—well mulched, and each root given its full place in the earth. On my former visit it had just been struck by lightning, but only a narrow strip down one side, hardly noticeable. It was a lovely healthy tree, in its barren setting. I gathered some of the berries and carried them to you on a large green leaf—can any receptacle be more beautiful? You had remained in the car with Andy under the knoll near where our beautiful Christmas wattle once grew above the fence of the cultivation paddock. You said that you could not bear to go up to the old place. You probably had suffered more than I during those years when we all were young—and now only 3 remained—and Tal [Hume Talmage Franklin] was so soon to go too . . . The mulberry tree was cruelly struck by lightning a second time so that now only a crumpled stump and a few leaves survive.

The house had long ago been carried away—part of it is now in Andy's home, some of it in his shearing shed or shearer's hut. The bed plates remain. Strange that the frail little pisé dairy survives almost intact with its block which supported the separator. Near-by can be traced the deep dam or surface well so carefully guarded by a stockade and gate; and the platform built out in it for the pump by which we watered the vegetable garden hard by.

I remember that the big flood, which carried away not only the orchard but your big vegetable garden entire, left all kinds of fish in holes . . . on the flats. Some of these we collected in buckets, and there were varieties which the oldest hands had not seen and did not suspect as inhabiting the waterholes. Some beauties, almost orange, with great profusion of fins and whiskers we kept in a tub until washing day, when Mother made short work of them.

I surreptitiously released them in the muddy dam just mentioned. Many years later when a particularly drastic drought dried up everything but the one or two permanent waterholes, in the mud at the bottom of this dam I saw something glinting salmon red and found the same (presumably) five red fish I had released and long ago forgotten. Not a hint of them had ever been seen in the time they had lived there. The water was grey with mud—never clear; but they had never been seen in the clear water of the intermittent creek. I showed them to you and you took them in a bucket of water back to the waterholes from which they had been dislodged . . .

As an eyebrow on the hill remains the little outcrop of rocks, rare, for the neighborhood was deficient in the beauty of rocks, such as abound about Sydney or Talbingo. I cling to these of old as a spot of beauty as they sheltered a few little rock ferns— the only ferns on the place, which was free from even the universal bracken—and, coming from the mountains, I missed ferns sorely. I made this little cluster of rocks support all the dreams of England. It was a castle where knights were bold, & the mistletoe hung in the hall, & the drawbridge went down with a clatter: and there running at an angle across it still was the pace-wide ledge exactly like a crumbling staircase or a miniature ancient ruin . . .

What an insupportable fate must be that of a ghost condemned to wander for ever through old scenes empty and desolate of all human connections . . .

I miss you terribly. Since you no longer are here life is like a house from which the roof has been lifted forever.

1 July 1936   Lovely day—worked in garden—Mother went to Hurstville to a meeting.

In evening I went alone to Savoy Theatre to see the New Theatre League present Clifford Odet's 'Till the Day I Die' & 'Waiting for Lefty'. A gallant & lively effort—full of performance as well as promise. Got home at 1 p.m. [sic; clearly 1 a.m.].

The publication of All That Swagger *in late 1936 put Franklin centre-stage. It was* My Brilliant Career *revisited, and more successful financially. The novel won the S.H. Prior Memorial Prize which had been established the previous year. The prize money was £100 and Franklin received another £50 for serialisation in the* Bulletin *immediately prior to its publication in book form. The novel attracted good reviews and Miles received hundreds of fan letters; 'People seem to be rejoicing like frogs after rain at something really Australian at last', she told Molly Menken, Rose Scott's niece, in January 1937.*[43] *All That Swagger was broadcast on radio in 1942, reprinted regularly in Miles' lifetime and published in England in 1952.*

The novel is based on the life of her paternal grandfather, Joseph Franklin, who is the model for Danny Delacy. Joseph had arrived in Sydney from Ireland in 1839 with his wife Maria (née Hogan)

43 Jill Roe op. cit., p353.

and infant daughter Elizabeth. The novel traces the family through four generations. It is Franklin's tribute to her Irish background and her pioneering Franklin relatives.

15 July 1936   Mr K.S. Prior called up about 'All That Swagger' and said it had won the prize [S.H. Prior Memorial Prize]. In afternoon I went to Mitchell [Library] also to Peace meeting King St. & thence to Shalimar Café to F.A.W. [Fellowship of Australian Writers] meeting—Hilary Lofting & others reminisced about Brennan.

In morning went to Dentist & called on Miss G [Gillespie] on way home.

20 August 1936   Pottered, read MS of 'Cockatoos'.[44] Will take some work to put the 'blood & tears into it'.[45] I skeletoned it out when I was so fatigued & Mother so sapping that it was like working only half conscious.

August 1936   On Wednesday evening 19th I was stealing into the back of the meeting of Fellowship of Australian Writers and was seen by F. Davison, who pounced on me with vim and wanted to make a fuss: tried to make me come up and sit beside Mary Gilmore!!!! I am not yet so far gone in senility as that. I had to be very firm with F.D. I said if he mentioned my name I'd immediately go home. In fact I thought it safer to go there & then. So he was very gracious and promised firmly not to mention

44 The first draft of this novel was written prior to Franklin's departure for the US in 1906. It was published under the Brent of Bin Bin pseudonym in 1954 just before Franklin's death.
45 See entry for 6 and 7 October 1943.

my name, & kept to it, so my flutteration ceased and I sat in peace. Mrs Cassidy on my right, Peace Moore[46] on my left. Bertha Lawson pressing over my right shoulder & Tom Inglis Moore over my left—the room was so crowded.

F.D. is kindly to all, charming in his manner, & his observations have grace & literary quality . . .

Mr Montgomery Stewart gave a fine evening of poems tactfully selected to please as many current members of the Fellowship as possible, & winding up with 3 outside humorous pieces which he rendered very well indeed. One likes him, he was a lovable entertainer, bright & witty & kindly. But memory goes back by contrast to the greater power and originality of the last lecture-recital on poetry that I heard from A.G. Stephens. Mary Gilmore, of course, was well to the fore—her bust in Gallery—paid for by herself—was dwelt upon, & the flowers sent to her birthday & the 2/6 a head party going to be given in September in her honor. (A good idea presents itself: any parties that people think they must give to me—why not give an extra one to Mary Gilmore—she has so many that one more would not worry her, and she has information concerning me that is news to me) . . .

I was utterly dismayed when I knew that I had been awarded the prize. It is a score for the Prior Memorial judges because I took particular pains to put the judges off. I had the MSS at a certain stage of finality but I wanted to read the thing once again & make final changes. There were the whole five copies & I thought how dreadful if there should be a fire in our flimsy cottage & the whole thing go. I had sent a copy to Miss Henry—the third copy or second carbon. It was tied up in used covers of brown paper—shabby to begin & Miss Henry gave it very hard wear. The MSS

---

46 Wife of Tom Inglis Moore.

looked as though they had been to every publisher in Australia. I thought, with a grin, this will put them off, and, as a final touch, I took out my lively title and substituted 'Advance Australia'— the most trite, stupid, chauvinistic title I could think of. Any novel with a title like that will immediately suggest to the judges why it is so worn out travelling around, thinks I, with another grin. In case the house should burn down while I was at work upon them I parked this MS with the Bulletin. They have a fine building there, and in the first competition an article in the papers showed that Mr FitzHenry was the kind of man who could be trusted with anything in office routine. I chuckled when this title Advance Australia [words indecipherable] led all the rest in the printed Bulletin list of MSS received in the competition, so glad I had put no title that could be associated with me.

I was as sure as I am of death & dissolution that my contribution would not even receive honorable mention. I prepared the copies for overseas and got them off a day or two before the prize was announced. I wanted to go to Angus & Robertson with one copy for the Australian edition.

And then one day I was called to the telephone and someone asked me was Captain Bligh there. I could not catch the name at first and then I said you mean the film, 'Bligh of the Bounty'. Then the voice said it was the Bulletin and I said is it someone at the Bulletin office? Then Mr Prior divulged himself, and I said I did not know his voice. He asked did I know anyone named Gillespie. I said yes. Where does he live? Annandale. What is his name? Archie. Do you know Mr M.A.E.Gillespie[47] and Mrs Bligh at Hurstville?

---

47 Mae Gillespie, Miles' former schoolteacher, lived at Hurstville.

I had given my nom de plume as Captain Bligh, and MS to be returned to Mrs Bligh, c/o Miss Gillespie. I knew, of course, as soon as I heard the inquiry, 'Is Mrs Bligh there?' that my MS had not got by as unnoticed as I had intended, & suddenly felt ill with shock: were they going to humiliate me in some way about it?

I said then I could make no admissions or denials over the telephone, that I had endured too much badgering about Brent of Bin Bin to put up with it.

He said there was a manuscript there & they had tracked it to me. I said, why bother about it if it was something by me & there was any doubt about it; throw it out and give the prize to something else. He said unfortunately he couldn't do that. I did not like that word <u>unfortunately</u>—what did it mean?—the antagonism of the Bulletin which deliberately killed my monkey book[48] etc. etc. etc.

Mr Prior was peremptory in his tone and told me to come in that day. I finally said I would go in on the morrow. Next morning I called Mr Prior and asked him had he really telephoned me yesterday. He said yes, of course, that he regretted that he had not asked me to call him back in ten minutes. I said, then it was not some hoax or leg-pull? No, he said, I'd actually got the prize.

---

48 Miles Franklin's *Bring the Monkey: A Light Novel* was published in Sydney by Endeavour Press in 1933. Franklin's comment may refer to the *Bulletin*'s review of 24 May 1933 which recounted the story and made two critical comments but said nothing positive. One comment was that it had 'a thin plot, and the Mayfair wise-cracking is overdone'. The other comment contrasted the weak characterisation to that of *Old Blastus of Bandicoot*, in which the author had 'created so many vital and original characters.' Considering the *Bulletin* was financing P.R. Stephensen's Endeavour Press which published the book, it is a trifle paranoid to say that it 'deliberately killed' it.

But said he, we want a better title. I should think so!!! I admitted that I had written the story, but that I had not intended to win the prize and was much embarrassed by so doing. I agreed to go in and talk it over before Mr Prior left for lunch.

That dreadful prize, I said. I wish I had never written the book, all my views as stated here. Mr Prior seemed a little taken back. I said I had already sent the book to England and America—had received one offer on rough draft which I did not like. He said it would not matter so long as the Bulletin could have Australian book rights and serial. £50 for serial and £100 prize. There's £150 for a start said he, as if the paltry sum were a fortune. He was in a hurry to be gone and so delivered me to T.D. Mutch and C. Mann. Mutch was winningly enthusiastic—said he would give ten years of his life to be able to write some of the pages. Cecil Mann was very anxious to fall in. I had long marked him down as a follower. Mann said there was another manuscript that he liked equally well, did not know how to decide, but on second reading it went off, whereas he liked mine better than at first reading—that at third reading he had liked it better still and looked forward with pleasure to reading it in proof, and was bored with the idea of having to proof-read the other; and so he thus became satisfied with the choice. Mutch, some time previously, had told Ida Leeson that there was one manuscript that towered over everything else and Ida Leeson, by the locality, had suggested that it was possibly my work.

Mutch had to leave and I was left alone with C. Mann. He put his fingertips together and suggested that some paragraphs might have to come out for fear of displeasing the RCs. Good gracious! I thought.

I took the manuscripts home to insert the final corrections. When I got away with the manuscripts, oh, the relief, and I felt that I did not want to publish at all, that I was too nervous to

endure the fuss, whether the book should be a success or failure.
And I felt it was such stuff that it could never interest anyone.
Mr Prior had told me they planned to put extra pages in the
Bulletin and print the story in full in four issues.

When I pondered on this I did not like it. If the public could
get it in four issues for 2/- they would not buy it at 6/6 and I
should have few shillings to collect. So I wrote thus to Mr Prior.
Then they began to call up from the Bulletin and I had to escape.
Mother, of course, made the situation killing to me. I have had
to endure contempt for business failure with my books, but now
as soon as I try to hold off for a while to make up my mind Mother
is at me again. 'I despise people who don't face things.' Continual
jibes in this key. Why don't I go somewhere else so that she won't
have to be bothered with my telephone calls? I intercepted
postman and stifled telephone and shut door in face of reporters
to kill off the notice as much as possible, but still Mother jibed.
I verily believe if she could discredit me as a criminal and she be
a heroine, so noble and perfect as she is, to have the tragedy of
such a daughter as that would be, that she would be better satisfied.

Even the dead fish [Charlotte] Hall cackled and said, 'Wouldn't
you think your mother would be proud of you instead of being
so cross about it?'

'The Cattle King, the Story of Sir Sidney Kidman' by Ion L. Idriess
(Angus & R. 1936).

Already in its 7th edition, and deservedly so, for here is what
the Australian public wants and understands, and here it wholesomely, or at least innocuously, gets it. Those Australians who
have the jejune notion that a worthy novel must be 'a good ad.
for Australia', and who would be mystified by the information
that that fact would defeat the novel as literature, and thus
ultimately also defeat it as 'a good ad. for Australia' can see in

'The Cattle King' an excellent illustration of 'a good ad.' at work. This story—a kind of biographical-novel—patently has been written as a good ad. for Sir Sidney Kidman, and by that purpose has been weakened to boredom for the sophisticated reader.

How one takes off one's hat to Mr Idriess and envies him for his rich store of distinctively Australian material, his familiarity with his continent as a whole. Enviable too is his natural ability to tell a story—to spin a yarn. In Mr Idriess Australia has the son I so often wished might appear. I used to ponder on the Australian yarn and its special characteristics as I have heard it from a hundred old-timers. How they would open their beards & out would spill tragedy, comedy, farce and that entrancing lore which is Australia—ours! our very own distinct and different! and we too unevolved, too much in European leading strings to realise it, to reap it and revel in it as part of our spiritual entity, our national personality. Then along came Ion L. Idriess before it was too late— the very apotheosis of the Australian yarner; book after book, unflagging; simply, vividly, narratively yarned, with all the old yarn spinners' disregard of scholarship.

Now he has tried the biography of a man in that unique field which he so intimately & widely knows, and it fails of distinction because it is a good ad. for Sidney Kidman. A musical comedy star attempted a role in full opera with the result a foregone conclusion.

Idriess has no soaring imagination to water the desert and lighten the darkness. The bush passes before us who know it in an unmistakable canvas but scarcely with sufficient conjuring of the senses to arrest outsiders. It is a book firmly within the frame of Australian actuality and experience. No lift. Normal Australians will not find here anything to alarm or astonish them.

Australian decency, Australian custom has ensured that. That typical Australian decency of neighbor to neighbor, where a neighbor is the most precious thing in life is part of Mr Idriess' equipment. He is too decently Australian to tear out the vitals of a subject he knows & peg up his hide & interpret his private life in terms of mid-European decadence and perverted imaginings of sub-consciousness which have not been so rankly fertile in our disinfecting sunlight, our so sparsely populated spaces. This militates against a tour de force of exhibitionism, and decency is rarely exciting. Biography because of the decency in subject & artist must necessarily be tame in such circumstances.

But what a novel could be written of one of the early squatters —handled without gloves—one of those vulgar, brutal old successes from whom gins heavy with child have swum the Murray in flood to be safe until their parturition was over.

This book has a line on its jacket—'Conquering a Continent'. The limitations of the portrayal are invested in a sense of satisfaction in achievement. Had it been considered as the rape of Australia—rape as distinct from gracious development—it could have been greater. Taken from Australia's angle, the last, lovely, sensitive, continent being denuded of her precious vegetation, beaten back to desert by ignorant, greedy commercialism —such a theme could have had an element of poetic tragedy to lift the book an octave higher, to give it an octave lower in viol notes that transfuse the emotions of the adequate reader of an adequate chronicle. But no, it is a book entirely of surfaces—the surface of the cattle king & his life, the surface of Australia being denuded by his success, which success a former generation termed the Kidman blight.

c. August 1936   So Zane Grey (S.M. Herald July 31st 36) has said, 'The best Australian book I have read is "Up the Country", by Brent of Bin Bin. It is a classic.' Next day (Aug 1st) the S.M.H.

in its second editorial mentioned this, but hedgingly. Brent is still too big for Australian critics. They deprecate him, walk 'round him and peck at him. He must have smiled wryly to know that his countrymen had to be told by a Zane Grey what is a major fact in Australian literature.

A.G. Stephens once said, apropos of another writer, that Brent took this and all other Australian writers in his stride. If this is so, why? Brent certainly is the only novelist of magnitude who is interpreting Australia from the inside, on Australia's own terms without regard to outside conceptions and conventions. He artistically keeps within his Australian field with enough of allusion only to suggest that he is conversant with others. There is a hint of his acquaintance with Freudianism and other philosophies but he refuses to strain Australia through such an alien, for Australia, such a distorting lens. He seems to be one of few who has it in his bones to realise Australia's own personality.

Now for the other major novelists to place beside him, and the reason why they are not entitled to be placed ahead of him.

'Pageant' by G.B. Lancaster. A lovely book, beautifully written, a large canvas full of fine strokes, a book written with sensitive regard for Australian scholarship, but it came after Brent had blazed the track, not before: an early settler rather than an explorer.

Helen Simpson: one of the giants. Perhaps she would have wiped Brent out of his field had she not relinquished it. The lively vitality and inherent understanding of the Australian scene in 'Boomerang' show what we lost, what England has gained. Again in the third division of 'The Woman on the Beast' in a sketchy, impressionistic effort, she indicates what she could have done to take Australia by the back of the collar and shake her to a sense of her asininity, her pathetic enslavement to an old sectarian controversy—a worse importation than the foxes and other noxious weeds. But H.S. left her country for her own great literary success.

[Later note, probably March 1940] on re-reading thought less of Boomerang than I did on first rushing through it. Its melodrama and disjointedness appeared and the Australian chapters were not so good as I first thought them.

All salutations to Henry Handel Richardson, one to whom her fellow writers in England and America pay distinguished homage as a great novelist of all time. Such a tribute can only be discredited or confirmed by time. We must acclaim her for the glory she has directed towards Australia. But her painting of the Australian scene does not well from the bone: one coming here adult could have done equally well, or better. The tributes to her work are for the presentation of the slow disintegration of an intellect—an exile from Europe in Australia—Australia is involved merely thereby. The story could have been set elsewhere with equal effect.

Vance Palmer is an honest self-respecting workman, commendably imbued with the importance of being a man of letters—almost as much so as was Geo. Moore. Palmer, however, retains the decency imposed upon Australians by the neighborliness of a small community. Moore had the ruthless disregard of friendliness, the jungle beast determination to survive like that of wolves around a dead moose where only the strength of ruthlessness can attain prominence. In the fierce struggle to emerge, reticence about friends, self, amours or anything else in the way of decency goes overboard. The result may be richer in the human document sense if not in the human grace and spiritual amenities field. Palmer is so careful that his work is lifeless. It does not remain to haunt the reader. His admirers, as all admirers worked-up by a coterie, apologise for his lack of vitality by imagining that it has been sacrificed to polish. This is nonsense. A blemish can be found in each 1000 words.

'A House is Built'[49] has composition acceptable to the University. It is beautifully written and carefully proof-read. I noted hardly any typographical slips. There are lapses in Australian scholarship— a pity because this is a work of Australian scholarship rather than pulsating inspiration. It rests with dignity on its craftsmanship rather than on its emotion. It is conspicuously lacking in emotion. All its big scenes take place off stage. A crisis is well brewed, the reader turns to a new chapter expecting the curtain to go up on a climax, but it never happens within sight or hearing.

'Tiburon'[50] is a fine novel. It is in the Brent tradition of taking in a whole community—it leans heavily & perhaps unconsciously on Brent's forerunning. The humor & character drawing are immense. The book lacks Brent's sprawl, emotion, illumination, infatuation, but a writer so young who is capable of this piece of work is a notable and most promising recruit to our ranks. How she will develop is of immense importance to Australia.

Louis Kaye's 'Tybal Men'[51] was full of promise but too little of performance. I am unacquainted with his subsequent development.

Hatfield & Idriess are amassing a lot of valuable source material while it is available.

'Landtakers' by Brian Penton shows a determination to be clever and modern at any price. There is a small boy's zest in wallowing in the gruesome. The old pioneering days are presented

---

49 By M. Barnard Eldershaw, published 1929.
50 *Tiburon* by Kylie Tennant, published 1935.
51 Louis Kaye, pen-name of Noel Wilson Norman, *Tybal Men*, 1931.

through the medium of Europe's preoccupation with sadism and other perversions. The weakness of this novel to me in one hurried examination was that by the time I had skipped two-thirds through it, it was still impossible to remember which character was which. But there is power of a kind in the attempt, and, as the writer is only beginning, he is to be watched with interest.

'The Montforts' by Martin Mills[52] had some fine émigré chapters. The writer has since become a permanent émigré and is enlivening London literary life and finding appreciation there.

[Later note] March 1940. On re-reading 'The Montforts', it is much better than I had remembered. It is perhaps the best expatriate novel we have, as 'Back to Bool Bool' is the best repatriation one. The writing in 'The Monforts' is pretty good despite the plentiful use of <u>very</u> and a haziness about pronoun & which is its antecedent. But there is one thing about the book, give it the closest attention and it is impossible to disentangle or to remember who the characters are. They are and remain little more than a list. This time I read from the American edition and in this had the family tree, but found it difficult—in fact impossible to elucidate. It is, in this edition, entitled 'The Madeleine Heritage'. Why the American publishers make many of their changes in names when they are not for the better is beyond me—this novel is a case in point. One character, I forget which already, brought home many pairs of boots. That is a good touch. I brought back 4 pairs & had 3 other pairs same origin—now nearly all gone & I can now find nothing that is comfortable though I have paid such prices as I never dreamed of paying in USA or London.

---

52 Martin Boyd's early fiction was published under the pseudonym Martin Mills. *The Montforts* was published in London in 1928 and in America under the title *The Madeleine Heritage* the same year.

The man who wrote 'Herridge of the Swamp' and 'Strawbane of the Mulberry Hills' seems to have disappeared.[53]

Christina Stead is a prominent fact as an Australian. Her 'Salisbury Tales'[54] has the massivity & dullness, & preoccupation with perversions of the Teutons. 'Seven Poor Men of Sydney' interpreted Sydney in terms of the cliques of Bloomsbury. Sydney is described antagonistically, as by an alien, one not spiritually harmonious with environment, by one who loves her not—infatuation missing. One who had Sydney in her blood un-prejudicially, so that it was more basic than any detractions, just or otherwise, would betray her love. Deepest & most deserved castigation would be shot with gleams of infatuation.

F.D. Davison is a lyrically artistic major fact: he has the proper infatuation for Australia. His works so far are pocket editions. They lean more towards the picture small enough for a private wall than to great canvases demanding the wall of a public gallery. The miniature & the mural must each be judged in its own class. His staying powers are on the way to fulfilment and I hope in the direction of the born insider's preoccupation with Australia.

But nearly all of these writers are past or on the meridian. Some of those who are not are permanent & irredaimable émigrés.

Brent must finish his related series so that we can see where & how he stands, and so that he can be placed or displaced as the biggest fact among current fictioneers who are attempting to interpret Australia in her own terms from the inside. His 'Back to Bool Bool' is practically the only novel portraying the modern

---

53   William Gosse Hay, 1875–1945. *Herridge of Reality Swamp: A Novel of the Convict Days* was published in 1907 and *Strabane of the Mulberry Hills, The Story of a Tasmanian Lake in 1841* was published in 1929.

54   The reference is to *Salzburg Tales*, first published 1934.

THE DIARIES OF MILES FRANKLIN 59

Australian scene with scope and insight. There is no major critic
to replace A.G. Stephens and recognise this. Practising reviewers
are all too timid. They want to hear of what outsiders say of him.
This is known only in stray remarks because he was published
surreptitiously. Helene Scheu-Reisz of Vienna acclaimed him as
one of whom Australians were justly proud because he had written
the great Forsyte Saga of his undiscovered literary continent.
C. Hartley Grattan referred to Brent's tremendous Chronicle.
London Punch acclaimed him in delicious verses. The Bulletin
was too scared to mention him. His countrymen walk around
this big independent bird & peck & cavil at him, & by their
detractions expose their own limitations while waiting for the
tinkle of the London bell wethers to change their tune.

29 November 1936   Mother on her old warpath of wounding.
Willie Gibson called in morning & Ruby in evening. Worked in
garden in afternoon to calm my nerves as Mother had put all
ability even to write a letter out of me.

4 December 1936   Went to Hordern's[55] at 4 to sign books.
Miss West, Mr Smith, Mr Hartley, Mr Fenton & Goldstein (head

---

55 Anthony Hordern & Sons Ltd, Sydney department store. This must have been
one of the first organised book signings in Australia. In her letter of 20 April
1949 to Angus & Robertson, Franklin stated that Ida Leeson had recommended her as the first author in a series. She said that when she arrived there was
a queue of between 60 and 80 people, and she netted the store £30 profit for
her two hour session. (Ref: Angus & Robertson archives, Mitchell Library, ML
MSS 3269)

of restaurant) were all very nice. The only time I have ever been
pushed by a stunt & it was wonderful how the book sold.

_c. 1936_   Feeling as if my heart was dead, so went with Mrs
Fogden to movies—'Geronimo' & 'Ninotchka' . . . 'Ninotchka' is
unrelieved rubbish. Tries to be comedy-farce but doesn't get above
slapstick & is intended as a broad insult to Soviet Russia. Garbo
as Ninotchka is an example of what can be done by advertising,
in reversing the glare of the spotlight & the subject being rendered
sacred by seclusion. They have built up a personality as a queen's
is engineered, & Greta G has no more in her than a queen, but
the public has been bitten. She is a very plain awkward woman
too skinny to act peasant roles but has all the peasant gaucherie
& ungainliness.

12 January 1937   Well, yesterday at 1 p.m. I met C.H. Grattan
by his invitation at the Claremont, Darlinghurst and had lunch.
Then retired with him to his flat at 43 Elizabeth Bay Road, where
he kept me talking until 5.30, though I suggested leaving several
times . . .
    Here is a fine intellectual capacity—clear-cut, self-willed, self-
organized to reach its goal. He is not a conformer: he will not
pander to those in authority to get to the top of good things. He
stated that it does not matter what a man is personally: it is the
work that he leaves behind that will count. But, thinks I, he can
also leave behind the stink of his misdoings—like Byron. This—
C.H.G's—is the sophisticated metropolitan idea. Here, our
environment still keeps us too far from specialisation—from
selection. We still have to live more in the round, even if it is only
as charwomen and rouse-abouts. We still have to be complete

men and women: we cannot hide in the jungle of mass population, and develop one or two facets only.

He is a small fattish man with fine, almost cinema features, a really beautiful brow, clear, straight-gazing brown eyes without self-consciousness or shiftiness, a too small mouth (which my mother calls peevish) with his own teeth. This alone would set him apart in a British assemblage as a beauty. Handsome hands, well kept and not disfigured by work like mine and Bishop Burgmann's. Legs rather bandy—biggish bottom.

He has escaped exhibitionism but not cynicism. I hope he is not a post-war pervert, like some of the London intelligentsia. If his spiritual reach matched his intellectual grasp he would be a giant.

He had many grouches, in fact he was more grizzle than grace. Funny points were that he had written me that he wanted to be let alone and to meet all sorts, even the young men that nurse a drink in a bar. Now he is cross because he sees nothing else. He is sick of meeting a useless clutter of people . . .

He is wearied by meeting so many mature and elderly people and hankers for those of his own age and similar interests.[56] He talks much of his youth in the way women do when losing it. He has more grey hairs in his head than I, and many more in his soul. According to our primitive standards it is womanish for a man so to insist on his youth—part of the she-mannishness of sophistication. I remember W.J. Turner practising youth when he was middle-aged. Post-war cynicism produced many shop-worn puppies who were blatantly senile in adolescence, and others who began to insist on their youth in middle age . . .

C.H.G. accepted Dal [Stivens] as young and of promise. I said he was imitative. C.H.G. adduced that all young artists were.

---

56 Grattan was 34.

Then he said he considered Penton the most hopeful of the Australian writers, he was young, only thirty (I believe he is more), had done good books and would do more . . . At any rate C.H.G. likes P. best of anyone he has met yet. I deduce that Penton is cultivating C.H.G., but poor Penton looks to me so evil that he will put his foot in it presently.

At this moment in our discussion Mrs Penton called . . .

She was patently <u>distrait</u> to see me intimately with C.H.G. I was very friendly and at ease with her. She tried to recover equanimity and respond to me, said she wanted to ask me a question, which of course would be was I Brent of Bin Bin. I said jocularly not while Mr Grattan was listening, but that some day we'd meet alone and she could ask me what she would. I said to tell her husband that I had meant to speak to him on Saturday night but that he had disappeared, that it was affectation for people who knew each other well by sight not to speak. She delivered her errand and went speedily without recovering poise. I asked C.H.G. why she should be so flabbergasted to find me there. He said it was because I referred to her husband being at the dinner on Saturday night, from which she was absent, while he had another female companion. But he had to be there to move the resolution against censorship (which I seconded) and could have made that his 'alibi'. I rather believe that Penton and his crowd have been decrying me to C.H.G. as the lowest limit, he probably aiding them with a 'debunking' stone or two, and then to see me there so intimate was bouleversing . . .

Mrs Penton had called on behalf of K.S. Prichard, who summoned him to dinner that evening. C.H.G. was to dine with V.P. [Vance Palmer] but said he would take him also to Susannah. I was excluded.

C.H.G. referred to K.S.P. as a fine woman but as utterly foolish and behind the times in taking up the outmoded proletarian attitude on literature. Said her Saturday night speech was dead except for the list of men's names who were ready to stand with her on the censorship question. I also valued her statement of how little she got on her books—a matter which should not be blinked and suppressed by writers in a genteel pretence of having more than they are paid.

He has seen Kylie Tennant, author of 'Tiburon', says she is a homely little thing, and politically involved . . .

He mentioned that M. Barnard Eldershaw ('I can never tell those two apart') had looked at him coldly on Saturday night and that was because of his review of their book. I said surely not, it was merely that they had colorless manners, one by preciosity the other being really proper and academic. He said it did not matter, that 'A House is Built'[57] was valuable in its place but not of great importance and those two have fired their bolt—will do no more. He agreed with A.G.S. [A.G. Stephens] that K.S.P. is an imitation of Lawrence, especially in her short stories.

When I talked of 'Capricornia'[58] and said the English rejected it because it was so Australian he asked was it as Australian as 'Such is Life'.[59] I said no, but it was as Australian as 'All That Swagger'. He said '"All That Swagger" is not particularly Australian, it is universal'.

He has not yet been able to see anything in Brennan (neither can I); also considers Hugh McCrae an 'exploded balloon'. I believe this may be true—without having read him—because of his disciples.[60] Baylebridge, yes, something there but so removed from

---

57   M. Barnard Eldershaw *A House Is Built*, 1929.
58   *Capricornia* by Xavier Herbert was published on Australia Day 1938. However, it had existed in typescript and later in proof since *c.*1933 and had been rejected by several British publishers and twice by Angus & Robertson.
59   Novel by Joseph Furphy written under the pen-name Tom Collins and published in 1903. Much admired by Franklin.
60   One of whom was Franklin's bête noire, Mary Gilmore.

contemporary form and involved that he has not yet made up his mind. Has not yet bothered to get in touch with N.L. [Norman Lindsay] because he dislikes him so intensely. Thinks that B.P. [Brian Penton] shows N.L.'s pernicious influence . . .

He says what we suffer is a dearth of facts scientifically assembled to support our windy idealism. This is a good and penetrating thrust. But I led him on to enlarge it and felt he knows the world by facts. Facts, facts. Yes, but a factual world that discounts the dream world would never rise above the dust. There never yet was a fact but it was hatched from the brain of a dreamer. Take flying. Think of the facts that were adduced of old to show that iron ships could not float in water, let alone in air! If the winged dreamers were not enslaved by the wingless grabbers—well, that would be paradise, and there never will be heaven in this dimension, for the dreamers are forever checked by the grabbers whose flag is facts. They know how to plunder and exploit and then when gorged and dyspeptic cry to the dreamers for comfort and diversion.

14 February 1937   Grey cool day. Norman took Mother, Jack [Franklin] & Mrs Wilkinson for a drive after lunch. I was hoping for an hour's peace but in comes Ruby Brydon—never a moment with the house of peace now. After tea Norman departed & I went to town, called on Metta [Lampe] at Metropole [Hotel], thence to hear Mrs Holman at Murray's on Spanish Relief & back to Writers at 9 p.m. when I got tail end of discussion on Brodziak pornographic play. Brodziak looked like a Jew who had been reared in a basement & suckled on cigarettes.[61]

---

61   This could refer to Leon Brodzky, 1883–1973, an Australian who spent most of his life in the US. He published the play 'Rebel Smith', set in Queensland, in New York in 1925 under his pseudonym, Spencer Brodney.

There was of course another writer, very much centre-stage in Sydney's, and Australia's, literary community at this time. Mary Gilmore, now 71, fourteen years older than Franklin, had had a long career as a poet and journalist and social activist. She had, at least in her own imagination, been everywhere, known everyone and done everything. Two books of reminiscences had been published in 1934 and 1935 with much success. In February 1937 she hit the jackpot when she was made a Dame Commander of the Civil Division of the Order of the British Empire. This was announced in the New Year's Honours List which was published on 1 February. It was the first time that such an honour had gone to an Australian literary figure. Mary Gilmore, DBE would rankle Franklin just by being Mary Gilmore, DBE. The dislike was not mutual. Gilmore seems blithely unaware of Franklin's scathing opinion of her. To rub salt in the wound, Franklin herself was offered an honour in April 1937 but, unfortunately, it was the OBE, which she declined. For all Franklin's excoriations of the 'English garrison', she would have snatched Miles Franklin, DBE with both hands.[62]

2 *March 1937*   Upon the urgent request of Mrs Dobbie I dropped in late to the Women's Club to the reception to Mary

---

62   Morris Miller, scholar and bibliographer, wrote to Prime Minister Joseph Lyons in October 1934 suggesting that Australian writers be included in the Honours List. He suggested two names: Mary Gilmore, 'worthy of being placed high up in the British Empire Order. She is one of the grandest personalities in Australia today and is fittingly recognised as a national poet'; and Bernard O'Dowd, 'the doyen of Australian poets'. Lyons replied in December saying that O'Dowd had refused an offer of a knighthood and that he, O'Dowd, had thought that Gilmore would also refuse an honour. Miller, in November 1935, suggested A.B. Paterson as the only other writer at present 'worthy of higher recognition'. He thought Miles Franklin worthy of a lesser award. O'Dowd's view that Gilmore would not accept an honour delayed her award. Paterson was given the CBE in 1939. (Ref: Mitchell Library Aa93/1)

Gilmore, Dame. It started at 2.30: I arrived at 3.30, and slipped in to a back seat, despite urgent calls to go in front. Mary Gilmore was on the platform saying that they had spoken of things she had done that everyone knew about; she would now tell them of many things she had done which they did not know about. It seemed to my half-listening ear that most of these achievements were might-have-beens. 'I could have been the first woman to stand for Parliament', also something to do with the University Senate, and so on. Then Mrs Dobbie said a very celebrated woman had slipped into a back seat as was her way (applause), but they would like Miles Franklin to say a few words. I said I had not heard what had gone before but had called to congratulate Mrs Gilmore in person because, having more letters than I could deal with, I had omitted to write to her.

This dameship, I said, reminded me of one of the first; that given to our darling Melba of everlasting fame. It was in 1919 when the opera season at Covent Garden was resumed after the dreary war years. Melba was the great star. People waited in queues incredible hours for a seat and at last there were cries of Dame Nellie! Dame Nellie! whereupon an old man remarked 'Gor's truth! have they dames in opera now as well as in pantomime!'

I often thought, only that dear King George was incapable of unkindness, he had taken this double-edged way of punishing women for plaguing for titles of their own, as it was such a terrible old name. However, writers get very little recognition in Australia, and as Mrs Gilmore had had the fortitude to win this title I knew she would have the fortitude to wear it and I hoped she would live long and happily enough not only to wear but to reclaim it . . .

On March 4th Mrs Dobbie rang up to thank me for my speech. Said it was the only breath of brightness in the afternoon. Said she M.G. should have been created Dame Ananias Gilmore, that she was a dreadful, <u>dreadful</u> woman, that her egotism amounted to mania. That there wasn't a bit of truth in her claims to notoriety and that her reminiscences[63] were all lies and stuff, also her work for Aborigines, and that no one ever knew what had become of Mr Gilmore.[64] Everyone says the same, that she broke up the new Australia,[65] and I know how she walked along the street with me telling me stories of myself that never happened, also how she wrote to Brent of Bin Bin and said she would help his book, and I heard her from the public platform depreciating him in favor of Dorothy Cottrell. Well, if she is finally rated by her yarns and verses and not by her medals and busts and painted portraits, posthumous justice will be done, but at present she and the crowd she dominates are prolonging mediocrity in our artistic development. What is one to do? Fret not thyself because of evil doers.

22 April 1937   Had fire in sitting room to listen to Lottie Lehmann concert and 'Black Horse', V.P.'s [Vance Palmer] drama.[66] Mother noisy & interrupted at all crucial moments in the singing. Went to sleep during play so there was peace.

26 April 1937   On Saturday afternoon 24th, when I got home from the Propeller League's meeting the appended telegram was waiting for me.

---

63 *Old Days: Old Ways*, published in 1934, and *More Recollections,* published in 1935.

64 Mary Cameron married William Alexander Gilmore in May 1897. They had one child, William Dysart Cameron, born 21 August 1898. In 1911, William went to North Queensland in pursuit of economic security, first working on his brother's property. He was joined by his son in 1914. Reunions with Mary were rare, neither husband nor son attended Mary's investiture as a Dame of the British Empire in 1937, and both died in 1945.

65 William Lane's Utopian community established in Paraguay in 1893. Mary Gilmore went there in 1896. The accusation is a canard.

66 Vance Palmer's play, *Black Horse*, was published in 1924.

To: Miss Stella Miles Lampe Franklin Grey Street Carlton
Sydney
Please communicate with official secretary Government
house Sydney matter
personal and urgent
Military & Official Secretary to the Governor General

I telephoned the Military and Official Secretary to the Governor
General. He said could I come in next day. I said no. Could he
see me this evening? He said decidedly not, he had five Anzac
engagements. I had one myself. Then he said Monday. I said could
he make it Tuesday, or couldn't he tell me on the 'phone. Much
too private for that. His tone became ever so slightly, hardly
perceptively peremptory, 'After all, this is a command.'

He said he had 250 people to see on Monday morning from
eight o'clock onward and did not want to keep me waiting. I said
then he was the busy one; to name the hour. He named 10.30,
and instructed me to come to the side door and ask for the
Military and Official Secretary to the Governor General.

Off I went this morning. On the way I took a look at the
Cenotaph and the Anzac offerings. How cleverly sentiment is
pumped into the man of war. Macquarie Street beautiful with
its feet in the sea.

Surely Government House, in a soft cosy small sheltered way
must be one of the most beautiful sites in the world for a home.
Not a soul about, no one at the gates, no sign of life in the
gardens—a solitary policeman in the distance striding away, who
never even looked at me. No one in the little house farther from
the entrance. No one anywhere. An enchanted castle could not
have been more deserted. That was surely a record in informality,
the proud symptoms of a free people.

Found a very side and very inconspicuous door, so informal
was it that it was open and two men inside, one working at a

desk and the other standing about. The one seated had a narrow forehead and hair on end like bristles and looked like a non-com in mufti, the other like a very unstylish Johnny of about shop assistant weight, (i.e. London shop assistant) but kindly.

Is this the side door?

Yes.

I was asked to appear here at 10.30 and ask for the Official and Military Secretary. My name is Franklin, I'm sorry I forgot my cards.

That doesn't matter at all. The secretary is engaged for the moment.

That did not matter, said I, and sat down and continued to read an article in 'Harper's'.

The young man announced my arrival and in less than a minute I was ordered upstairs. The young man took me with gentle remarks up a delicious little side stairway into another side room. There was another man with the Secretary. The Secretary waved me out with the young man into yet another side room and my chaperon talked amiably about the beauty of the weather.

The man ahead of me was telling the Secretary how to send his communications to the newspapers—two in the morning and one (the Sun) in the afternoon, and not to the Labor paper[67] as they would not want it. I wonder if this is true and who was this man to state that the Labor paper would not want this matter. The Labor paper might not want to print much of such stuff but should certainly want to receive it the same as other papers to see if it contained important matter. Labor is not anti-governmental.

'Well, Miss Franklin,' said the Secretary. 'Come in and sit down—a pity to bring you all the way from—now where is it that you live?'

'Carlton.'

---

67 Probably the *Australian Worker.*

'And the street and number?'

'26 Grey Street, but Carlton will find me.'

He referred to a dossier. 'You are Stella Maria Lampe Franklin, are you?'

'Yes, those are some of my names.'

'Quite like royalty, isn't it? Well, Miss Franklin, in connection with the coronation His Majesty wishes to make you an Officer of the British Empire—that is to give you the O.B.E.'

Whew, when I recall the disrepute of this decoration among people on active service 1914–18! It was a synonym for failure, incompetence. The unimportant senile nincompoops were fobbed off with it. And I was 'commanded' to Government House for the first time to be thus insulted!

There was no need to offer me anything. I have never put myself forward officially, have never touted in any shape or form. Most Australians deserve this sort of thing for their servility. What complicates the matter in this instance and also makes it particularly insulting is that Mary Gilmore, who has been a most egregious tout and self-booster and politician [and] has also written some verses and undistinguished memoirs (which in all parts that I can check are unreliable), has been given a higher order, and it may be thought that it was for her literary work.

I was quite passive for a moment and then asked, 'From whom does this emanate, by whose recommendation is this offered me?'

'Oh, it's wonderful what we know—you know, when people do good work—your good work has been taken note of.'

It had been clear to me in the second time of asking my name that he hadn't the slightest inkling that it might have been as a writer that I had operated and was summoned there.

'I cannot understand it,' I said in a very low voice, for I was depressed into my boots. 'I have never put myself in the way of such a thing. I know no one at Government House, have never received any notice or recognition from that quarter, and I don't know a soul in the Federal Government.'

'It's wonderful how people take notice of good work. What is your principal work now?'

'Looking after my mother principally. I am a recluse and so wish to remain. I am not able for many shocks since I acquired an active service heart in Serbia.'

'You were on active service?'

'Oh yes, under the British Red Cross with the Serbs.'

'Oh, then it is your work there.'

He was being automatically kindly to another of these servile colonials who run around after baubles like foundlings for a silver coin.

'Well then, with your approval—His Majesty could not confer this without your approval.'

In light of this gentle informality I hated to be unfriendly, but it was no use, I was outraged right through by the Australian jacks-in-office failure to be self-respecting in demands for recognition of true Australianism.

'As you are so busy,' I said, rising, 'I need not take up any more of your time. I refuse.'

'You refuse!' he said in the gentle-to-colorlessness [of] English surprise. 'May I ask why?'

'Because to accept would be to reduce letters to the level of charity work.'

'Is that quite definite?'

'Absolutely. I'm insulted and wounded right through. I don't know when I have been so hurt. Do you want me to write my refusal?' I was longing to leave a limerick with him.

'Oh, no, not at all! It is entirely confidential.'

'I don't see why it should be. Everyone knew that Asquith refused a peerage, also Gladstone.'

'I must insist that this is entirely confidential.'

Of course this system of bribing boobies to uphold caste depends on muzzling the recalcitrant with blither of 'good form'. If it were known how many worthwhile persons refuse these brands their power would be lessened.

'Well, I waive a discussion on the expediency of that for the present,' I said. 'In this case I <u>want</u> it to be secret. I don't want <u>anyone</u> to know of the terrible insult I have received. I hope you <u>will</u> treat it as confidential.'

He promised in the mild inoffensive English way that it was entirely between him and me.

I wonder what complexion he will put on it—if he is not entirely indifferent.

Just think what might happen [to] a similarly recalcitrant mere female before the officer acting for the crown (State or Dictator) in Russia, Germany or Italy! I love and appreciate the democratic free manners of my own dear native land, but I want to know who was responsible for this blunder against Australianism.

The highest Order to a Mary Gilmore for literature is to demote, to devalue the Order, or, on the other hand, to impale Australian literature on the spear of its own mediocrity. And yet there can be such a difference in standards that Sir Robert Garran could observe to me <u>apropos</u> Mary Gilmore's decoration, 'You must feel with this recognition that Australian literature and Australian women have come into their own.'

Gadzooks!

I hope the Military and Official Secretary of the Governor General is really as quiet and indifferent as he seemed and that I shall not be slyly penalised in some way. If so, there must presently be a struggle by all genuine self-respecting Australians to repudiate these petty honors given out to please the sycophants, and no decoration taken except one really and honorably Australian.

I turned back to the Secretary and shook hands and said, 'You can't help it. It is not your fault that the only time I ever came to Government House I should be so hurt, but I must discover who is responsible.'

He again assured me it was confidential.

I wish I had a friend to whom I could go and be sure both of truth and judgment in asking am I merely conceited to resent being rated lower than Mary Gilmore as an Australian litterateur.

In any case, supposing I am so low in the scale as to be lower than Mary Gilmore's slipshod verses and lying autobiography, no rubbishing official had the right to attempt to brand me so, publicly.

Though I should be in letters so low,
Still I resent this attempt of a foe
And can't be commanded
Like a sheep to be branded
The public my rating to show.

I came down and out, and the two men in the side-door office were so perfunctory in response to my 'good morning!' that it must have been unnecessary and excessive formality on my part to offer it.

I re-emerged into the exquisite, the adorable day and walked away from the lovely, deserted silent place. Not a soul of any sort was to be seen during my retreat. The sunshine was so exhilarating, so endearing that a sense of humor restored my equilibrium. There was something deliciously absurd in the whole incident, that is, if it has no grave aftermath. Perhaps I do dishonor to our freedom and democracy to feel this slight suspicion. I wonder.

Frank Clune was one of the most successful and prolific Australian writers of the 1930s. He was active in the Fellowship of Australian Writers and he and his wife Thelma were friends of Miles Franklin. In June 1937 they set off by car to Adelaide driving through the towns of the Murrumbidgee, which for Franklin was 'my country as Wessex in England was called Hardy's'.[68] From Adelaide they flew to Alice Springs and back again and drove home along the coast via Melbourne. Although Clune made many trips researching his books, this journey seems to have been a holiday and an opportunity to give Franklin a respite from caring for her mother, who by this stage needed constant supervision.

8 June 1937   Frank Clune and Thelma arrived at 8.30 a.m. & had cup of cocoa in Mother's room. Set out at 9 o'clock. Showers in morning—ran out of rain a little after Goulburn. Halted by wayside for a snack in car. Retained my opinion of Bowral and Moss Vale as shabby arrested-mental-development looking townships . . .

9 June 1937   Lovely hilly far-rolling country between Cootamundra & Junee, with lovely clumps of box. Occasional silos . . . Junee had an attempt at gardens in middle of the street—white cedars and splendid kurrajongs.

In afternoon left for Wagga Wagga. Beautiful country—rolling and wheat in all stages of advancement making the landscape a park, dotted with kurrajongs and occasional box. The sky to our left made a glory on the horizon—mountains of tinted snow—cauliflower cumulus or thunder heads—and that liberating eternity of light, which is Australia's. The trees along the wide rich lanes were a park-like avenue devoid of underbrush. The young trees shaped like rounded puffs of dark clouds.

Arrived in Wagga over rich flats and across the Murrumbidgee, grown old & wider. Had afternoon tea about 4.30 in a café, and

68   Jill Roe op. cit., p364. Letter of 22 July 1937 to Carrie Whelan.

F.C. drove us along the main street and put up at Bellair's Commercial Hotel. Dreadful turkey for dinner and unpleasant seat in middle of room where the draft of a defective door played upon the victims in line with it. Noted an awful piggy fat young man who gorged—smitten on a poodle-like wench with coarse legs and a falsely delicate face—well-designed to survive with & hoodwink such as he . . .

Light glared through my transom (such a nicety as a shade or glass would be deemed unnecessary) and there was hot & cold running water in the bedrooms, so sleep, of course, was impossible to anyone except the deaf or very, very insensate. Went to bed at 11 and to sleep after 2 a.m., when the gurgling in water pipes died down . . .

13 June 1937   In these drumbuilt houses [in the town of Ganmain] noise is inevitable. Close a door normally and it reverberates to the farthest corner. Add to this the procedure of people who have no conception of any need for comfort or refinement, people who would think any demand for it by anyone not in extremis, or not his Majesty or a baby, an abnormality amounting to perversion.

For one man to catch another in bed at any hour after 6 am is a vast and evergreen joke to be celebrated by Falstaffian guffaws and chiacking as though he might have been caught enjoying baby's pap or powdering his nose or putting his hair in silk rags to make curls.

This is all good training for more Gallipoli heroes. Men thus trained could be expected to outstrip other warriors, as the Russian ballet has been able to beat all other soldiers of Terp[s]ichore through intensity of training & segregation from other experience. But to train warriors to out-do other war lunatics of Europe— is that the only ideal permissible to an Australian?

16 June 1937   Called on Father Hartigan ('The Boree Log'). He received us with friendliness and we had a pleasant chat & the usual photographic entertainment. Father H. is a fine physical specimen—makes a commanding padre. Likes Australian literature within the limitations of his generation & the Paterson School (lesser). I was delighted to find that he is one of the Brent of Bin Bin suspects. He looks the part magnificently. He said he had received letters asking had he not collaborated with me in these books, if he was not solely responsible . . .

. . . and thence off to Leeton. Pretty Murrumbidgee country, rich plains and little ridges. Endearing number of native pines preserved in beautiful groves & extensive scrubs, as it was at Uncle Gus's [Lampe] thirty years ago. We were in the irrigation area of canals and drains. Leeton was approached through lanes of trees. Everywhere the sugar gums (poor conies among our trees, but better than nothing, & a surprise to find even these among a people so barbarous & suicidal in regard to trees) with foliage like painters' puffs of green clouds on the end of long straight boughs (result of pollarding) with a dado of light between the upper & lower branches—the saplings as usual of spear pointed grace.

Here was a laid-out town which became beautiful as we neared, because it is furnished with lovely kurrajongs—aristocrats— good trees of individuality & native character. Ah, I had forgotten —here is a town laid out by the great W.B. Griffin—now immortal. No wonder it was unusual, and, alas, so rare in New South Wales.

We drove to the Hydro Hotel, commanding as a gentleman's country seat, built on an old castle site—suggested by the two great mediaeval towers that remain. But this is a newly inhabited land and the towers are exactly like the bastion silos of dub grey mud, but these on an eminence are separated like a noble gateway and ornamented with gothic frills—which enhance them, redeem them from silo plainness like curls rescue a girl.

Thelma introduced me to the grandeur of the hotel's new furniture and ecclesiastical hall carpets and colossal balconies and verandahs & laundry arrangements . . . Thus to lunch.

This was a lovely hotel but had its blemishes. The hall or lounge light is so mediaevally dim that one could not see to read by it, the dim religiousness of the light probably made Creet[69] forget where he was & thus the carpet of fleur-de-lys & crosses on a red ground, & the writing room upstairs was without a fire except in the evening. Fires & radios & all such lures are to draw victims to the bars. Frank says if he ever finds a light of more than two candle power in a hotel he will photograph it. It should be given a jubilee medal. Added to this night dimness, hotel builders go out of their way to induce day darkness. At Ganmain —one common example—Hydro another—the windows in sitting rooms were darkened so that to see one had to open them (French lights) & have a fierce cold winter draft . . .

At 2.15 p.m. Mr Lindsay Black came & drove Thelma & me out to see Jim Gordon (Jim Grahame of the Bulletin) and wife and family . . .

Mr Black took us also to his house and to my surprise and intense delight a curlew trotted out to meet me. It was as though a fairy had come to make me happy. That sweet darling moved like a spirit. And it seemed as if its delicacy must be endangered by its boisterous companions, two fox terriers. Not so, it sleeps with one of them and when they are too lively chitters & remonstrates and they obey as if it were a human voice.

---

69 Pierre Creet, hotel manager.

The sweet creature let me put my hand on it and I revelled in its fairy gait on its long legs and tiny feet, its magic-lantern eyes & laced breast. So silently he trots I'd fear to step back & break one of his delicate legs. And then as if to indulge my infatuation he opened his beak and gave one wail—only one, but enough to bring back the orchestras of my childhood when nights were delicious with the curlew music. 'A thousand curlews to wail an angel requiem.'

18 June 1937 Arrived at Griffith . . . Scenic Hill is a bird sanctuary and public picnic ground. Hope the birds don't mind such a contradiction in facts. It is a lovely plateau covered with bleached natural grasses & pines extending like a tongue into Riverina plains. Far back to the south east was the Governor's-Hill contour of McPherson Range cupping a mighty sweep of fertile irrigated plains. Where once the lonely, ill-paid boundary riders (and the swaggies if any wheel their blueys out back today—or they are old age pensioners & live in colonies of shacks instead of solitary tents) did their 6000 acre paddocks under one or two squatters now is a closer-settled area lined with irrigation canals and smaller drains and water wheels. The salt bush & myall have given place to Europe's citrus trees. All-weather (alleged) roads run where Tom Collins' bullockies once strained beneath the lacerating thong to an ensanguined libretto. There are signs of advancing municipal organization in the long avenues of sugar gums & kurrajongs. The ibises, the shags, the small grey herons find permanent water. As the scene darkened, homestead lights twinkled over a vast panorama of homesteads. Men attempting to cultivate rather than to sack the land—reapers rather than wreckers. And everywhere the bleat and blare of radios where once plovers & curlews wailed. Another age, another story on the palimpsest of time. Explorer, surveyor, pastoralist, agriculturalist, a people now set to a different tempo, another rhythm, but no more reason. Whither Australia? The magic, mournful, merry, glamorous land . . .

. . . we left for Hay.

A rolling season, a lowering sky opposed to richly muddy earth as we departed. The road was threatening and sloppy & grey, a grey flat world showed weirdly in Ponty's lights.[70] But as I could not see it clearly I just sat and didn't even think.

We entered Hay over my Murrumbidgee. The post office at night seemed to be of white out style of architecture. Got to C.T.A. hotel Hay rather late, such a crib! Were taken down a passage little wider than a door into these asbestos rooms. The builders of Australian hotels are magic acousticians. Frank & Thelma were 3 doors down on the other side of the passage yet I could hear their every remark. It resounded as though we had all been confined in a billy can.

20 June 1937   We arrived in Mildura while there was still light to see the hotels' water towers—one of silo architecture and the other like a colossal gipsy pot elevated on an iron scaffolding. We betake ourselves to the Grand that looks like its name, and most unpublike. Palms and gardens and a glorious view of the Murray with, of course, as in so many towns from Chicago to Baghdad, a stymie of railroad tracks and miscellaneous obstructions.

The drawing room looks like the drawing room of a large private house but free from private clutter. We have rooms on

---

70   Frank Clune was driving a Pontiac.

the broad balcony from which splendor we gloat and dote on the Murray. The Murray that has swallowed the Murrumbidgee and Lachlan. It is locked & weired and, reflecting the magic Australian light, is like a great mirror among the dying trees that have glorified its banks for a thousand, perhaps for ten thousand years. Here is a tragedy of enterprising engineering progress . . .

We inspected the Carnegie Library on which has been built a memorial block tower which forms an entrance hall . . .

Ponty, all muddy & uncombed, was berthed beside a big black Rolls-Royce as spick and span as a sample in a window. Ponty did not suffer by the contrast. Breed (style) was in her every line. She looked like a lissom, high-spirited young woman who had had all sorts of adventures and was due for many more through her competence and daring. R-R looked like a bland and portly old Director of Companies who would be helpless without a valet to care for his shining broad cloth. There was no use in him eyeing Ponty suggestively. All his money would not tempt her from knightly youths who could share her adventures, and while her It lasted she would have her way.

We retired. Hotel noises were outdone by the vast Government clanking of railway engines sorting their families. Up and down, thud, bang, collision, crash—encore—da capo—ad lib. I was out betimes on my balcony but found the Murray entirely veiled in a heavy white weeping fog. Nothing visible but near-by palms.

21 June 1937   We go in company to visit the Workingman's Club. It is a guzzlers' paradise. The subscription is five shillings per annum. There is a more exclusive club at two pounds 2 shillings but the members all belong also to the Workingman's. Such an opportunity to guzzle finds all men equal in the gullet, & democracy, equality, brotherhood flourishes in beer.

There is a shire population of 18,000, a town population of 7,000 to draw from. The paradise has a double bar which is twice the length of a cricket pitch . . . It is furnished with a resplendent rail to breast, and resting board for the foot. A foolish male attitude catered for grandly. Beer five pence & three pence per glass, a sixteen-ounce schooner eight pence. At Christmas every member has a bottle to take home. In August there is a Club party with free beer that lays the members out. Paradise indeed, for the strange, mad male love of water made dirty with hops & ferment. But there is no after-hours or Sunday trading. The employés are envied of pubs' employés that the hours are delimited. A good swim during the day but bang at 6 p.m. We saw the bottling department and the latrines commodious & near at hand . . .

In this kind of co-operative guzzling the profits go to local charities instead of to individual vulgarians, often to squander in other countries. Here enlargements and extended amenities were in course of construction including a funny segregated little cubby for wives & other women connections of members. Humph! American men seem to be the only ones in the world that are not terrified of decent women or perhaps it is that they are merely more indulgent, & that, because they have more to give in general than men of other nations . . .

Arrived in Wentworth . . . We went down to the lock and weir and walked across. A lovely part of these locks is the bridge. There we saw the spit of land between the Lachlan & Murray-Murrumbidgee where Sturt met the blacks like a man and a gentleman—here was a glamorous sight. The place seems haunted with that historical event. The tribes still stand there as in a mirage, the atmosphere is instinct with long-gone presence. The voices seem to be almost within hearing. There is one of the most wonderful spots in Australia. Again the dying monarchs in the backed waters—things of beauty that it would take generations to replace. But who cares but myself? And why should I care so passionately—it is a burden. Far stretching roads, wraithlike into our land whose enchantment widens with the plains. Out here its dust absorbs water like blotting paper becomes a pulpy paste. Or it rises in clouds that will bury everything. The silence is equally absorptive—oblivion in two dimensions . . .

24 June 1937   We return and have a charming lunch with the Heysens [at Hahndorf, South Australia]. He is very handsome. Beautifully dressed as an informal country gentleman. Sixty but does not look it—pink of skin and as free from wrinkles as an Englishman—blue eyed. He had grey knickers not as clumsy as some plus fours, nice golf stockings, grey coat & very natty blue fine jersey full fronted to match eyes . . .

We had lunch in a fine room of two fireplaces (but one smoked too much to use & the other had to have the fire confined to one corner), fine rugs & interesting articles. Lovely flowers really tastefully arranged in the vases. Home of a man of means & taste.

We saw the studios—Norah's[71] & Pa's—fine big places—transformed stables & barns—grand rugs and easels & work benches. Hans's was of red gum—magnificent [and] as heavy as marble. How satisfying are things that show the craftsman—the work of hands that have had time & material directed by intelligence, skill & taste.

26 June to 28 June 1937   We got in [the aeroplane, at Parafield, Adelaide]. I had looked forward to this with delight for weeks and here we were at last . . . It was a lovely Lockheed

---

71 Nora, born 1911, daughter of Hans Heysen, won the Archibald Prize in 1938.

Electra . . . & Pilot Hughie Hughes was a precise little chap—one to take his work exactly and give confidence. The sinking moon was a pale disc on the left. Yellow dawn on the right. We were flying at first at about 500 ft as Peter Donegan (24), the nice young mechanic, told me. The farms north of the city were perfect geometrically at that altitude & in that light all was as smooth as a billiard table—red earth and green growth. Perhaps that is how it looks to the creator & that is why he lets it go on so long. The sun came up in a mist—a steam engine ran with a great plume of white behind it—exquisite. The sun grew bolder under the right wing tip. All was exquisite and inspiring.

Our seats were perfect, each with an air vent, a little window, a pocket for odds & ends, & we were each handed a morning paper. 'I hope I don't disgrace myself by being sick,' I observed.

'You won't be sick with me,' said Pilot Hughes, rebukingly.

We saw St Vincent's Gulf—exactly—and marvelled at the exactitude of the old cartographers. A new world, a new dimension, enlargement, release as we went due north with these young men, successors to the brave old ostlers and coachmen.

By 7.30 the sun was all up washed & clean for the day—and what a day! His light dispersed the semblance of perfect flatness and showed the ridges and hollows and larger irregularities of surface. We were going at about 97 miles an hour before 8 a.m. Spencer Gulf & Pt Pirie on our left wing tip . . .

The Flinders ranges showed in their glorious blues. Lake George on the left. There were no end of buried, or dormant or dead streams to be seen by the lines of trees—and so pretty their color on the fawn drab earth . . .

We dropped suddenly & my ears filled. Peter said that was because we were dropping at more than 300 ft per minute, and to blow out my cheeks. We swooped around and landed at Farina for breakfast. Boy scouts with goats. As the machine banks one loses the earth and is suddenly projected into an eternity of space—no trees, no earth—no horizon to border eternity. An ocean of eternity.

Farina is a defunct lake. All over it were the wheel tracks where the Lockheed had bogged on a previous trip because of a little rain. There were tracks where a car had tried the surface now & again, but Hughie had not risked his machine & kept them all there . . . eating the provender they were carrying, & bunking on the floor of a terrible hotel till it was safe to lift again. The lake had small tufts of growth on it which when examined had the beaded nature of seaweed. 1¾ miles from the drome to the town proper. Farina has a race course. The machine took a drink of petrol from a tank on a Ford and rose again. Lovely blues to the S.E.

Mt Searle. Mt Termination Hills. At 10.15 we saw Lake Eyre South. There was actual water and the ghost of water in places. A grand sight. Marvellous colors. It was as though the old lady who had made the Milky Way had let fall here a tin of cafe-au-lait. Every color of red-to-brown chocolate and cream (alkali) scattered out on that vast level surface. It looks as though an ocean had died there, or alternatively as if an earth had worn down till all that was left of its hills were sand & quartz & fields of gibbers; that the streams had sunk underground to be indicated by still-remaining trees. A world elusive that can be bare as dust one month and massed with flowers the next. In other lands do the deserts bloom—ever? Or, it was like a chocolate sea with milk islands & promontories—seas within seas. Red Stuart's Creek Hills. Hookey's Waterhole. Shepherd's Waterhole. Gibbers. Airmen say that God thought it such a poor job that he shied stones at it . . .

At Oodnadatta we saw the Afghans' camp and saw the Aborigines. And a cemetery with 10 graves. I remember a palm

or two. One pub; about 50 pop. We raced into the town in the
car that came out with a Mrs Wilkinson . . . We saw the Railway
Station. Oodnadatta a vast gravel bed. Mulga, gum & gidgee
creeks, blue bush & sea weed in dots on the desert. Afghans had
a goat corral & I heard the kids' childlike cry that reminded one
of 1917 in the Balkans.

Gibber jasper fragments, starts as small as gravel & increases
to boulders. Red heart of Australia in very deed—sq miles of
color. All sorts of blue—red from rust red—stone red to rose
red. Clay pans like ice cakes, hard as . . . soap stone.

Finke River shining like silver on the tail of Lake Eyre. Also
Coopers Creek (The Barcoo). Away to the right the Simpson
Desert. At 12.30 saw first sight of MacDonnell Ranges called so
after the Governor of South Australia by Stuart on same trip in
1865. Very ancient rock still high above the silting sand. At 12.45
crossed the 26th parallel of South latitude. South to Northern
Territory. Charlotte Waters. [word indecipherable] Hills dark &
crater like & just like the grubs we used to draw on our maps at
school. Continual red like sand waves of powdered raddle. Trees
fairylike and lilliputian; clay pans like soiled mother-of-pearl
shells. Some of the hills with flat tops like old tin houses gone
rusty. The Finke runs north & south, a wriggling two-tailed river
without a mouth. The land is marked by a number of lines of
trees as if long ago before it was worn flat it might have been as
full of rills as the Boogongs which have squirmed out of sight of
the relentless sun and the thirst of a wind with 'a clear fetch of a
1000 miles'.

1.05 p.m. saw Chambers Pillar on left discovered and named
by Stuart 6 April 1865. More hills like black slag. James Ranges
on left. MacDonnell Ranges higher & blue in the distance.
Relieving break in the Red Heart of the Centre. Took Stuart
8 days from Chambers Pillar to MacDonnell Ranges. We did it in

less than 80 minutes. Lovely blue ranges—color, color. Over Heavitree Gap. Ranges east & west clear and distinct. And there was Pilot Hughes making a lovely round circle surely a mile in diameter and as round as the earth—right out round, what a gorgiferous view we get of the ranges and Alice Springs below, on the Todd River, looking like the tiny model cities of the Housing & Town Planning Council, especially in the miniature & fairy reproductions of the gums.

And down we come perfectly with great élan onto the red bull dust . . .

We went down to the actual Alice Springs with its rocks and lovely trees . . . Saw the Alice, another river of sand, dotted here & there with fairy gums—miniature & shapely eucalypts—snowy white from tip to earth.

We saw the race course, and the gorgeous blues and reds of Mt Gillen and its escarpments and the hush and magic of the atmosphere of dry inland country, wide and empty. It has a presence and a fascination that has the power of awe . . .

We set out with Jas. Rice, the town's storekeeper, in the front seat of his service car . . . It was another gorgeous sparkling, inland June day. The landlady handed us a suitcase of grub apologising that she was short of bread, and at 9.30 off we went, due north like the Overland Telegraph . . .

One cannot take in a locality in one pressed flight in a car. All is blurred and telescoped, but as life itself is that with speed, awaiting the steadying influence of selection—it was typical. Names flash past. Curves, creeks & bogs . . .

We left the road and turned into the bush, high with spear grass & shrubs and thickly dotted with ant hills, hidden from view, that thundered on the under parts of the car till I expected it to be disabled. We followed a truck track of a previous year for some time and then steered by the horizon till we reached another underground river. Hanson Creek. It was some hundreds of yards wide with many gum trees growing in it. We proceeded some miles along this and halted opposite Central Mt Stuart. We left the car and crossed the Hanson. It was heavy walking over coarse sand. By scraping near the farther bank we could reach a soak. There [were] still some miles to be walked through the irritating spear grass & my tailored skirt was not wide enough for my stride. I decided to stay at the foot of the hill & let the men complete the climb. I did not want to take the last ounce out of myself. I was fatigued but far from spent. Had I been normal I could have had a comfortable snooze & become a new person, but no, such bliss was impossible to me. I made myself a couch of shawls in the shade of a bloodwood tree & investigated the flowers, some of which were beginning to bloom.

Central Mt Stuart was somewhat whale backed in shape & composed of rubble. The lowering sun poured down splendidly upon it and on the shrubberied plain. The atmosphere was divine. Magic was all around me. I had my soul to myself in the silence— the glory of the exact dead centre of my Australia. It was a wonderful experience. The shadows grew longer, a little breeze whispered that it was June and that when the bright sun went the night would be crisp . . .

Frank & I reached the car . . . The sun sank clear, to the left of Central Mt Stuart. How lovely the transfused radiance. The silence, the wide emptiness, how frightening to an alien abandoned in it. Little wonder such became delirious and stampeded in circles. The vast palpitating presence of the atmosphere flowed all around like an ocean. I loved it. I was at home here as some pilgrim reaching the goal . . .

We drove out to the drome & H. Hughes came circling in skimming near to the tree top . . . The Lockheed Electra took her fuel and came to life again, breathing red bull dust like an excited dragon. It went up from her stutterings into the beautiful morning, like a stationary red cloud. We circled gorgeously again, seeing the town below, and grand Mt Gillen with its shale razor edge north & trees south. Up into the young day leaving the hills like caterpillars on the plain and the earth like ebbing waves of sand ridges when it went off the boil away back in oblivion. There were the small hills like giant ant mounds & the buried streams staked by trees . . .

We got in at 3.30. Thelma waiting with Ponty.

Back in Adelaide, Franklin visited Lucy Spence Morice, niece of her hero, C.H. Spence, and acquired some Spence manuscripts which were donated to the Mitchell Library later that year. The Clunes and Franklin left Adelaide on 2 July and returned to Sydney via Melbourne where Franklin was able to visit her old colleague from Chicago days, Alice Henry. Franklin arrived home on 9 July.

19 July 1937   Wrote review of 'S is L' for Aust N. Review.[72] Went to town at 3. Shopped. Called at Bulletin, Mitchell [Library]. Went to Repins for evening drink. Newsreel. To English Speaking Ass. to hear C.H. Grattan on 'Henry James'—& home.

23 July 1937   Mrs Jenkins called on Mother during afternoon. I am so tired I'd sell my soul for peace & quiet, freedom from financial hopelessness etc etc.

---

72 A new edition of Joseph Furphy's *Such Is Life*, abridged by Vance Palmer, was published in London in 1937. Franklin's review appeared in the September 1937 issue of *Australian National Review*.

28 October 1937   Mrs W. [Wilkinson] in outrageous temper—snapped at me. Ivy Vernon came for day. Ethel Nerly Norris & 2 girls came also. My heart is giving out with fatigue. Oh, if I could have peace & harmony. I hate incarceration in this family life. Oh, for a flat of my own wherein I could shut myself. Never, never, any peace. Hope is dying at last in me. I am weary & defeated.

8 November 1937   H.M. Green has a nice temper in these lectures. He is kindly—as lacking in malice or acid as he is in brilliance. No fire. A true mediocrity. He always reminds me of someone who is deputising for a superior, as though a professor had said, 'I cannot keep my engagement, but I'll send my man along. He's a decent little chap and has been so much with me that he knows as much about the subject as I do.' He is so much smaller than his subject.

23 November 1937   Today arrived a poem from M.E.F. [Mary Eliza Fullerton] entitled 'Comet'. How I wish I could read it to you, Father, you would revel in it. Not a soul have I anywhere within hail who could absorb its texture. I remember once when I had come to a state of nerves you looked up from your reading in the corner & asked me what was the matter & I said I was sick to death of confinement with people who had no interests that were beyond an animal's. You said you had had 80 years of it. That when you were young any interest in poetry or higher things was regarded as sheer lunacy & of course I knew what you were at present undergoing. I went out that day and when I returned on my desk I found your Bible in which you had marked, 'Be still & know that I am God'.

Mrs C.P. Gilman once said to me that the movement for woman's emancipation was going wrong if it merely made life easy and idle for her. What she and the race needed was the release of woman's potentialities. That a woman kept on a pedestal or in a boudoir just because she had been, was, or might someday become a mother was to worsen her position. She is even more deleterious than the one kept down as a beast of burden.

Well, something along those lines has happened [to] women in these Sydney suburbs. Contraceptives have limited child bearing, and besides, women quickly become ex-mothers, and then what are they—simply nothing; they have no thoughts in their heads, no civic pride or ambition—not one playground or closet for the kids after a generation of woman suffrage, as a character in 'Back to Bool Bool' put it.

I retired to my room while Ivy A. [Abrahams] ironed and Wilkinson cleaned. She (W) flurries and scurries over and over the same thing and thus seems to be a martyr at cleaning, which in this cottage is no more than one day's work from 8 a.m. to about 2 p.m. including lunch. That was Mrs Couldrey's record for months, and mine was similar. They began to make fun of the serviettes with holes in them. Such ladies were used to better. 'You can't please some people,' said Ivy. 'No, they want things done their way,' said W. 'You should have started the ironing after breakfast and not helped me wipe up.' 'But that only took 10 minutes,' said Abrahams.

If Abrahams was so smart, well and good, but she was laying out that she must leave at 10 a.m. to be at her appointment. She was out last night too, and will have all next Saturday off, and Sunday afternoon. It was impossible to write in this atmosphere, so I appeared and said I would do the ironing myself so that she would not be incommoded. She went off and sat down and came back when I had finished, asking could she do anything. I was then ironing or re-ironing the runners and tray cloths (and these were sound linen) that she had just rubbed over and which were not fit to return to the sideboard. 'I wish you would have ironed these things instead of making fun of the poverty of the serviettes,' I said. But she wasn't the least 'feared'.

'I think she's out of her mind,' said Mother. In that case, God help her, she'll never get back into it for it must be too small to be seen except with a microscope.

At the same time a dishcloth with one hole in the lattice disappears, I ask what happened [to] it. 'Oh, Ivy took it home to her mother,' said W. A day or two previously when I had said, 'I wonder what Ivy's people are,' W. said, 'They don't have to scratch and scrape,' said it pointedly. It was nice by then to have W. to contribute a dishcloth. What is one to make of such minds? They need depicting, showing up against the opportunities which they cannot seize, the potentialities of life upon which they batten like vermin but it would take genius backed by sheer hard work to make them interesting.

We wonder what W. was. Mother insists she was a cook in a restaurant. She may have been a waitress but she shows no acquaintance with good usage even from the flunkey angle: nearly butts one over in a doorway if she wants to get through, and a flunkey would defer. She also uses her fingers continually instead of a handkerchief to wipe her lips—it makes me sick. She is not a bad little soul if she hadn't such a sour temper. She is selfish but not so commandingly so as Hall, nor so hypocritically so as Abrahams.

Thus goes my whole morning and my heart too tired to force my brain, besides, this afternoon Mother is ramping to go to Hurstville, and this evening the cake will have to be iced after she goes to bed.

All the airing laundry has to be watched against the rain too.

29 November 1937   Mary Gilmore had telephoned on Saturday that she wanted me to see her article on my poet[73] before it was typed so I repaired to Claremont[74] at 3.30. Found her flat just like the one in Phillip Street.[75] Every room littered and unkempt like an old bachelor's quarters who has only an occasional char to char up a bit. The bare boards made it look as if she had just dumped in or was going out . . .

The only other time I went to her flat and at her earnest solicitation, she told me how H. Lawson was madly in love with her, and that she wrote his stuff. I suppose she will say <u>she</u> wrote the poems presently. My first impression of her ignobility is confirmed. I wonder am I wickedly compromising to yield to her, like a mother with a child, just to further my poet. I'd never do it for my own work. She told me that she had rewritten the first half of 'Man Shy'[76] and that was why it was so much superior to the latter part, and that Davison put in the bull fight upon her suggestion to make variety. When we met at the Australia [Hotel] she told us that she had got G.B.L. [G.B. Lancaster] to write 'Pageant'. This is mania.

1937   There are authors—Thackeray, for instance, and others that make their readers glad that they have several books extant.

---

73 Mary Eliza Fullerton, 1868–1946. Franklin was instrumental in securing the publication of her poetry in the 1940s. The article by Gilmore titled 'Poetry: and an Australian poet' appeared in *Australian National Review*, February 1938.

74 No 2, Claremont Flats, 99 Darlinghurst Road, Kings Cross, home of Mary Gilmore.

75 In early 1933, Mary Gilmore moved from Trenton House, Phillip Street, to Kings Cross.

76 By Frank Dalby Davison, first serialised in 1923–25 and published in book form in 1931.

One settles down with them comfortably like returning to a dear place of resort—one is delighted to find the author is himself again. There are others of the tour de force order whose novelty ceases to charm—a trick seen through an originality that does not sustain itself. I hope E.D. [Eleanor Dark] is not going to rob me of my delight in her thus. There is in this [*Sun Across the Sky*[77]] her vividness, her sheer braininess, but I said that 'Prelude to Christopher'[78] could not be repeated. Miss Dark is overworking the monologue interieur. I must read 'Return to Coolami'[79] to see where she is going & how.

'Plaque with Laurel', M. Barnard Eldershaw (Harrap 1937).

This is a careful clever piece of work by our literary phenomenon, a collaboration so wonderfully fused that no joins are discernible. By two educated women who take writing seriously, and who are placed so they can do so, the craftsmanship is competent—their prose is good. Here they have set out to observe Canberra and it is carefully observed, but it is cold and stiff: there is none of the warmth and illumination that invests a work that comes from deep inner compulsion. They do not love Canberra—do not feel it or really know it—they wear it like a stiff new suit that has all its tailor's creases retained.

9 January 1938   Mary Fogden & I went to the New Theatre League's production of 'Shickers Limited' & of 'Waiting for Lefty' by Odet. Had seen the latter before at St James's Hall. These were spirited performances of plays that have fought their way abroad.

---

77 Published in 1937.
78 Published in 1934.
79 Published in 1936.

They were given with youthful gusto that almost amounted to defiance & bravado, where neither were called for, or, if justified, the more by apathy than opposition.

The bravado or sense of doing something startling is the result of the ominous fact that the third play of the trio 'Till the Day I Die' was banned at the behest of the German Consul. It is splendid that this group put on these plays and bring to our segregated nation a strain of what people are doing to keep the way open for freedom of speech overseas. The significant lack is that there are no Australian plays to mirror & criticise the conditions here. This group would accept nothing but criticism of their milieu: it is a pity that they would not start by simply mirroring it. I feel that the national-spiritual-sociological weakness of this group is that they are fervent imitators of Russia's experiment without making any contribution themselves though they are placed in happy isolation and primary wealth in a whole continent of their own with the ready-made inheritance of a greater tradition & habit of political freedom than any people extant. Their weakness artistically is monotony—the narrowness of evangelism. Their pieces are all on the one theme and all produced fortissimo. This wearies a discriminating audience, but they are an illumination in the waste of drab piffle put on by the other theatre societies. Selah.

12 January 1938   Hot day. Mother spiteful. Norman morose. Ivy A. [Abrahams] in tears. I took Lily to town & did chores: typewriter, looking for washer for Mother etc. Life Hell—can't write, nothing to hope for—even death has ceased to be a refuge.

22 January 1938   Went to Fellowship of Australian Writers party at Feminist Club, 77 King Street, in honor of Frank Dalby Davison accepting the ranking of MBE. It was a shoddy affair.

Met F. and T. Clune again for first time since we parted at end of our Adelaide trip. Thelma was her dear loving welcoming self. I consorted a little with Mr and Mrs T.I. Moore and Mr and Mrs L.C. Rees. Dulcie Deamer in an ultra gown 'with a big behind and her nipples wagging' as F.C. growled in my ear and Thelma remarked that it was lovely to have me with them again as I did not care what Frank said.

I couldn't disregard poor little F.D.D. by staying away from this; and he was patronising to me. Said that there were others should have had this honor ahead of him and mentioned Palmer, Shaw Neilson and Barnard Eldershaw. He related how he was summoned by Bracegirdle to Admiralty House and how Bracegirdle said that if he did not accept it would be regarded as a rebuff and writers would be offered no recognition for an indefinite period to come. Here is to be discerned the sequel to my behaviour. They evidently were touched by my scorn and sought someone else to debauch with their colonial honors. They were cunning in their choice. This was a sop to literature to keep its Australian-ness in imperial leading strings. It is the ruination of our national dignity. The Gilmore dameship has put Australian literature back a decade by putting a seal—a badge on its mediocrity and lack of values from which to erect standards.

28 January 1938   At 5 p.m. went to see Ken Hall at Cinesound, Ebley Street. He is just like Australian film pictures. One sees that their faults are inevitable, inherent in him as well as in the material, but one must also understand his superhuman difficulties. He was kindly to me because Frank Clune had told him to soft-pedal. He has evidently had no contacts in the polite or polished sense. Called me interchangeably Madam or Lady or dear Lady. Same level of manners as Baume, but not as handsome, nor so blatant in egotism, nor perhaps so gifted, or so mean.

His reader was ringing him up and told him he had at last got hold of a book. By Cronin (Bernard). He had had a three years' search. I could have got it at the Mitchell [Library], I said, or I could have written to Cronin. He said with unbelievable naivety, 'I did not know that Cronin was available' and of the Mitchell, 'Now I might have found it there, I never thought of that. I might have found it there.' Written down this looks so moronic, so illiterate that surely he was not sincere. If he was it shows where we are, or aren't, in this great art—or even in the craft side of it.

He said he was searching for a big Australian story. And he searches among the Thwaitses [F.J. Thwaites] and (lesser efforts) of Cronin. I said Cronin had done a good book in 'The Sow's Ear'.[80]

Great searchers that they have never sought even as far as me, even to discard me. I could see that, like the 'Military and Official Secretary to the Governor-General', he knew nothing of me, good or bad, except Frank Clune's introduction. They don't understand Australia scientifically, spiritually, mystically or intellectually, nor approach her with the ecstasy and infatuation of the artist. The idea is to imitate Hollywood in a get-rich-quick rape of a new field. The approach is to bung into her through the box-office. There is no realisation of the patience and delicacy needed for long sensitive gestation to work this strange, sparse, arid, intransigent material into art forms, reverently preserving the essence of its differences and special qualities. No, the idea is to deface it into the semblance of something else. Trade rape instead of the seductive wooing of art.

And what did I get out of it? Nothing but that at my time of life I had to make the approach and I could go away and submit

---

80 Published in 1933.

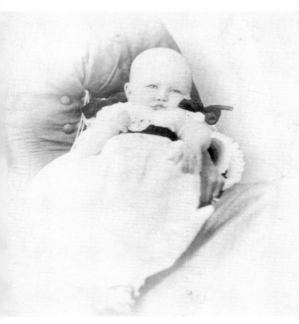

Left: Miles Franklin aged four months,1880. (REF: MITCHELL LIBRARY PX *D250/1, NO. 1)

Below: Old Talbingo Homestead, the home of Miles Franklin's grandmother, Sarah Lampe. Franklin was born here on 14 October 1879. The Homestead no longer exists. (REF: MITCHELL LIBRARY PX *D250/4, NO.1)

The Franklin family at Stillwater, near Goulburn, 1894. Left to right: Miles, Linda, Mervyn, Norman, Mrs Franklin (holding Laurel), Hume Talmage, Mr Franklin, Pat O'Rourke. (REF: MITCHELL LIBRARY PX *D250/1, NO. 3)

Sarah Lampe, Miles Franklin's grandmother, c. 1906. (REF: MITCHELL LIBRARY PX *D250/2, NO. 155)

ısannah Franklin and John Franklin, Miles Franklin's parents, 1919. Following the ⁞ntemporary fashion, the negative of this photograph was enhanced at the time it ⁞as taken, to rejuvenate the image. (REF: MITCHELL LIBRARY PX *D250/2, NO. 39)

Hume Talmage Franklin and Norman Rankin Franklin, brothers of Miles Franklin, 1901. (REF: MITCHELL LIBRARY PX *D250/2, NO. 28)

Above: Miles Franklin as
probationer nurse, Sydney, 1900.
(REF: MITCHELL LIBRARY PX *D250/1,
NO. 66)

Left: Edwin Bridle and his wife,
Australia (Trallie) Little, 1908.
(REF: MITCHELL LIBRARY PX *D250/3,
NO. 171)

Facing page: Miles Franklin,
2 April 1898, aged 18 years, just
before she began writing *My
Brilliant Career.* (REF: MITCHELL LIBRARY
PX *D250/1, NO. 8)

Above: Miles Franklin (second from left), Chicago, 1912. (Ref: Mitchell Library PX *D250/1, no. 49)

Right: Rose Scott, c. 1903. (Ref: PX *D 250/3, no. 117)

Above: 26 Grey Street, Carlton, Sydney, the Franklin family home from 1914, and where Miles Franklin lived from 1932 to 1954. (REF: MITCHELL LIBRARY PX *D250/4, NO. 12)

Left: Miles Franklin with Peter, London, 1932. Peter was kept as a pet in the household where Franklin lived. He features, under the name of Percy, in Franklin's thriller, *Bring the Monkey*, 1933. (REF: MITCHELL LIBRARY PX *D250/1, NO. 80)

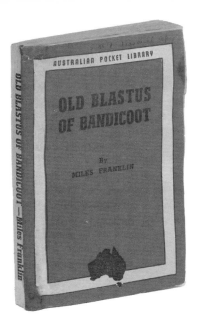

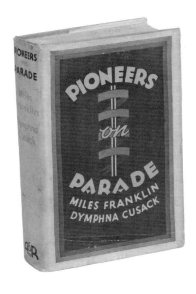

The Australian Pocket edition of *Old Blastus of Bandicoot*, 1945, which sold 25 000 copies in its first year of publication, making it Franklin's most successful book commercially; the first edition of *Pioneers on Parade*, 1939, written in collaboration with Dymphna Cusack; and the first edition of *Bring the Monkey*, 1933. All three books are held in the Miles Franklin collection, Mitchell Library.

something to compete with the Thwaitses and with the surety of the Thwaitses being preferred, and perhaps of something being sucked from my ideas. With my family burdens I find myself over-fatigued and too enervated to plunge out on a chance like that of a lottery. However! At least I told him to have no more of those damned gangsters as in 'Thorobred',[81] that they were alien to Australia. He agreed and said they were burlesque. If so the intention was not realised and they were mere 10th rate imitation of spurious USA.

January 1938 was the sesquicentenary of the founding of the colony of New South Wales in January 1788 and was celebrated as Australia's 150th birthday. There were celebrations around the country from 26 January (then known as Anniversary Day)—pageants, exhibitions, vice-regal garden parties, receptions and a number of titled overseas visitors, 'too many overloadings with overlords' as Franklin said. The Aborigines and the convicts were by and large airbrushed from the story of the nation. There was a Women's International Conference, held in conjunction with the sesquicentenary, which opened on 1 February. Franklin, in conjunction with Dymphna Cusack, would satirise the sesquicentenary celebrations in Pioneers on Parade, *published in 1939.*

<u>2 February 1938</u>   Went to opening of Mitchell [Library] Sesqui exhibit.

Opened by Evatt and Ifould, thank God. Ifould crowing while Ida Leeson did work in the way of androcentric society, but at least he was not an exterior overlord. Hartley Grattan resplendent in white 'traphies' suit and accompanied by a Mrs Arnott (?). He was

---

81   *Thoroughbred*, a film produced by Ken G. Hall, 1936. Script by Edmond Seward.

in fine plume because praised in S.M.H. [*Sydney Morning Herald*]. I had met Lena [Lampe] at door. Mrs Holman first time out after illness. Saw little White assistant librarian from Canberra and told him I'd do review of 'Capricornia'. He gave me 500 words in April number.[82] Spoke to Mr and Mrs Lloyd Ross, to Mackaness and Mrs Burley Griffin on the wing. Jack and Beattie there, so they and Lena [Lampe], I and Mutch and his niece Mrs Doughty went to tea in Gardens, leaving enjoyment of exhibition for another day.

On way back Ida Leeson came to meet us and she and Mutch talked, thought Exhibition was being boycotted—would have collected more people if Governor instead of Chief Justice had opened it. Mutch said Australians won't come to anything unless they can see the vice-regals or other lords. Well, they must be educated; people so servile could be disciplined to anything. It would be worth while to have a lord or two in a cage as a bait, but let the natives learn to walk and talk and open things (their minds if possible). 'Those royal dolls,' as Editha Phelps said in London, 'they open and shut their eyes, they open bazaars—but they are expensive toys, they are so fecund, and their fecundity has to be supported by the State.'

3 February 1938   I . . . departed to the Sesqui at home at Admiralty House[83]—A generation—a lifetime since I went there with Rose Scott—ah, the difference in my outlook and expectations then and now.

I went by train and by Carabella Street, where I had long ago such fun in Mary-Anning [working in domestic service]. The royally situated place on that point, like the manager's stage box

---

82 Xavier Herbert's *Capricornia* was published on Australia Day 1938. H.L. White was editor of 'The Book World' section in *Australian National Review*. Franklin's review appeared in the May 1938 number.

83 Sydney residence of the Governor-General.

with everything under one's view. We went through the entrance hall and the drawing room into the garden again—no house intimacy for this collection of <u>worthy</u> females—the same lot as at Government House.[84]

Their Excellencies[85] standing in the drawing room to exchange paws. I forgot to note the color of the gloves, being embroiled by the spectacle of poor old pot-bellied women ahead of me dipping their knee to the female of the species. Such <u>disgusting</u> servility! Why don't they pull their forelocks and be done with it. I felt myself growing even more erect and I said to Dymphna [Cusack] who was following me, 'Don't you bend your knee'.

'Not me,' said she.

The aide, finding Dymphna too much for him, bawled 'Miss Cossack' and made me chuckle. It was all so in keeping with the whole show in so far as it concerned women writers that her name should have been mangled and she go in under an alias. Serve us right for doing articles for a book that had to be foreworded by two outsiders![86]

Dymphna and I explored the heavenly-contoured grounds and I suggested that we should join forces in showing up things as they are—with a light touch if possible.[87] She seemed to be delighted—asked did I mean it. Of course I don't know what she

---

84 There had been a reception at the New South Wales Government House on the morning of 1 February.

85 The Governor-General was Baron, later Earl, Gowrie; his wife was Zara née Pollock.

86 *The Peaceful Army: A Memorial to the Pioneer Women of Australia, 1788–1938* was published in 1938 by the Women's Executive Committee of the 150th Anniversary Celebrations. It was edited by Flora Eldershaw and included an article on Rose Scott by Franklin. There was a foreword by Lady Gowrie, wife of the Governor-General, and one by Lady Wakehurst, wife of the Governor of New South Wales.

87 The genesis of *Pioneers on Parade*, written by Miles and Dymphna Cusack and published in 1939. It satirised the sesquicentenary celebrations.

will say behind my back but shall presently hear or deduce. Afternoon tea in a tent . . .

I left early to call on Emily Fullerton at 56 Carabella Street. Had tea with her and attended evening session of Women's Conference.[88] Sat down near to the stage this time.

Mrs Moss in chair, a grand-looking old dame like a countess at least, lorgnette and all. Lady Stamp [word indecipherable] first. Her dress must have been improvised by a charlady in a hurry. It was all ugly as could be. Color—material and lordy, the cut! She was a short plebeian, stout, methody style of woman—no caste in accent—slight hint of midlands or something equally lower-class. Fundamentalist wants to put marriage back to the Bastille. She spoke dull common sense about marriage and references to her own—happy of course—style in spouses seems to be deleterious to happiness in marriage. Gorgeously platitudinous, is for limited divorce and for self control.

Followed by Dame Enid [Lyons]—near at hand her face is trivial—brow unintellectual and small, pretty nose, a neat face being spoiled by fat. She has no depth or originality but is a smart politician—just that—as much yes–no as George Reid.[89] Adept in pulling out the well-worn stops that bring applause and laughter.

She talked and talked for an hour or more, on and on and blew over it a vast wheeze from the bellows of motherhood—sure of popularity. Other women condemned as freaks and

---

88 Women's International Conference, 1–4 February 1938, held in conjunction with the sesquicentenary celebrations.

89 Sir George Reid was given the sobriquet 'Yes No' because, as New South Wales Premier at the time of the referendum on the Federal Constitution in 1898, he advocated a yes vote while at the same time pointing out the proposed constitution's defects.

perverts have gone before and made it possible for her thus to air herself on the public platform. She lectured the reluctant modern mother on many points but never once even skirted the fundamentals of war and poverty—never once. She talked all the time away. Why should this stuff be called a <u>conference</u>? There was no discussion.

Enid DBE[90] would be very popular with those who believe in breeding regardless of the results being wasted in slum dens, brothels or war.[91] At any rate there were not so many nonentity-personages 'featured'.

4 February 1938   Dressed and got myself off to the official dinner to wind up the Executive Committee's Sesqui beano—female department[92].

Feeling deadly depressed—can it be all due to frustration and fatigue or is some dread growth sneaking upon me . . .

We eventually got settled down in the Australia's [Hotel] banqueting hall. I found myself at a table on the outskirts but in a line with the one at which Birkett was seated and that other which Barnard-Eldershaw helped to fill. Mine had three empty places. D. Cusack was at it and a Mrs Bowden and two other nondescripts whose names did not transpire. Bowden had been fifteen years in New York and picked up a little from that. Criticised the place cards as being behind the times. Her idea of advancement would be for us to have same gadgets as USA. The dinner was

90 Lyons was actually GBE—Dame Grand Cross of the Order of the British Empire, a higher order than DBE—Dame Commander of the Order of the British Empire. Franklin's bête noire, Mary Gilmore, was DBE.
91 Lyons had 12 children.
92 Australia's 150th Anniversary Celebrations Council—Women's Executive Committee and Advisory Council, chaired by Florence Muscio.

very good. The roast fowl was plentiful and well-cooked and the pommes Saratoga a work of art. The Sorbet (sherbet) was feeble. I did not sample the wine.

Dymphna [Cusack] was forcedly, egotistically and bitingly brilliant. One can easily tire of aggressive brilliance. She is at one with me in resenting the Australian lick-spittling colonialism, but her interest may not be so purely Australian as Irish-Catholicism, and Australia genuflecting to the Cardinal instead of to the English Governor would be out of the frying-pan into the fire.

Dame Maria [Ogilvie-Gordon] gave toast of Australia and Dame Enid [Lyons] responded. That was fitting, our most distinguished overseas guest and Australia's leading woman. The Muscio only spouted once.

Dame Maria was most satisfactory on our long long coasts, and our long long views, and the uniqueness of Australia and our rocks (seen in Blue Mountains) but Lordy, she had no more intelligence than a hen when she touched on sociology.

She said how splendid it was to have two excellencies in every state, that what Australia needed was many domestic workers from the home land. Domestic workers should be trained and come out, and then what was needed was social leaders, and there, you have their excellencies!

Well, I'll be damned!!!!!!!!!!

Dame Enid in a lovely silver frock, fat hams of arms—ribbon order across ponderous bosom, face all gone to fat, responded. Big cross conspicuous on chain around neck. She was pleasant and entertaining but bored me to rib-platting extent.

Her speeches and Alice Grant Rosman's books are analogous. The first book you read with pleasure and delight, saying that A.G.R. deserves her success, that in such stories there is nothing too heavy for the primary perusers, and at the same time it is sufficiently deft and entertaining for more advanced minds. The second one makes you yawn so that you never perhaps will read a third. Well, I had to listen to Dame Enid for the third time, and now have no respect for her.

She is merely the glib male politician in skirts, no matter how many children she has. She could add on a litter of sextuplets without altering that, or being anything fundamentally intellectual in motherhood.

Dame Mary Gilmore running around said to me didn't I think the women wonderful.

'In what way?' I asked.

This great conference.

'Yes, but the Government paid for it.'

Yes, she supposed the Government did.

'Well,' I said, 'I wonder what they would have done unaided.'

There was no use in talking to this lot of oddments. Not a working woman in the official sense present. The Government (male) to keep the women from nagging allotted them some of the funds to have a party on their own—indulgent—to the tame and privileged women who enjoy what rebel and martyred women have won. Bah, the whole thing was futile intellectually and spiritually and for any influence it would or could have on the real issues women face today as women in addition to those they face as citizens regardless of sex.

A few touts may get a dameship out of it and thus be more firmly bound to the English Garrison.

I dawdled a while taking stock of the animals. Dame Constance [D'Arcy] is like a mask, she is not so big as inelegantly shaped. Lordy the size of Lady Huntingfield—no fat there—a great, stiff tall Clydesdale of a woman, plain of feature and plain of hair. I thought of speaking to her having been 'raised' on her pop's poetry[93] but was intimidated by her stiff, quiet size. She towers like an armored dinosaur—there is nothing billowy or pillowy in her body, besides, one cannot separate these people from the sycophants and hangers-on.

Mrs Brookes—Deakin's daughter, another tall woman but more on giraffe lines. How did their husbands approach and capture either of these?—I'd like to see them, the hubbies.

I had the foolhardiness to speak to Mrs Brookes because Deakin had always been enthusiastic about me. I don't forget that he once offered to send me home from Melbourne in the State Railway carriage only that I had already accepted a berth from the steamship.[94] Mrs Brookes cannot take after her father—she is of the dead-fish personality—the English personality at its nadir—total lack of appearance, charm or anything else. No doubt she is respectable, able and worthy.

And then, good Lord, I saw a loathly sight. Her Excellency, Lady Gowrie, a very attractive, unassertive looking woman was backed against a wall well out of the fairway talking to a few women who had bailed her up, but the departing crawlers not passing her at cross angles, merely away at the side, bowed their knee in a bob like the Catholics when they cross the line of the altar. Even the R.C.s do not genuflect unless they directly face the Holy Idols, but there were those sickening creatures.

Ye gods, what can an Inky S [Stephensen] do against such a state of affairs as that? A Mussolini could do what he liked with such crawlers without even the aid of castor oil. Selah!

---

93 Lady Huntingfield's father was Judge Ernest Crosby of New York. The reference to poetry is unclear.
94 This presumably was in 1904 when Franklin was in Melbourne. Federal Parliament at that time met in Melbourne.

The defect of these affairs, in addition to the fact that they touched nothing fundamental, was that the women of Australia did not perform enough themselves. There were too many overloadings with overlords. If a local gets up to do anything she is sneered at by all the others out of jealousy—where all are equals—the charwoman ideal—prominence is resented. And in truth the locals instead of giving what they have with simple unaffected dignity splurge too much, trying to provide the luxury & pomp to which the visiting overlords are accustomed, & thus trying to be what they are not, fail in essentials. The result is striving for official favoritism like harem favorites instead of being Franklins—those who never paid fief nor owned an overlord.

17 February 1938   Oh dear, what a sad, wistful, agonising little bit of ephemerality is life. I can't bear my emotions of relinquishment & nostalgia: they are as poignant as my youthful power to feel.

25 February 1938   Life is hell surely enough. If only I could sleep I could conquer it instead of being defeated by it. Norman home, sick, a fearful cough, spitting and snappy. He has had, poor fellow, nothing from women but Mother's criticism & then her senile torment; & his wife mad as a hatter from her terrible pathological condition—that and wrestling with rough shearers— and he puts me in the same category evidently. I have to listen to his limited dogmatic statements on everything—me that has been where I've been etc. To be reduced to this level & that of the small-witted (Mrs W [Wilkinson]) & defective (Ivy A [Abrahams]) is pure, long-drawn torture. Night before last Jack [Franklin] went out to see a mate off the premises & kept me nervous till 11.30

awaiting his final noises & Mildred next door was out till 12.15 saying goodnight to a swain & she has a voice like a nail on a can—so exhausted & ill yesterday morning with my back, could have slept but household bangings kept me awake. Last night things quietened down at 10.30 but a flea kept me awake & after chasing it at 2 a.m. sleep was chary. No one in the house but me has these acute disabilities to noise etc. and I get neither sympathy nor understanding. They all snore all night.

This diary business has been a relief—a bastard relief for a desire to write, frustrated by interruptions and disharmony (arising out of uncongeniality) until my brain power is too scattered & irritated & finally exhausted to concentrate on anything extensive: but it is only a substitute; and now I am sick of it, and my small space will be over-crowded with the results. Must burn them all in case I peg out, but should I live & ever be free & my wits rested, some of the literary notes would be useful to me. It's all a puzzle & an exasperation. If only I could have been free of my family for this last ten years! An uncongenial family, if one is affectionate & sticks to them, congeals one in a special hell shut out from friends. I showed Norman 'The Peaceful Army'[95] yesterday saying he might be interested, and he never deigned to open it. If I say a word one of the half-wits or Norman interposes and overtalks me. If ever I tell him of anything overseas he gets up & leaves the room. His only interest is to ridicule people—me or anyone else. All people have that tendency, but in Australian segregation and isolation it grows out of proportion & results in a lot of soulless cocksure ignorant ridiculers of their betters.

I used to feel ten years ago that I was in a very long tunnel with the light faintly glimmering ahead. Then I lost the light but kept on hoping it would be seen again around a turn. Now I feel

95 *The Peaceful Army*, op. cit.

that the tunnel has fallen in and is my living tomb. It doesn't matter that I was too ungifted to come to anything but it is weary & uncomfortable to myself.

28 February 1938   Rather a field day. Heart protesting. Dressed and left before 1 o'clock for Em Fullerton, 56 Carabella St. Took her some zinnias. Walked from there to Dr Booth's Memorial College of Domestic Science [at] Kirribilli. What a lovely situation. I savored every inch of the way. Miss Stenhouse the Principal, a very correct youthful looking New Zealander . . . met me at door and I was let loose upon about 15 girls, minimum age 17. Horrors! Some of them were pretty enough—all pretty in the bloom of youth. But they looked me over superciliously—another old hen. Some went to sleep, some grinned to each other privately, whether for or against me I don't know or care. I don't think I interested them, but D. Cusack told me later in the evening, if they looked at me like stuffed owls—they were interested. She is used to addressing girls of high school age.[96] What would these girls care about the arduous and unglamorous life of C.H. Spence? However, I was there & had to struggle through. They laughed pretty often, but it was heavy going. I was given an hour, could have done that & more to an adult, intelligent audience, but I wound up in 40 minutes. One girl came up afterwards & asked questions, & another wanted to see the second picture of Miss Spence again.

The difficulty in addressing young people is the proportion of chaff. Before they are 40 most of them will be dead altogether— gone like chaff and there may not be one of the whole collection worth anything. But there is also the possibility that just one of

96 Dymphna Cusack was a school teacher.

that tiresome mass of developing flesh may contain a soul & mind—an eager, devouring mind like that of C.H.S.: or there might be one of my own power to feel & remember; & it is in the hope of that one & to that one, one struggles to say something.

This was a fantastic ménage. The principal seemed like an embalmed example of what a refined, genteel, very, very, English lady should be. Dr Booth has conjured up this outfit in this delightful dwelling divinely situated for these pampered creatures to play at housekeeping . . .

I found out from the Principal that the girls don't do their own cleaning altogether, only certain parts as set lessons. She admitted there was only one girl who might have entailed financial struggle to be there. Too many of the others' parents found it a place to dispose of their daughters for a couple of years more . . .

Dear, dear, a depressingly ladified circus segregated in this privileged situation, while war ravages China & Spain, and all the world trembles on the brink of explosion.

30 March 1938 In evening at Feminist Club heard Flora Eldershaw on 'The Australian Scene in Literature'. An extra-ordinarily brilliant, able, generous & judicial paper. She dwelt lightly on early writers & said that with B. Penton & H.H.R. [Henry Handel Richardson] Australian writers ceased to be picaresque & became humanitarian. Our situation had been boisterous & commonplace but never sinister. Australia to her writers is more than a setting—it is a force & their books are often a portrait of Australia. K.S.P. [Katharine Susannah Prichard] has a grim power— a sadistic force. H.H.R. greatest of all.

Dalley ('Max Flambard') satirical. But these writers were all grim—made Australia grim. Coming to 'Jonah'[97] the grimness

---

97 Novel by Louis Stone, published in 1911. It was republished in 1933.

had been watered down by mediocrity & was the acme of commonplace. Novels of the small town, 'Tiburon'[98], 'No Escape'[99] and 'Redheap',[100] thus named in ratio of intensity. 'Redheap' most brilliant & robust of the trio.

Spoke of Penton's vehemence & lavishness. Healing power of the Earth in Eleanor Dark though the earth with her is no more than a background. 'Pageant'[101]—period more than a setting. It was difficult to believe that the Victorian age had bloomed so luxuriantly in Tasmania.[102]

She said that when we came to Miles Franklin's 'All That Swagger' the transition had been made from grimness to joy in the land. In this book & in Brent of Bin Bin's three[103] there was no grimness. I noted from 'Up the Country' Bert's joy in his lovely country. I noted from 'All That Swagger' the passage about the Canberra view being as beautiful as that towards Mt Olympus. Danny was as sweet as a nut. It was a period book too but here you also had the sense of hardship.

Dalby Davison & Vance Palmer Artists—finest example of how to take the country easily without self-consciousness & special pleading—they let it speak for itself—veracity & simplicity. I noted from 'Man Hamilton'[104] & 'Children of the Dark People'.[105]

---

98 Novel by Kylie Tennant, published in 1935.

99 Novel by Velia Ercole, published in 1932, winner of the *Bulletin* novel competition.

100 Novel by Norman Lindsay, published in London in 1930, banned in Australia until 1958.

101 Novel by G.B. Lancaster, published in 1933. It won the Australian Literature Society's Gold Medal.

102 'Pageant' is set in Tasmania and traces a family from 1826 to the twentieth century.

103 The three Brent of Bin Bin novels published at this time were: *Up the Country*, 1928; *Ten Creeks Run*, 1930; and *Back to Bool Bool*, 1931.

104 *The Man Hamilton*, by Vance Palmer, was published in 1928.

105 By Frank Dalby Davison, published in 1936.

'Jungfrau'[106] was a story independent of place.

Mentioned the 'Doughman',[107] & Christina Stead. Her novel was life seen through a temperament—& through a glass darkly.

3 April 1938   Went to hear George Mackaness at Blue Tearoom[108] on 'The Future for Australian Literature'. The terrible thing about him is that he is just wrong, a go-getter—unethical, limited artistically. He has been forced a little beyond Thwaites, whom he assured me was the hope of Australian literature when I returned last from London & USA. He recommended us to copy J[ack] & P[hilip] Lindsay's success. They had got on to a paying vein & others would do well to emulate them. One man here who had done so was Timms—boosted Timms. His next book going to be better even than 'Conflict'[109] is in Stewart times. All his harping was that we should think internationally about Australia, so that our novels would be understood & accepted by publishers in New York & London. His idea of internationally is un-Australianly. He said 20,000 copies of Frank Dalby Davison's 'Children of the Dark People' had been printed for schools. Must judge our literature not in Australian terms but in terms of worldwide literature of importance.

He (Mackaness) is a mediocre go-getter aping the cloak of a doctor of literature. He is a cloven-hoofed clod-hopper on the artistic side. He is totally tone-deaf as to what is intrinsically Australian in Australian literature.

---

106 By Dymphna Cusack, published in 1936.
107 By Robert Desmond Tate, published in 1933.
108 The Blue Tea Room was in Rowe Street, Sydney—an artistic area of the city at this period.
109 *Conflict* by E.V. Timms, was published in 1934.

When Franklin returned to Australia in 1932, she had been out of the country for over 25 years, since she was 26. In no time it was as if she had never left. She plunged into the local literary scene, 'confounding their politics, frustrating their knavish tricks', as the anthem has it, and standing up for literature with a 'bias, offensively Australian' as her old friend Joseph Furphy had put it. She passionately believed that great literature was firmly rooted in the culture of the writer, once remarking how quintessentially English Shakespeare was. She flayed those who urged Australians not to write about Australia for the risk of appearing parochial. No one commented on the irony of a cultural nationalist who had spent the best part of her life overseas.

8 April 1938   Discovered Kylie Tennant in person of Mrs Rodd of Christian Socialists—dear little husband to encourage and balance her. He is a school teacher. She is not bad looking but was frumpishly and very shabbily dressed. Excitable, did not seem to me to have a copious intellect. Did not seem up to her gifts as exposed in 'Tiburon'—that book, of course, is plainly derivative from B of B.B. [Brent of Bin Bin]. She now has to justify it in a more independent work.

30 April 1938   The night of the Sesqui Prize Play.[110] It was preceded by a cocktail party at Tom and Peace Moore's to which I was invited but did not go because I was so beaten out & unhappy after 2 days of Mother's power to wound & misrepresent, which remains in zenith, though her intellect wanes to nadir. I went

---

110 *Men Without Wives* by Henrietta Drake-Brockman, Sydney Players' Club at St James' Hall.

early and paid for my seat, which was in Tom Moore's party. I chose one on the side & went on reading 'Australia Felix'[111]— dull, dull, heavy book—unnecessarily extended by extraneous detail. When the party arrived Mary Gilmore eclipsed me; it was like sitting behind a big chair. I did not bother to talk to her & she cannot talk to me—seems uneasy with me; or do I imagine that, & is it merely that she can only talk of herself & there was no time for that here.

The Drake [Henrietta Drake-Brockman] came in, grandly attired and a fine looking woman—good size & shape & pleasant face. If she were a queen or a governor's lady how the servile would slobber over her looks. Displayed in front of first row on chairs were a series of dull-looking old people—evidently relatives or friends of author. In interval I crossed & sat beside my hostess Peace for a few minutes & was introduced to an ugly little man, brother-in-law of the Drake or the lion of the hour. Ah me, if he has a family resemblance in size & shape it is the Drake's beauty that has attracted her gander.

Violet Roche[112] talked to me in interval and then C.H. Grattan came in second interval, to grouse about P.R.S. [P.R. Stephensen] and say he is mad. C.H.G. was sitting beside the Drake and any notice from a society person goes to his head rather, and I suspect that that is why he was so enthused with the play: though he made the reservation that he would have to see the third act.

I was depressed that it was such a poor audience. There were plenty of vacant seats yet this was the prize Sesqui play & also by a young & beautiful society woman who had money and

---

111 By Henry Handel Richardson, 1917. The first volume of the trilogy *The Fortunes of Richard Mahony*.

112 Violet A. Roche, editor of *The Australia Handbook*, published quarterly by Australia Hotel Co., 1925–1936.

connections to get all that was going in that respect. There was no sort of official recognition or even any excitement among theatrical groups—it shows how utterly indifferent and careless the public is, how unaroused or else entirely indifferent or lacking in cultural interest from the angle of self-respect.

It was Ruth Draper's first night and no doubt all the servile non-thinkers were there. If Australia were anything but a milch cow for overseas artists & imperialism, it should have been said, 'Ruth Draper's show was not so full as expected because we had an important first night in Australian Drama'. But no, it had no interest either as Australian Drama per se nor from the Government-official angle. A great exposé of what we are. So much for the national angle of a national event.

Tom Moore was buzzing about—no time for me when he has sweller fry—but that is the way to get there—and why not? My standards have led me to the grave only—whereas his may give him a little glory & ease beforehand to fill the megrim hours.

As to the play. Of course it is old fashioned in form & put on cheaply & poorly with none of the aids in setting of its era. The story is that of Ma Bates who with her drover husband has made a home in the N.W. & struggles against [word indecipherable] & all other pioneering arduosity. It started as a biographical play of a young woman arriving from the city & dispersed itself into Ma Bates's & other people's affairs. The author is sincere & evidently knows her territory and vernacular. A good setting & professional acting would no doubt improve the play but not redeem it completely—it lacks power. Ma Bates is supposed to be a good rough diamond, 'rough as bags', but the actress[113] did not suggest that. She had no weight physically or mentally. She attacked the

---

113 Doris Williams.

part by shrieking her way through it in the one key, I was wearied by her powerless importunity. I was in the front row & that is very hard on the play—halfway back I might have been glad of the shouting. The girl cast for gin[114] did very well with an unfamiliar role. Ma Bates's husband[115] was a triumph of type-casting, except for his unfried skin. Moustache, hat dress, bearing, he was enchanting. He had the bushman's soft easy way of talking. The others, & this I should say was in the acting, not in the lines, were inclined to be stagey & exaggerated—a tinge of Dave[116] in their presentation—people who think that bush people are caricatures.

The play at an end there was the usual school break-up of flowers & other presents. The Drake, the producer,[117] Old Windeyer[118] (as patron of Dramatic Company) and Elliott Napier as final judge of plays took the stage. Windeyer was offensive and dull. As Dymphna Cusack who had slipped up to front & into seat beside me remarked that women always have to suffer these insults about their sex appeal. He had said something typical in bad taste about the Drake's beauty. He has the ugliness & unpleasing personality of other Windeyers. I remember the awful night he debated with F.E. Baume & kept spitting into his handkerchief and examining the results. Ugh! I shudder again with disgust to recall.

After him came the Drake, fine appearance, gracious & adequate to the occasion, but no thrill—just something lacking.

---

114 The reference is to Channa, house-gin at Kooli Crossing Cattle Station, played by Molly Ramsay.
115 Played by William State.
116 Bush characters Dad and Dave, created by Steele Rudd.
117 S.R. Irving.
118 Richard Windeyer, barrister. He was 70 in 1938.

Then came Elliott Napier (to whom I was delighted to hear the Drake refer as Napier Elliott) and who looked more like a disintegrating golly-wog than ever. This sort of mediocrity is always in the places of authority. Then the poor old producer was called upon to make his bow and I lit out with D. Cusack and her mother for supper and home very late.

29 May 1938   Beached—or shoaled? Shoaled I think. Life has been complete hell for weeks. For example Mother took a notion that she could not see. I think there is some failure of mental manipulation of muscles—part of her increasing senility and she is more ramping restless. As far back as April 16 she wanted to go to see Miss Gillespie. I thought it better for her to rest in view of the fact that the next afternoon was to bring Ken, Lena and Oscar Rossitter. Old Mrs Jenkins came in and I thought that would hold Mother: but no, she invited Mrs J. to go too. Mrs J. very pleased. I could not get a taxi (a wedding was on) though I had to go to phone every few minutes.

'Poor old thing,' said Mrs Jenkins. 'It must be terrible for her to be all alone.' I said didn't you come in? and as you came my brother fled because he could no longer endure a house so full of old women. The two Ivys [Abrahams and Vernon] were dancing ceaseless attention on Mother, so was Jack [Franklin] and my whole afternoon went in it. 'I suppose it is because she can't see,' said Mrs Jenkins. I said we had the word of two specialists that there was nothing the matter with Mother's sight—that it was remarkable for her age & no speck on it. It was too late when a taxi was eventually free and Mother raved at me, 'Yes, you'd like to imprison me' etc. etc. I was trying to write a Sesqui novel in conjunction with D. Cusack; me doing all the lay-out & typing and sending it to her: and with Ivy V. & Ivy A.—both fussing morons and Mother irrational I was distracted and ill. However I plugged along.

I said now some literary men do good work when drunk, and Nature does not care whether a man depletes himself by an excess of industry or worry or an excess of alcohol: the result is sometimes similar. So, despite being bemused with fatigue, distracted & tormented beyond using intelligence or generating inspiration, I'll write on & on & see what happens. Result was D.C. gave me credit for interesting matter, but is she a judge?

15 June 1938   At 1.30 a.m. Mother knew me, at 3.30 she went into coma & passed at 1.30 p.m.

Susannah Franklin was 87 when she died. For five and a half years, since her return to Australia, Miles Franklin had lived with and cared for her increasingly irritable mother at the family home, 26 Grey Street, Carlton. These last years of Susannah's life were trying for Miles when her mother was probably suffering from a form of senile dementia. But it would be unfair to judge Susannah by these years. She had been a good mother, supportive and courageous— and Miles well knew this. Miles always lamented the waste of her mother's talents in domesticity. Susannah's death brought guilt, sorrow and a feeling of profound loss.

Susannah's death did not really change Miles' domestic situation as her nephew Jack was now living with her and her widowed brother Norman moved into the Carlton house in April 1939.

Both had, it seems, been regular visitors previously, staying for some days or weeks at a time.

7 July 1938   Ruby & Aunt Lena came & we went through Mother's things—a mortally unhappy day & put me right back.

In evening went to hear Flystad & Tauber at Mrs Morgan's. Tauber sang vile tripe & Uncle Gus [Lampe] rang from P. [Peak] Hill in middle of Flystad.

26 August 1938   Broke fine but soon began to shower. Did some washing. Williams's man finding borers all over house.

   Nor [Norman] home in time for tea. I read 'Waterway'.[119] Feeling just panicky with nerves because of my financial helplessness.

3 September 1938   Fine day. Suffering. Complete nervous collapse. Tried to sleep but see Mother dying or struggling about in her last days. H. Henry came & advised me about building at 8 p.m.

27 September 1938   Fine day. Got sitting room straight. Awful grief again to go over Mother's things—She kept carefully everything—wonderful. Ruby called in afternoon. X. Herbert and Sadie called up in evening. I finished typing Aunt Lucy.[120]

30 November 1938   Nice warm day. Cleaned the house throughout & cooked for D. Cusack who came at 5.30 for the night. We talked till 12.00. Jack's [Franklin] second day at work.

During the first part of 1939, Kate Baker, keeper of the Joseph Furphy flame, moved in with Miles Franklin at Carlton, bringing with her from Melbourne her collection of Furphy documents. Together

---

119 By Eleanor Dark, published 1938.
120 Aunt Lucy is a character in *Pioneers on Parade*, written in conjunction with Dymphna Cusack and published in 1939.

they worked on the manuscript which would win a second S.H. Prior Memorial Prize for Miles later that year and which, with revision, would be published in 1944 under the title Joseph Furphy: The Legend of a Man and His Book.

6 February 1939   Worked on Furphy. K.B. [Kate Baker] ratcheted till 11 pm & gave me a sleepless night. During afternoon she read 'Pioneers on Parade'. It patently absorbed & titillated her.

13 February 1939   Hot day. The fatigue of trying to get K.B. [Kate Baker] to hear is killing. She has no idea of literary procedure or construction & one can't yell a notion into her deafness.

14 March 1939   Showers. D.C. [Dymphna Cusack] came to go over final version of 'P. on Parade' & to my surprise did give suggestions for about ½ a doz. phrases. She soon got tired of trying to talk to K.B. [Kate Baker], said she could not wear herself out. She stayed the night. I retired at 12. Rat kept me awake. Up at 6 a.m. Very tired.

21 March 1939   Worked on Furphy and read 'Happy Valley' by Patrick White[121] & crept to bed soon as tea was over. Not able to sit up. Mrs Morgan called at 8. I got up in wrapper and gave her 'Happy Valley' to read.

---

121 *Happy Valley* was Patrick White's first published novel and appeared in 1939. The author never allowed it to be reprinted.

*18 April 1939*_____ Wind made it a cold day. Worked on Furphy. Harry came in afternoon. The interruptions are constant. I never work for more than 15 [minutes] unmolested. Very wearing.

*9 May 1939*_____ Went to town at 3 to do shopping & get proofs at A & R.[122] But I was so exhausted I had to sit in the News Reel theatre till time to meet Cousins. D.C. [Dymphna Cusack] came too. She is no help—lazy—thinks she is such a genius that she need not slog. Got home at six & read proofs till 10.

*13 June 1939*_____ Mother, Mother, a year ago today—it was a Monday then—you were still with us. Your mind was clearer than mine. It had all its old clarity and surety. I asked you about people in Goulburn whom I had forgotten, whose names were in an old paper, and you knew them as firmly as forty years ago when we were there. Father gone, taking his memory, and now you were really gone too—the anguish of it, and how was one to survive in the poverty of past knowledge that was ahead? All your intransigence gone, gone was all the irritability, the tortured & torturing struggle against failing strength. You rested in a clear calm like a ship in port with her engines quiet. The slight moideredness—so very slight by comparison with other old people's—that sometimes was evident, had gone. You had your youthful alertness and amiability. You were now pleased even with me. A lot came that afternoon. I decided to have afternoon tea in your room so that they could all be around your bed. 'If there is not enough other food and cake, tell Mrs Wilkinson to

---

122 Proofs of *Pioneers on Parade*, written in collaboration with Dymphna Cusack.

give the people bread and butter,' you said. Still concerned with your generous hospitality, which made of your home a free boarding house. You were never caught without provision, never unpunctual, never flagged. I have never seen a like combination of courage, industry and organizing ability—(wasted). I sat with you that night. You said several times that you were leaving no trouble behind you, that everything had been attended to. (It certainly had.) A few details worried you—Jack [Franklin] foremost. You seemed comforted when I promised to do my best. You worried that you were leaving me with such terrible old furniture. You had wanted often to get me a new modern suite & a new typewriter. I had been firmly against it fearing there might not be enough money to see you out.

'You will be alone in this old barn!' you said.

'Stay a little while with me, and comfort me,' you said.

And I am tortured by that, fearing that you did not realise that I never left you at nights at the end. Thirty-six and more hours without sleep did not affect me at all, so bad a sleeper am I, and anguish took sleep's place then. I offered to read the Bible but you declined decidedly.

'This can't go on. The end must come, the end must come,' you murmured at intervals.

You had such fortitude. Steady & calm, it never failed in any trial. Why can I too not have fortitude? 'The end must come.' Why, oh why was I too awkward to talk with you about that vast, imminent journey? Why are those to be left and those at the moment of going too constricted, inhibited, to talk to each other about it? Are they both too anguished and overawed about the fell mystery? Is there anything beyond the grave? The anguish will not abate. When we entered the desolate place after the funeral, Norman burst out, 'Well, she's gone. She reared us on nothing—fed and clothed us & tried to educate us.' Then grief broke his voice & he turned away. He felt that remorse that sickens me too that you had nothing from life but the fortitude and effort you brought to it. Nothing but trials, disappointments and griefs. But Norman and I have had nothing either but struggling unavailingly with insufficient strength. And what had poor old Dad but his own triumphant soul—and that, after all, is the only kingdom.

27 June 1939   Oh, the hellish desolation: I <u>can't</u> go on living.

17 August 1939   Went to town, met Aunt Lena [Lampe] for the Irene Castles film, lunch at Cahills[123]—saw the modern art show at D.J.'s [David Jones] & home to cook dinner. In evening went to committee F.A.W. [Fellowship of Australian Writers], afterwards supper at Repins[124] with N. Cayley & F. Eldershaw & home.

3 September 1939   In evening went to New T. [Theatre] League to hear L. Rees' play read on Eureka Stockade.[125] Came away with Louis Esson & saw S.M.H. poster that France & England were at war.

Sadness & despair.

(A letter never sent: I have forgotten why: perhaps because I did not want to depress Mary [Fullerton] by reiteration of my sadness. M.F.)

Dearest Mary, The burden of my wretchedness from grief lifts a little today so that I indulge myself in a chat with you. Ah, that

---

123 A chain of restaurants.
124 A coffee house.
125 *Lalor of Eureka*, 1937, by Leslie Rees. It won a Melbourne New Theatre competition.

it could be a two-way affair as of yore, you in bed, I in the comfortable chair cosying my feet under your eiderdown.

Yesterday I attended the Henry Lawson pilgrimage, organized each year by the Fellowship of Australian Writers. The gathering is at the Lawson group by Lambert, which is set on that high point beyond the Art Gallery in the Outer Domain on the way to Mrs Macquarie's chair.[126] On one side is the wall of the Botanic Gardens, on the other Woolloomooloo Bay with the big ships tame at the wharfs. Lovely! Lovely is the world and many of man's works thereon when he is not erupting in the mad-bullness of his maleness as in Europe again today.

Mrs Bertha Lawson was there and his son Jim (hers too of course). Jim has the gleaming eyes of his dad, the slenderness, and a real old drawl such as I have not heard in such perfection for many years. He is an Ancient Mariner: starts off to anyone who will listen, regardless: if that one escapes he goes on with the discourse to the next at hand without a break—original, unclassifiable talk such as made A.G.S. [A.G. Stephens] describe him to me: 'Well, Jim's dopey—just dopey.' I was enjoying him at a first go, but so many came up to congratulate me on winning the Prior Memorial Prize (K.B. [Kate Baker] and I got it with 'Who was Joseph Furphy?') and to suggest tea together afterwards that I was continually disconnected from Jim.

It was the usual ceremony: Bart Adamson, H.M. Green, Arthur Crocker, Rod Quinn and Tom Moore spoke, and some were on the air later, also another man from Dept. of Education, longwinded and schoolmannish, to whom no one listened.

---

126 George Lambert sculpted the Lawson monument in the Domain, Sydney. It depicts Henry Lawson standing, as if he were about to speak, flanked by a sheep-dog on one side and a pensive, seated 'swaggie' on the other. It was finished just before Lambert's death in 1930 and unveiled in July 1931.

I had accepted tea with Mrs Henry and Jim, with Tom Moore, and Inky [Stephensen] and I forget how many others, but I espied old Billy Miller (Linklater), 50 years in N.T., worked with the Watsons—so I ran after him and passed him to Inky, and when I got through only Tom remained, held up by Duncan MacDougall. All the others had walked out of sight. So we three walked into town. Tom and I talked in a café till 6 p.m. when we went to Market St. to hear the recorded ceremony over the air. Tom asked me to another meal while waiting for his wife, and they both asked me to the pictures with them. I sat between them and it was such a relief amid the gathering war clouds, and we laughed at slick farces in peace.

I seized the opportunity with Tom for your poems, but he wanted to talk about our entries in the Prior Memorial. It was this way. Some time before on August 7th Farmer Whyte had a nice tea party at the Hotel Sydney to which he had asked me to round up such people as Tom, Dymphna [Cusack] and Xavier [Herbert]. There were others too, who made no impression on me. Tom and Farmer Whyte both arrived on this occasion together with the announcement that the Prize had been won by some vast thing on Macquarie, and the announcement would be in the coming Bulletin. I knew of the Macquarie opus from its author M.H. Ellis. He has been 15 years on it. Researched Macquarie through Scotland and his clan, and tracked him through his military campaigns in India. Went to all the places in pursuit— 250,000 words by a raging enthusiast—outclassed everything that was put in. Soon as I knew it was in the swim I knew it was all over for our puny effort.

So that was that, and I wrote to Kate.

But there was no announcement in the Bulletin of that week. Yet another Wednesday went by and then Mr Prior telephoned me, and asked me to come in as soon as possible. He took me into his confidence, so this is private. The judges, Frank Davison, H.M. Green, and Louis Esson, had brought in a unanimous verdict for Ellis' Macquarie as this year's winner—were so sure of themselves that they said so abroad. Prior said that, knowing Ellis, he would not be satisfied until after the MSS had been to some authority on the subject. The judges persisted that it was a great work, particularly Green, who considered himself as good an authority as any. Prior said, knowing Ellis (he is a Bulletin staff member) he still insisted on extra judgment. It went to Ida Leeson. She worked on it for a fortnight. She said it was undocumented and full of inaccuracies—altogether in an unfinished condition. He said Ida was firmly against it as the prize winner. The prize has been collecting for the three years since I won it with 'Swagger', and Prior said they now <u>had</u> to find something.

The judges said if Macquarie was ruled out there was nothing fit for the award this year. Furphy was ruled out because about one-third of it is extracts and letters from Furphy—not all my own geniass.

Prior said he consulted Ida about this and she said that without seeing the Furphy effort she considered that any book by Miles Franklin would be a hundred per cent better than Macquarie, that literary merit did not go by size, and so on. So Prior called the judges to him again and said they had to make some award. So they gave Furphy the normal award of one hundred pounds, and the accumulation to be carried forward till next year when Macquarie finished will have another chance.

I think Mr Prior did very well indeed to settle the matter that way. I was glad of the prestige as Kate thought that Macartney or Furnley Maurice might have been better than I to handle the material. I had a difficult struggle for my way of doing it, even to the naming. It was no easy task, as no one knows Furphy. No use [in] writing of him as if he were someone with a large acquaintance (literary) awaiting news of him. If I had not won this Kate would have thought that I had misused the material, but now she thinks it splendid. Also she needed the money. Poor little thing was talking of going out to do a day's cleaning to make ends meet. It will be a crown on her long devotion in collecting the stuff.

Prior said that the judges' placing ran thus:

Macquarie, first

Furphy, second

Australia's (6) Major Poets, third (Tom Moore)[127]

Bulawarra novel by Eric Lowe

A Big Tome on Papuan Administration

Another Novel by an unknown.

Louis Esson has told me that they arrived at judgments separately and independently, and all agreed on Macquarie and then Furphy with no question. After that nothing worth anything, that Tom Moore lacked originality. The two novels very dull but just about worth publishing. The Papuan thing merely administrative but commendable for the effort.

I have been out today with Ellis and now am to meet Green to hear what he has to say for himself. Ellis and I have long been chums. He was born on the Paroo[128] or some spot near there. Had to support his family at 17 and since 11 has only one eye. Spoiled the other with scissors. A nervous shy man. I do hope he gets the prize next year—all those years of work! And so generous

---

127 Tom Inglis Moore *Six Australian Poets*, with a foreword by C. Hartley Grattan was eventually published in 1942.
128 Paroo River, south western Queensland.

and nice to me. Says his book is too unfinished in its present state to be a prize winner. He has read thousands of MSS in the Mitchell [Library]. Despite that and having only one eye he has generously offered to do an index for Furphy for me because he has had practice in his own work.

Eric Lowe's novel, not this one about Bulawarra but the one called 'I sold my Horses', was second after 'Swagger' in the last competition that drew a prize.

Tom Moore spoke generously too, said that I was a popular winner, and, as for himself, after himself, I was the one person he liked best to win it. He is a nice big generous-minded creature to discuss things with.

4 November 1939   Hot fine day—Nor [Norman Franklin] always sour & depressing. I am very tired of him. He would behave better with strangers. Never says a kind or cheering word to me.

24 November 1939   Worked in house & garden, so exhausted I wish I could reconcile myself to relinquish the struggle & die. If only Norman would go away for a week & give me respite from his unsympathetic presence.

25 December 1939   Cool day—grey. Jack [Franklin] & I went to Lena [Lampe] for dinner. Then Lena & I went to Ruby Brydon for tea. Will & R. pleasant & kind. But oh! I was exhausted & such a day of dud human beings—not one remark of wit, intelligence, culture, wisdom or knowledge—truly without vision the people perish. And Australians' lack of vision is doubly feeble being vassalage to England & the world. To bed exhausted & depressed at 10 p.m.

30 December 1939   Cooking & cleaning—curse it. If Nor [Norman Franklin] & Jack [Franklin] were worth it or kind to me I would not so much mind, but they are a useless self-indulgent pair.

31 December 1939   Beatrice & Jack came in afternoon & stayed for afternoon tea. Then Jack & Norman calmly announced that they were both off to town to see N[ew] Y[ear] in. It was then too late for me to make any arrangements. I had to see the N.Y. in alone with what equanimity I could summon. Went to bed at 11 & did not wake till 2 a.m. There had been no sound in the street— all must have been out.

1 January 1940   Had to stay in and cook & char because of Jack & Norman but the Fogdens invited me to join them so at 2.30 I departed. Bert Swales driving Mr & Mrs & May [Fogden] & I. We went to National Pk & took a boat & rowed well up the stream & had a picnic. Oh, such sad memories since Eva & Tal [Hume Talmage Franklin] had a picnic for me in 1924. Then too we had a boat, & Geoff Henry & I each had an oar. Not so many ferns now along the stream, but the law saves some of the native flora from the savages. Mother & Father, Aunt Sara & Miss Gillespie as well as Tal & Eva gone since then, of that special picnic. Beattie Bridle was very charming that day. I recall a little Geoff kept putting his hand in mine & leading me about affectionately. Poor old Mother used to complain so bitterly that all her mates were gone—mine all going fast.

28 January 1940   Very hot day. 105° in Sydney. 98° in our back room at 4 p.m. Damn the cooking 3 meals a day for useless men. I was so weary I could not think out improvements in text of 'Swagger' after a night of 3 hrs sleep & Jack [Franklin] in and out all day—no hope of rest.

They sleep in day & roam at night & disturb me. I loathe people living with me.

24 April 1940   Grey morning but warm day & cleared up. Left Ruby cleaning house. Mrs Fogden & I met at Stn. & met May [Fogden] at Manly wharf. Went across to Manly to see Q. Mary. Lunch at Manly. Saw HMS Australia coming in. Mauritania etc. The Harbor was full of action & beauty. Those big boats never would have come but to ship our boys to the shambles. In afternoon Mrs F. & I went to Minerva to see Steinbeck's 'Of Mice & Men'. Hurried home & got dinner for Norman.

5 May 1940   Awoke to light rain. Cooked dinner. I simply can't get strength for writing & Norman is a strain so sour & self-centred—never a pleasant or intelligent word or thought on anything. His lamp of life has nothing but vinegar or bilge.

7 May 1940   Showers all day.
Usual household chores & cooking—deadly tired. In evening went to F.A.W. [Fellowship of Australian Writers] committee. Free

Speech the issue—Nearly all nit-wits & against it—FitzHenry a competent quibbler. One Stephens female said there was a war on & we must not criticise the Govt.

18 May 1940   Ida Leeson rang up & I went to dinner at her house to meet a Mrs Lachlan or Loghlan from Columbia University (38,000 students). Very unprepossessing—not of gentle folk evidently. But I wanted to get her point of view—difficult because Florence Birch twittered all the time to me personally with small-talk gentility playing the ladylike hostess. Home at 11.30 & dropped in on the Andresen's party for Mildred's 17th birthday. Oh, dear, what some people think is pleasure!

24 September 1940   Pottered—wasted day—exhausted.
     I can't wait on Jack & Norman—I resent their uselessness & unkindness & selfishness and self-indulgence & ignorance. Never to meet anyone from month end to month end with a spark of intelligence or knowledge of things interesting to me.

3 October 1940   Jack nasty and selfish and insolent—Norman instead of helping me to discipline him as usual helped to insult me. Nor says no one ever has done anything with J or ever will, & he (N.) slobbers around him as the extension of his own ego & in response to flattery from Jack. It made me quite ill. Mother broke me down & 2 years of N & J have completed the wreck. Went to Dr Booth's Anzac women & their knitting and garment work & slobbering worship of royalty—there was not one gleam of brain in anything said. Went to newsreel—sickening, sickening of wreck of London and instruments of war (male madness) all around the world. Home depressed to cook Jack's dinner.

20 November 1940   In morning wrote to Mary [Fullerton].

In afternoon met R.T. Baker at Metropole [Hotel] & the little dear gave me a Doulton Waratah cup.[129]

From there I went to Mutch at Par. Hse & had tea in room of Member for Yass.[130] Two men Baxter & Chester came in to talk business chicanery with him. Mr Mutch gave me tea. He renewed his offer to work like devil & give me all material if I'd do H. Lawson biography with him.

25 November 1940   Mother's birthday—gone are some of her contemporaries who used to gather for it—Miss G. [Gillespie] prominently. Awful day—I felt so ill—trembling at knees & elbows & as if blood had gone thick in veins. Lay down during afternoon. In evening went to Minerva to see 'Design for Living' with Noel Coward present in person. Went early & sat in gallery to see the hoi polloi arrive. The only members of my acquaintance were D. Deamer, Ruby Illingworth, Connie Stephens Robertson, Mrs Vernon Coles, & Adam McKay's niece. Only other I recognised by sight—Andrea [Dorothy Jenner], gushing on Noel. Noel dark & dissipated with on & off stage technique perfect. Never raised his voice yet every word he said in curtain speech easily heard as if he were [in the] next seat, in last row of gallery where I was.

Slight shower while we were in theatre. Home at 1 a.m.

---

129 Franklin would offer tea to special visitors in this cup and ask them to sign her visitors' book. The cup was presented to the Mitchell Library by the Misses Bridle in January 1956.
130 George Edward Ardill, of the United Australia Party.

November 1940   Once again the cicadas announce that it is summer. I heard them again after 17 years that December morning of my return. Some fell on the deck of the Tahiti outside the Heads. It was a glorious Sydney morning bulging with bush fire smoke and warmth. My shipmates, finding the insects, said: 'Let's try them on Miss Franklin.' They expected me to start from the whirr, but I put the lovely creature on my neck, as I love the clinging nip of beetles & cicadas. 'Oh! Are you an Australian!' they exclaimed.

12 December 1940   Grey day. In morning X. Herbert called me on telephone & talked for 60 min. about himself. I have all his frustrations & perplexities & more agonies but would not think of thrusting them on a colleague so extensively. Glorious male ego—no wonder it achieves. I got a cushion to put under my elbows.

In evening Mrs Fogden & I went to Carlton movies 'Florian' & Deanna Durbin in 'It's a Date'. Deanna is not lovable.

1 January 1941   Woke early to a heavy grey still morning. Began to rain ever so gently at 8 a.m. Fed my bantams after a breakfast of warmed potatoes and tackled 'Give Battle'. Rain went off.

Left at 5 p.m. to have dinner with Ada Holman & her sisters on Ocean St. Dear me, I used to go up that St to dear Miss Scott when I was young. Blocks of flats are thick where in those days were enticing carriage drives under great trees leading to unseen houses by way of splendid shrubs, trees & flower beds. Some showy Scots in their national costume on the train from the sports at Kyeemagh [Sydney suburb]. I got home well before

12 after a fair dinner & a dull evening. Ada is alright, but spare me the sisters.

16 January 1941   Pottered—depressed and enervated. Shall I ever recover or would it be better to give in & die. I haven't the strength to char up the garden & house.

24 February 1941   Warm day. P.R. [Stephensen] rang up and said he & Winnie were coming out. I scurried to prepare something. Must be over a year since I have seen Winnie. She is now an echo of P.R.S. Oh, dear, says Germany is 'modern'. Ye gods! Modern mechanisation of ancient barbarism. He is predicting that Britain will be defeated. I pray not. He says X.H. [Herbert] is a treacherous plotting scoundrel: that he will never write another novel: that 'Capricornia' was a jumble when he (P.R.S.) took it in hand.[131] I wonder.

9 April 1941   Today, exhausted, I fell asleep. The bliss of sleep. If only I could sleep like that for an hour every day I might recover mental & spiritual vigor. I dreamed that Mother and Linda[132] were still with me. What warmth, how rich it made me— how rich! I awoke to the chilling fact of my poverty. For normal uses we are rich while those of our family and personal drama— our own generation—are alive and in touch with us. We grow

131 Stephensen had assisted Herbert in the revision of *Capricornia* which was first published in 1938 by the Publicist Publishing Company with which Stephensen was associated.
132 Ida Lampe Franklin, but always known as Linda, was Franklin's sister born in September 1881. She married Charles Graham in 1904 and died from pneumonia in August 1907, aged 25, while Franklin was in Chicago.

poor & poorer as they drop off and leave us lonely. Loneliness is an acute form of poverty. Father grew richer rather than poorer with age because he never gave way to grief or loneliness but exulted increasingly in the wonder of being alive per se—some secret he had captured till he realised he was part of eternal life—not in the mere saying of it but in realising it freely.

The warrior dies rich for he dies young and therefore unlonely. Perhaps that is why men worship Mars and they do not shrink from meeting and dealing violent death.

19 July 1941   Lovely day. Did bit in garden and chores in house. In afternoon Paul Haugh came & cut down the two front trees for me. I gave him large bottle of fig jam, about 40 lemons and 'Mutiny of the Bounty' by Nordhoff & Hall.[133] Gave him tea & we had a chat. He was gentle & friendly & kind.

I spent the evening reading 'Flush' by Virginia Woolf. The sensitivity of her writing is delightful as well as its lucidity. It would be nourishing to talk with her over this. She should not have let us who loved her down by committing suicide as it leaves her open to such accusations as detract from the value of the lovely searching behind the veils that she did.

10 August 1941   Fine again but clouds at 5 p.m. Did nothing. The desolation got me down. If I diverted the courage it is taking to go on living to facing the fact of dying perhaps I could go in peace. I wanted first to straighten my papers & MSS. Why don't

---

133 Charles Nordhoff and James Hall first published in 1933 in America a novel based on the mutiny on HMS *Bounty*. It went through many editions and was the basis for the famous 1936 film starring Charles Laughton and Clark Gable.

I simply burn them all and be done with the futile struggle? Went to FAW [Fellowship of Australian Writers] meeting & took chair for Green's lecture on Mary Gilmore.

21 September 1941 Lovely day. Mrs A. came to telephone in morning. I did up front room for blackout . . . In evening I went to F.A.W. [Fellowship of Australian Writers] to hear B. Adamson on our intellectual blackout. I had to take chair. Good full meeting. Had to be quite in dark after 9 because the wardens said light was leaking out of door down stairs. It was a nervous strain to impose any chairmanship in dark. The meeting was very good. Got home by 11.30.

20 November 1941 Had to put my nose down and write anecdote for Mr Finnegan's magazine & a message for J.B. Ferguson's MS. magazine. So tired by late nights that I had snooze in afternoon—dreamt vividly that I was on the way home from England & hoping to see Dad & Mum again. In dream realised Dad had gone but would see Mother, had that tense apprehension lest she might be gone that I had on 3 homecomings. Woke to desolation to find them all dead long ago & all the others gone & left me.

Norman Franklin died in hospital on 24 January 1942, aged 55. He was the last of Franklin's family. His death added to Miles' sense of desolation. She was also worried by the behaviour of her nephew, Jack, now aged 21, who was on the road to alcoholism.

Also, in early 1942 Australia seemed in a precarious position with the Japanese advancing, the fall of Singapore and the bombing of Darwin. It was perhaps some comfort that All That Swagger *was being broadcast on the ABC during February.*

*27 March 1942*____ Heavy showers all through the night & a real wet day. In afternoon Ida Leeson rang up to tell of the sensational charges in papers about the A. First movement.[134] Mrs Morgan came over to see if I was alright & to invite me to tea with her. I had to wade round to back door ankle deep in the water.

I cleared out big carton of Demmy's & Will's love letters[135]— never dreamed there were so many. Back they took me to the fragrance of youth & pre-war 1914.

*3 May 1942*____ Well, my diary, it is a long time since I said anything to you. Too desolated by Mother's going and more recently by Norman's to take up life again.

Last evening Xavier H. [Herbert] came to dinner and to spend some hours . . .

X said during dinner that he and I are the only story-tellers in Australia: the others might be attempts at literati but we were the two who knew the pulse of the people. When he is talking to another doubtless he and that other become the only two great writers & he is then as contemptuous of me as he is of F.D.D. [F.D. Davison]. He said a writer must not be political, must confine his art to pure story-telling with no political philosophy. X is a more inventive storymaker than I, but my core of faith is a compass to me. That is where X is weak. His book is a better story than 'Grapes of Wrath' but the Grapes have more power because there is vision & direction in them, whereas X's incidents become only

---

134 The Australia-First Movement was founded by P.R. Stephensen in October 1941. It was a right-wing nationalist movement opposed to Australia's involvement in the Second World War. Stephensen was interned without trial in March 1942.

135 'Demmy' is Demarest Lloyd and 'Will' is his older brother, William Bross Lloyd.

things observed—by a genius perhaps, but there is a lack in spiritual integrity. K.T. [Kylie Tennant] is similar but without genius. I wonder what a person of ample perception would say of me. The trouble is that I am, so far, bigger than my observers and I cannot use them as an adequate mirror.

24 May 1942 Warmish day. Busy in morning. In afternoon went to F.A.W. [Fellowship of Australian Writers] and did washing-up for the first afternoon for soldiers. Washing-up arrangements just as primitive and muddled as ever—typically British. Women who have no mind above charing in the end have so little intelligence that they can't manage that spaciously, the charing, I mean.

30 June 1942 Jack arrived at 12.30 and had lunch. The trouble with his eyes is enlarged pupils—from kidney trouble. Poor boy.

I repotted my hydrangeas. Corrected story about Nedda Rich & began to type it.

Feeling loss of Norman terribly. It rose to anguish. I could see him in the dark coat with the blue facings. He had so little in life & went through it so lonely & so bravely. Why this anguish of existence at all?

28 August 1942 Yesterday went to Mark Foy's[136] to the 40th anniversary of the enactment of woman suffrage in New South Wales. Mrs Quirk, M.L.A., chief speaker. After 40 years we have

---

136 Sydney department store.

only this specimen in parliament. They wasted time before beginning. We were bidden for 2.30 and it was nearly 4 before speaking began. Mrs Quirk M.L.A. tall and stout, real publican's widow figure. Majestically attired in an expensive black beaded gown & cape with white facings, so well cut and she so expensively harnessed that her figure instead of gross became fashionable. Her coiffure and make-up, even to tinted nails, must have been the work of a professional. Tilted fashionable hat, ropes of imitation pearls, four glaring diamond rings, artificial posy. She had a thick sheaf of quarto sheets: on each was a sentence or two. She discoursed on each of these as texts for an incredible time and then laid it down so that her victims could ache with boredom because of the number still to be endured. She kept on for half an hour. People were sneaking out in ones, twos & fives. The M.L.A. seemed quite oblivious of this. As an illustration of the worthiness of women's rule she instanced the 60 years reign of Victoria in which there was never any war or slavery!!!!! Then she fulminated about Florence Nightingale and her struggle. Told how Florence had hung about the doors of the hospitals in the Crimean war (couldn't the ass know that this was one war in Victoria's reign?). At length Florence got into the hospitals with her little lantern and rescued the men from the swarms of flies. Now flies & snow do not operate in concert. Flies disappear even in Sydney's mild snowless winters, and in any case go to bed when little lanterns come out.

Thus she lumbered along, her whole utterance on that scale of pomposity, spuriosity & ignorance. The chairman was frantic. She was whispering under the M.L.A.'s great bowsprit that the other speakers would have to be cut out as closing-time was approaching. M.L.A. seemed to be in a trance of auto-intoxication and unaware of emptying seats & bored & restive victims.

I leaned across & said to the chairman that I would be overjoyed to forgo my talk of 10 minutes into which I had been pressed because of Lucy Cassidy. The chairman thanked me with joy: she had never heard of me. I had paid two shillings for a tea mostly of uninteresting scone & 1s 8d train fare, an expenditure I could ill afford as well as the wasted day. In hopes of salvaging something I sunk off to do a few errands before half-past five. The M.L.A. had now gone on for 40 minutes and the notes in her hand weren't half done. I had nearly reached the lift with the other escapees when Lucy & Mrs Lawson espied me. Despite her lameness Lucy started in pursuit. She is taller & stronger than I. She clutched my coat & I could not without unseemliness prevail against her on the slippery floor. She returned me to the obsequies remarking in full voice: 'Miles Franklin that everyone wants to hear, sneaking off!' The victims were glad of the diversion. It did not break the trance of the M.L.A. Relief however was on the side of the beleaguered. M.L.A. took a substantial fit of coughing. The waitresses had long since surreptitiously extracted all the cutlery & vessels. The manager of the floor was found. At long last, with everyone on the qui vive like Sister Anne, water arrived, but it did not rescue the M.L.A. from her cough. So with long drawn-out apologies for having to desist in the middle of her speech, she subsided just as she was advocating the spoils to the victors in politics.

A few other battered war horses, rusty with faction & destitute of vision, had to have their airing & then I had to tackle a bored audience aching to be home. I spoke for five minutes only. Not one went out nor looked bored—I made a survey. Then Bertha Lawson presented the M.L.A. with some of Henry's books. God knows why except that Bertha having been unable to live with Henry as a wife is now having a distinguished career among the non-cognoscenti as his widdy. She took scarcely a minute in her speech: but up rose the M.L.A. again and made a seven-minute speech of horn-blowing acceptance. She said Henry Lawson was her favorite poem (sic). Her other favorite poem was Kipling's 'If' because every word of it could be applied to Jack Lang!!!!!

She was the equal as an empty windbag of any male, ignorant, self-seeking member of Parliament. Shades of Rose Scott. Poor Australia!!

5 September 1942   In afternoon went to Lawson statue & gave oration.[137] Clive Evatt asked me twice if I would be finished by sundown. Second time I said it was doubtful if I would <u>start</u> before sundown because I had a politician ahead of me. My oration was wasted on that crew with few exceptions. Jim Lawson has got fat—greasy hat band talked all through the ceremony. He is decidedly queer. Came home & had rest & back to give oration again over 2 F.C. at 9.45. Mackaness ahead of me talking about Moll. He is stupid—can't analyse a poet. Howarth was reading the poems—very badly I thought.

11 October 1942   Nettie Palmer at the F.A.W. [Fellowship of Australian Writers] lecture on Oct 11th aided feebly but worshipfully by F.D.D. [F.D. Davison] extolled the work of Louis [Esson]. It was one of those 'wakes' that the [word indecipherable] hold occasionally to acclaim each other: & which Mary Gilmore has brought to such a pitch for herself from her well-mobilised

---

137 The Lawson statue in the Domain, Sydney. An annual ceremony was arranged here by the Fellowship of Australian Writers. Franklin's speech was published in *Meanjin Papers*, 12, Christmas 1942, pp. 17–20: 'No Australian who has wrestled with the ardors and subtleties of resolving this continent in terms of literature will discount Henry Lawson. Few have equalled him: none has yet excelled him. His achievement remains unique.'

followers. When F. Eldershaw on F.D.D. (or Marjory B. [Barnard])
get through there is nothing left to say about a possible Shakespeare. Nettie was well in the tradition with poor frail old Louis.
He looks such a walking ghost & has such a just appreciation of
Australian literature that I do not begrudge him his hour, but it
was foolishly excessive. He was humorous about it. By Nettie's
and F.D.D.'s account Louis has had a profound influence
on Australian Literature by his criticism & plays. I was called on
suddenly to move vote of thanks & said I of course thought Mr
Esson a great critic because he had given my Furphy biography
the prize: spoke of his literary integrity, said we had seen his play
the 'Drovers' here & it had stood out, & so on. I never rested till
I got to the Mitchell to read his plays which I had entirely
overlooked at a first reading. Well, the 'Woman Tamer' is a push
& stoush drama, done humorously & on the right side of the
woman question at the time, which increases my appreciation of
Louis, but the verisimilitude might have been achieved because
of reading about the slum life instead of living it. D.C. [Dymphna
Cusack] says 'The Sacred Place' is emotionalised the wrong way.
I don't know enough to demur or concur there. 'Dead Timber':
a 'past carin'' kind of story but without Lawson's knowledge of
the bush. Louis mixes things. Is it drought, too much rain or
shiftlessness that is the root of the people's trouble? They can't
buy chaff, but it's a tale of mud, & it's always raining. The old
man shoots himself. In real life he would have more likely gone
to the pub to moan about the lost virtue of his daughter Mary
or at best have got as far as firing a shot wide of her seducer. It
seemed to be a dairy farm, there was mud; they wanted chaff—
& gave it to the steers to fit them to travel to market. As H.M.
[Green] points out the chaff would have gone to the milking cows
& the steers have been given a bit of scrub, & I added that with
all that mud they would have held the steers back for another
market day. Louis's knowledge of the bush is patently inadequate.

He has not done a sustained job like mine. I then turned to his criticism and found he had not mentioned Tom Collins at all. 'The Athaneum' far away in London did more for Australian Literature in that case. It makes me wonder if the 'Drovers' is in proper character.

28 October 1942   Anguish engulfs me. If I write it to you Mary [Fullerton] I may find relief because I am half extrovert. I need not send you what I write as Mabel [Singleton] says that as far as possible she now keeps all distresses from you. It is now passed sixteen months since my brother spent his last night in this old home. He never came back here for a night again. His little old room is hardly more than 6 ft by 6 ft. It is unlined, its iron roof bare to the view and the outer wall all stained where the rain has beaten through the cracks. It is in fact a bit of enclosed verandah; nothing could be more humble or limited but it has the charm of retreat. Its little window gets the morning sun: on hot nights it is cool. Father had it for his till nearly the end of his sojourn, until I left for London, and in his failing strength he had a fancy that he would be better in my room. So Mother told me.

The room was a favorite with me too. I wanted it. Once I got into it while some old cousins were with us for two months, and I tried to retain it by putting Norman in one of the larger rooms, but he said if he could not have his own room he would not come home at all. That was in 1934. He came home frequently from the South Coast for weekends—& always when Jack [Franklin] had a holiday. He came home to live with me on April 28, 1939. Into his little room, he said he was more to himself there. Jack went into front room shortly after Mother vacated it for ever. Once when Norman was sick with 'flu I got him into Lena's [Lampe] room—more space to wait on him there—and not so cramped when the doctor came. But as soon as my back was turned he upped & changed back to his own lair. I used to rest there on afternoons after sleepless nights when Jack and Norman were away at work, the scent of the lemon blossom was heavy in it. It had for years nothing but a dilapidated stretcher and no light but a kerosene lamp. I fixed Mother's electric bedside lamp for it & bought a new & comfortable stretcher and a new coverlet. Norman said it was a great improvement.

Now I could have it for ever, but God in heaven, it drenches me with anguish. I see poor Norman there in pain the afternoon he left for the hospital. I was not sufficiently aware how desperately ill and suffering he was.

I steeled myself to go into it today to clear out things because Jack is nearly a week gone to R.A.A.F. training school and if he too should come no more I could not face the ordeal of going through these mute reminders. I had of course cleared out the place fairly well long ago. Norman took most of his things from time to time after he came out of hospital & went to Ruby: Jack did likewise when he followed his father to Ruby.

Still much of both remained. Norman had kept Jack's tennis racket, cricket bat, bales & balls, also every letter that Jack had written him and some of Mother's. There were the tablets and powders that he had had to ease pain, his razor strop, glass and brushes. Still some shirts & socks and a white overall-coat—that he will never, never, come back to use. He was against piling up sentimental rubbish but there remained snapshots of Mother & Jack, a photograph of his wife, and her luggage slip with her name in her own writing still in it: there remain other suitcases that I have not yet the courage to tackle.

Norman's shaving mirror with the magnifying looking glass at the back I shall put up for men visitors to use—in memory of Norman; he was so generous in hospitality having been trained to it from his infant days. Often as little boys or as youths he and Tal [Hume Talmage Franklin] would give up their room and go to the hayshed to accommodate guests, invited or uninvited. His desk, a present from Mother, is still untouched. So pitifully few things he had after 56 years of delving in Australia! Life yielded him so little!

Jack said in departing: 'Get rid of everything: I may never come back.' If he too should come back no more ever again I could no longer survive. Why this anguish of suffering? It cuts like a knife & leaves me drained and helpless. There are none to grieve for me who has grieved so desperately for each as he or she went; and grief will not soften. Time instead of lessening or dispersing griefs has rounded them all up and intensified them. Grief is an illness and is particularly deleterious to the mental powers. It is a form of nostalgia.

14 November 1942   Sat. night.

Lovely warmth, 90 degrees at sunset on my thermometer, so I put on my N.Y. black chiffon & went off to 5 Phillip St. to see Beryl Bryant's new play house—great improvement on the old, incidentally. Disappointed to find her show was not on. Wasted my 2s 3d on 'Streamlined' by Mab Eldershaw . . . It was one of those things: réchauffé of dead West End commercial successes that served as vehicles for star actresses—the greatest of all being Marie Tempest, lately dead: Maggie Albanesi dead in her youth; Gladys Cooper, Madge Titheradge, Tallulah Bankhead, Edna Best & all the galaxy now dimmed by years & drowned by the films. This attempt did not anchor anywhere—a man had the part, a man from New Guinea. Why its name I could not determine. There was no sign of acting talent—completely inexperienced. It showed me that a play well read is preferable, less embarrassing to the audience than one acted without confidence & talent. The thing was milk & water imitation of London. The audience seemed en suite. Many young people & a goodly sprinkling of men in civvies. No one I had seen before. A different crowd entirely from Beryl's and thereby conclusions can be drawn. I sat like a ghost from some other society alone. Behind me were the chatterers as like to the chatterers as the London models from which the play was drawn, just the same ratio of dilution from the thing imitated. They were gabbling about 'The Hound of Heaven'. Then the male regretted that the old days were gone, 'no more sitting on cushions on the floor & listening to Dulcie Deamer discussing poetry & literature'. 'Who's Dulcie Deamer?' 'Oh, she's a writer, wonderful, but terribly oversexed. She's had an affair with everyone in Sydney. She's 45 and really a very wonderful woman apart from that.' The female was inclined to dismiss her as promiscuous on this evidence. The man declaimed any part in Dulcie's promiscuity. He went on to confess that his head was full of plays, that he fell to creating them at all sorts of hours. At the end I turned quickly to regard him. He was even more of a goof in appearance than I had expected—callow as a baby seal with a strange round face like a new born chick's if its bill were removed so as not to interfere with the complete roundness. A southerly had blown up & I was chilly coming home though I was wearing mother's velvet jacket given to her by Norman.

1942   'The Pea Pickers' by Eve Langley (Angus & Robertson 1942).

Well, Well! Wonders will never cease. Mary Gilmore thinks I wrote this or I plus my unknown poet.[138] Frank Dalby Davison

---

138 Mary Gilmore wrote to Miles Franklin on 26 April 1942 saying that she had 'felt Stella Miles Franklin's mind all through it' and later in the letter wondered whether the writer was 'S.M.F. plus the unknown poet S.M.F found' (Franklin papers ML MSS 364/3/8, p369). The unknown poet was Mary Fullerton. Franklin had arranged for a volume of Fullerton's poetry, *Moles Do So Little with Their Privacy*, to be published by Angus & Robertson in 1942, under the pseudonym 'E'.

has been extolling this book as lyrical so off to Angus & Robertson's for a copy. It repels me, as phoney. The girls are supposed to be so pure and lovely—high spirited youth. They are false. Only girls vagrant by nature or slightly moronic would take their form of adventure—or else what I mean is that the author has tried to glamorize and sentimentalise a sordid adventure. If these girls were so brave & good why did they do anything so lacking in self-respect & backbone as crawl under the Italians' cubicles and steal their food. In the bush, when left in an old woman's home in the midst of timber, why did they so gutterlingishly burn her chair legs? There are wonderful phrases of course. Tried it on Joan Browne.[139] She said the situations were faked. F.D.D. and constellation raving over it. He read a letter from M.B. [presumably Marjorie Barnard] dragging in Joseph Furphy, H. Lawson et al!!! If this book should go in N.Y. or London of course it will show that something has gone wrong with me—or will it?

6 September 1943   And I am left alone in the desolation of my family graves.[140] Anguish, desolation, nostalgia. It is sad beyond endurance to return to old scenes, but when the scene is empty the arena cold . . .

Each death in my circle, and particularly the going of those who have known or shared my childhood, drenches me with chill terror of the emptiness of this strange isolated land. It is as if I felt the tremors of the first exiles. We took it from the Aborigines. We do not yet possess it spiritually. We destroy, deface,

---

139 In a postscript to a letter to Ian Mudie of 20 July 1941, Franklin wrote: 'I did not finish this last evening because a lovely young writer, Joan Browne by name, came in and I handed her your poems and we switched to reading them to one another.' (Jill Roe (ed.), *My Congenials: Miles Franklin and Friends in Letters*, volume 2, 1993, p. 55)

140 In Woronora cemetery, south of Sydney.

insult, misunderstand it—whack it—but it resists. In the shock
of bereavement—the thinning of family support—I see a dark
spirit running over the land, a spirit akin to a sardonic smile,
with the same mockery that is in the laugh of the kookaburra—
that laugh which is loud, robust, hilarious, but aches with
a mystery so baffling that it is tragic. That dark smile that runs over
the land as if all the nostalgia of oblivion lay there unquenched
and unforgiving.

I must not again go alone. The gone-awayness is too sapping.
The sunlight caresses the gravestones and the wind sweeping
over them intones the very essence of that oblivion from which
we came and to which we go.

6 and 7 October 1943   'An Outback Marriage' by A.B. Paterson
(Angus & Robertson 1906).

Returned to the reading of this in connection with an ABC
talk. A.B.P. ['Banjo' Paterson] once sent for me to collaborate with
him on a novel. Rather diffidently or sheepishly he laid it before
me in a little flat on Bent or some street in that locality. He had
written it for George Robertson and <u>he</u> said—so A.B.P. told me:
'You take this to little Miles Franklin & get her to put the blood
and tears into it.'

I read it and started to infuse it but the attempt was abortive.
A.B.P. was cynical, and shrivelled all my inspiration. I never made
more than a page or two of suggestions. By that time his reception
of them put me back into my shell which I sealed up firmly as
far as any gift or revelation of myself was concerned. The
association then proceeded with my interested investigation of
the most sophisticated man who had so far attempted to woo
me sexually. It was an exciting experience—but is another story.
Today I reread his novel.

I have so entirely forgotten it, or he had so changed it before publication that I could not swear that this is the identical story but I feel towards it exactly as I felt towards that manuscript 40 years ago.

Paterson desperately needed money to swim in the set which he was in & because of the réclame his books of his verse and his Boer war adventures had brought him. It was as if he gathered up all his knowledge of bush life and carpentered it up into a longer tale than those in his bush verses. Reading it now I see its resemblance in design to Mrs Campbell Praed's successes. He has an heiress who is sent home to be educated. There is a bright new chum, Jim Carew. There are love affairs but the brightness seems forced & the fun mechanical. Jim Carew and a Gordon, of the family who are managing the heiress's station, go north to look for the next of kin to Carew's ancestral estate. This is done creakingly to drag in buffalo hunting in the north. That sort of thing queers the whole story. The novel is cynical and shallow. It recalls to me the idiom of the period in 'totties' 'stuffing', 'leg-pulling' and 'donahs'. It will be useful as source material though its incidents are exaggerated. I remember feeling the same way about 'Three Elephant Power'[141] when I read it about 15 years ago. The happenings were too manufactured to be humorous. I tried some of them on Norman. He was utterly scornful of them and never relaxed to the ghost of a smile.

24 November 1943 ... went to see the official opening of the Public Library. On the dais noted Metcalfe & missus: T.D. Mutch: H.V. Evatt and Mary Alice, Dr Mackaness, Mrs Hubert

---

141 By A.B. Paterson, first published in 1917.

Fairfax [Ruth Fairfax]. Also Sir William Dixson, recognisable from the bronze tablet of himself pairing that of David Mitchell. Dixson can see what is to come in epitaphic honor for him. I remember Rose Scott taking me to see her cousin David. They have made his jaw lizard frill like a valance tacked around the seat of a chair. I recall it as a bit of rubbed white hair that would have been tidier non est. Dr Mackaness beamed and bloomed—the only writer on the platform, unless H.V. Evatt, who was boss spouter because he is boss trustee of the Library. He (H.V.E.) pronounced months <u>munce</u>. He is not improving with success, neither is she. Clive [Evatt] also talked, likewise the Premier (McKell), Drummond & Governor Wakehurst: Lady W's profile, directive and imposing as usual. Drummond made a good working speech about the Library—poor man, deaf, but managed his voice with complete normality. Wakehurst, with his strangely flat very un-haw-haw voice, made the best literary speech because he used stuff from C. Foyle's article in S.M.H. & from English periodicals instead of depending on his own paucity. I noted H.M. Green and Cousins in the reserved seats. Those who live on literature instead of for it gain the honors and the cash. I was in the outer edges with the hoi-polloi as at the Sesqui parties.

5 December 1943   Always on washing morning the desolation is as annihilating as ever. There are the back steps, Mother, where we had our last activities together. There you helped me pack lemons for Maggie and Edward. There, a few days before your going, you sat in the sun to dry your hair after I had washed it— until then you had always done it yourself—always dressed it yourself so daintily and smartly, which took skill & intelligence because it was fine & silky—soft & straight. Up those steps is the last time I remember seeing you walk. There, on the back doorstep, when the house was first empty after your going; anguish drowned me in the realisation that never again would I do anything for you; never, never again would you do anything for me. The one constant anchorage of my life was gone. I cannot write—the tears blind me.

Father's memory is more of a benediction, less anguishing than yours—Ah, I did not see him fade and let go at the last— he was excited & happy when I bade him good-bye for the last time on earth.

Father was a worldly failure, who did not provide adequately for us, whose shortcomings put us to pain and confusion, yet there is blessing in the memory of him, while you Mother, so brave, so grand in fortitude and steadfastness, so undefeatable by hard fortune, still wound me from beyond the grave. You too must have been desperately unhappy, confined in a hopeless net of circumstance where your immense capability was wasted. Now there is nothing but this deadly silence. No one would understand. They would all say I craved to be alone. Yes, I longed for a place to withdraw from noise, where I could have repose to think and write, but not desolation. I needed an income so that I could have an office in quiet for part of each day, and pay for your entertainment and care, but I too was one of the financially helpless, unendowed with the ruthlessness and acquisitiveness to make money.

Someday oblivion will blot out my infinitesimal anguish. One cannot run away from grief. Distraction from it does not cure it.

Miles Franklin had a small income of about £3 per week from her mother's estate following the latter's death in 1938. This came from a property at Willoughby which her parents had purchased in order to provide an income when they moved to Carlton from Penrith in 1914. Apart from this source of funds, Franklin had royalties from her books and fees from radio broadcasts, talks and articles. She received £675 as a bequest from the estate of Alice Henry in 1946. Her best year was probably 1944–45, when her gross income was

£7 per week, boosted by royalties from the Australian Pocket Library edition of Old Blastus of Bandicoot *which was commercially her most successful book selling 25 000 copies in its year of publication, 1945. The male basic wage at this time was £4/19/- so this was quite healthy. Generally, though, she made little from writing. The royalties from the Brent of Bin Bin novels were fairly slim. All That Swagger was more remunerative, earning her around £55 in each of 1938 and 1939.*[142]

1943 M. Barnard Eldershaw, 'The Glasshouse' (Harrap, London, 1936).

A minor novel by the authors of 'A House is Built'. It is the story of a writing spinster of 35 making the voyage homeward to Fremantle from Antwerp via Lisbon and the Cape. It is a Norwegian cargo vessel carrying 12 passengers—13, counting the infant Alix, aged 15 months. Stirling Armstrong is an expatriate returning to Australia after years. Nothing is given of her life abroad except that she sold off her London flat and embarked. The incidents or rather, the lack of incident and adventure of such a quiet comfortable and respectable voyage are minutely and genteelly elaborated. The 13 passengers plus the doctor, the captain and one or two of the mates are carefully exposed in the orderly, ordinary, monotonous segregation of this placid voyage on a placid ship. The writer has made the most of her material that her inhibitions and limitations as well as her literary gift permit her to do.

---

142 Figures from 'How did authors make a living? Case-study: Miles Franklin' in M. Lyons and J. Arnold (eds) *A History of the Book in Australia 1891–1945: A National Culture in a Colonial Market*, St Lucia, University of Queensland Press, 2001.

The story suggests that Stirling Armstrong has read 'Back to Bool Bool' by that crude fellow Brent, who is ignored and 'butted' by the Stirling Armstrongs of our literary scene, as far as his size and virility allow, and then set out to do such a voyage literary justice by a 'litr'y' artiste. 'The Glasshouse' is elaborated into three books. The chapters are entitled 'Night Piece', 'Variations on a Theme', 'Silly Symphony' and so on, all very proper and derivative. What is lacking in originality is made up in meticulosity: elaboration of trifles takes the place of drive. Brent deals with the voyage—two voyages—the other from San Francisco to Sydney and with two groups of people widely separated socially & financially in a chapter or two and sweeps on to other affairs like a river full of freshets while Stirling Armstrong thinly spreads her people on the one voyage over a whole pretentious book. She is more polished, more preciose and self-conscious than Brent, but to read 'The Glasshouse' beside 'Back to Bool Bool' is to understand why A.G.S. [A.G. Stephens] said that Brent took all other Australian writers in his stride: that he deals by a paragraph or a chapter with what others spread over a whole volume. Robust and wasteful man!

These people progress as such people would. They are well-behaved to a degree though frequently distasteful to the superior Stirling by being common and fat, red in the face, through eating too much and through general banality. Stirling is revealed as a respectable middle-class Englishwoman (though she is an Australian born), a little withered and withdrawn, protecting her nonentity yet desiring its superiority to be recognised.

To while away the voyage—after getting past the chapters to improve upon B of BB—Stirling takes to C. Stead's device of Salzburg tales which she imagines about the passengers. She cleverly conceives the history of each passenger in turn: of Raymond Becque the consumptive Belgian youth being sent out to the sun. Of Corinne Cartwright—a spinster of Stirling's age with a kindly father and a bossy mother. Of Wolski the mate who is soured because he can't rise to a ship of his own & because his wife is expecting a baby and he can't get news at the port. Of David Priestly the vulgar fat fellow, fond of eating, who has a good voice. Stirling imagines his having been to Germany to study and the Germans discovering that there is no music in him, despite the voice, which they lay to the fact of his being an Australian. Stirling in this anecdote betrays that she herself knows nothing of music though she speaks of 'Mother Machree' as a vulgar song. (Is it so vulgar or merely saccharine & shoddy?) The passengers, by the way, are all returning Australians except the Belgian boy & the parents of Alix—the Devlins—who leave the ship at Cape Town.

The story thought up for the doctor is the liveliest, and, taken from its context & put in the volumes 'Coast to Coast'[143], would make the lauded masterpieces in those chaff bags look thin. The pages are carefully and sometimes expertly written but that does not rescue the work from being a secondary instead of a fundamental effort. There is not enough emotion or experience to give depth to its finely studied surface.

The stories are mostly slight. Sometimes they are slated to be imagination grafted on to the life as it happens on the ship. The life on the ship has a fine air of reality: it reads like an actual experience. But accepting it as fiction, the imaginary stories with which it is wedged sometimes gives an effect of tangle or scrappiness.

The story of the captain, the Norwegian Towald Kristiansen, is told as if real and not as a fantasy made up by Stirling. Stirling

143 *Coast to Coast* was an annual, later biennial, anthology of short stories which began in 1941, published by Angus & Robertson.

is depicted as falling in love with the Captain and he responding. This incident makes me understand why men sneer at old maids' writing: it is so clearly of wishful imagination only—romanticised.

(As Mrs Hamilton once said, 'Miss Franklin, what <u>are</u> we to do to save old men from themselves when they reach that last spurt of virility before they become senile?' That was <u>apropos</u> a man of 58 who had arduously worked himself to a position of honor and then fell in a year to disaster and disgrace & penury because he looked at an obscure & persee demi-mondaine and went off his onion just as that mediocre HMG[144] has thrown away his withered wife who has coddled him so long through duodenal.)

Stirling in herself gives a portrait of a genteel maiden woman who is genteelly sex hungry. An 'old maid' by many people is supposed to be one who has never attracted men (though where any woman would have hidden to escape is outside of my observation). The Captain, like all other ageing captains segregated on a ship among respectably, wholesomely inhibited people, casts an eye on Stirling as the only possible within reach for an hour or two. They make a few passes well within the dead-line, but Stirling, making a cult of sensitiveness, superiority & withdrawal, does not imagine outside of genteel or lit'ry bounds. There is a suggestion of Corinne also having an eye on the Cap to bring in a little Freudianism, but it is all so genteel that it is hardly noticeable. And at the end of the voyage the people disperse like a dream into their actual lives. This is all very well done—but—but—

Stirling Armstrong's portraiture is very good, if a little epicene, & she draws herself the most expertly of all. To quote, 'She was one of those writers who wither at the word "melodramatic"; <u>who eschew</u> (should eschew not be singular? I noted in the book

---

144 H.M. Green married Eleanor Watson in 1911; and Dorothy Auchterlonie in 1944.

the common solecism of aggravate for provoke) plots and coincidences and devices, heroes and heroines, and murder their characters with the greatest subtlety, off; who shudder at a word of inept praise and pick their way delicately among shades of meaning; who have an aesthetic reason for all they write and can discuss it endlessly with the <u>cognoscenti</u>, but are put out of countenance by a word of robust praise. At least, Stirling would have been one of these had she not been saved from the last enormities of earnestness by a sense of humour, and from the endless discussions by her inability to believe that any of her friends was a true <u>cognoscenti</u>.'

Exactly! Exactly!

Stirling also describes herself as faintly malicious. Yes faintly, always <u>faintly</u>. Faintly superior, faintly interesting, faintly <u>modern</u>. The book as a whole is faintly irritating as Stirling herself as presented by herself in the pages is faintly offensive. It is secondary writing—a picking and milling over a field where others have cleared the trees and scrub and pioneered the field generally. Not a crude performance, but, but . . .

People sometimes express curiosity as to what influence in this collaboration is Marjorie's and which Flora's: I should hazard a guess that this book is all Marjorie's & Flora just went over it when it was fully conceived, but, but . . .

These notes are a rifle fired at a mosquito, but, but I have nothing else on which to use my idle talent.

(Read this to Neroli Whittle on Dec 5 1943: wonder if she told Marjorie.)

February 1944   'The Persimmon Tree and Other Stories' by Marjorie Barnard (The Clarendon Publishing Co. Sydney, 1944). (17 stories). (Feb 1944. Lent to me by D.C. [Dymphna Cusack]).

On the jacket, with characteristic contempt for the text, the
artist has drawn an inland box tree with seagulls flying above it,
&, with it in the foreground, is an old two-rail cattle fence of fifty
years ago before rabbit- & dingo-proof netted fences became the
rule. In the distance seems to be an English country scene of little
squares of cultivated meadows with bowers of poplars and elms
here & there.

Marjorie Barnard seems to be as addicted to persimmon trees
as E. Dark is to pittosporums with a corresponding ratio in intensity
of emotion & expatriation. What is Marjorie about in her persimmon tree? It seems faintly unwholesome, faintly—well,
faintly faint. It ends with one woman secretly watching her
neighbors' nudity across the street and feeling that her heart will
break. Why? In the name of world cataclysm—why? Men writers'
obsession with female nudity is wearying but to have to endure
women's imitation of this obsession is too much. These women
suffer from loneliness, and, after suffering their self-imagined
self-superiority & [self]-sensitivity, the reader feels they deserve
the neglect of their fellows.

'Because she loved him she knew when he was distressed,
even when he had successfully hidden it from himself; and because
she had complete faith in him, sometimes she was afraid.' The
first sentence of the first story is typical of them all, and of their
Henry Jamesian airing of perceptiveness in epicene hair splitting.

'The Bride Elect' is another precious darling who couldn't
fit in, and didn't deserve to. In 'The Party' another lone inconsequential woman, so sensitive, so pitiful, is a bore to the
others at the party and to the reader. Why should so many women
be so neurotic & so dull? 'Beauty is Strength'—a banal woman
is at a beautician's getting herself plastered up to hold her husband
of polygamous trend: if she were at the mortician's it wouldn't
matter.

Some of the little yarns are puzzling. You have to hang on like billyo to keep the slender thread of them, only to find that you have lost it after all, and that it is not worth the effort involved. I struggled nobly, knowing how highly Marjorie rates herself as a writer, but the stories make no impression on me except an irritating feeling of frustration. One or two show more instinctive sympathy—'Fighting in Vienna' for example, but this is vicarious material of experience, showing M.B. as a writer who can work over material tilthed by others better than she can guide the stump-jumping plough herself in virgin territory. 'The New Dress' is very good; also 'The Lottery'. 'Habit' is a commendable piece of work showing, as it does, that habit is stronger in an old maid than a chance to marry. This story is a piece of hidden truth & a relief after the conventional and largely androcentric legends of elderly women being man-hungry. 'The Wrong Hat' is also good—but a very slight sketch. It is somewhat as if Margaret Trist's poor little unhappy girls had grown up and become epicene in the alembic of old maidism. Selah!

9 August 1944 Mild day threatening rain. Went to Uni to hear Marjorie Barnard make a venomous & cowardly attack on me, every detail of calculated malice to bring ridicule on me before University group.[145] After had lunch with Green . . . & coffee

---

145 Marjorie Barnard commented on this occasion in her book *Miles Franklin*, Melbourne, Hill of Content, 1967, p3: 'I was giving the Commonwealth Literary Fund lectures in Australian literature at the University of Sydney. Miles, somewhat to my horror, arrived to listen to my lecture on her work. I am a sincere admirer of her writing and gave a fair, even enthusiastic account of it, but when I read some passages in illustration the students were convulsed with laughter. This so hurt and angered Miles that she refused to sit down to lunch with me and for a time diplomatic relations were broken off. However, the crisis passed and the hurt healed.'

in common room among a lot of v. plain & undistinguished looking men. Then met C. Morrisby & K. [word indecipherable] for tea at D.J. Then ran into X. Herbert at door of A & R & went out for evening to Em Fullerton. Home by 11.30. Raining as I came home. Rained all night.

2 September 1944   Lovely day. In evening wasted time going down to Fogdens'. Dear oh dear, how ordinary the ordinary people are—never the glimmer of a thought in their heads. Sowed some beans: & the last of the gladioli including the 2 at 3d each: under lemon tree. Wrote long letter to Mary [Fullerton]: typed a number of her poems. Wish I could drive myself to my own work, but desolation paralyses me, also the long Australian struggle against the tide—one is never established but always at the beginning.

c. 1944   The Australian war novels are vivid, vigorous reporting but they all lack that rebellion against war, the disgust with it that informs the best war books from other nations. 'Flesh in Armour'[146] is pedestrian in its class of the after-the-war novels dealing with the lower orders. It is useful to illustrate what a drab sordid business it all was—even the amour of those times lacking in electric passion. 'Her Privates We',[147] the most clapped-up of the squad, is purely English. No matter how completely Australian-born the writer, his soul had never been touched by Australia's magic. It is in the irritating style that cannot put naturally egotism in stories about one's self but smatters them with a deadly & painful self-consciousness which is mistakenly lauded as sensitiveness. Sometimes this failing is coy and affected as Jas Barrie's. 'Her

---

146 By Leonard Mann, published in 1932.
147 By Frederic Manning, published under a pseudonym in 1930.

P. We' is a personal diary. Though told in the third person the first person is there all the time & in one place he lapses into one or I. It is a document of terrible unhappiness—disharmony.

22 April 1945 [Today] I attended the Conference[148] at the New Theatre League's shebang, 167 Castlereagh St. Bartlett Adamson in chair. Leslie Haylen spoke first. He has come on well on this subject since I chaired for him at the Fellowship when he first got into Parliament. He laid out a grandiose scheme for housing & presenting great drama, ballet & opera greatly, to be subsidised by the taxpayers and policed by artists and directors from overseas. But he also stated that in this circus was to be an experimental theatre devoted to Australian drama.

Following Leslie Haylen, Australian, were the importers and expatriates—some of the latter probably born here. There was Parkinson. (An ironical incident of radio talks some years ago was this man & Denzil Batchelor discussing Australian literature. This they had a right to do. Their egregiousness in this instance was that they affected to speak for it from the inside, referring to themselves as Australians, and that their pronouncements were colored with the garrisoned mentality.) Assisting Parkinson to make a galaxy was some Peter Bellew, who looked as if he had once acted Little Lord Fauntleroy delightfully and had grown fat and lethargic. A fellow with a fattish superiority was named Robt. Stirling. Patricia Bullen represented the Russian group.[149] There was an English looking man referred to as Mr Bissett, a humorous

---

148 Convened by the People's Council for Culture to discuss proposals for the establishment of a national theatre.

149 Peter Bellew was from the Kirsova Ballet; Godfrey (not Robert) Stirling was from the Musical Association; and Patricia Bullen was from the New Theatre League.

architect [Henry Pynor] and F.D. Clewlow. A short paper was read from some corporal, who named Tyrone Guthrie as his candidate for the imported director of drama. Clewlow blew with all stops out that, by God, he is behind the project with all that he has in him—the project of drama in Australia: pity is that on two counts he is an obstruction of Australian drama—(1) he's too old now ever to have any understanding of the core of Australia; (2) he has not an original mind. Illustration: he can gas furiously about a Synge or Lennox Robinson, established by the Irish patriots, but if he is confronted by a possible Synge or L.R. drama here, he can do nothing about it but evade it or stifle it.

There were many fine suggestions put forward in which anyone of ideals could find encouragement, that was for giving us drama from other lands. We need it. This was vociferously articulated by all speakers. The discussion showed up the same old lack of an Australian consciousness. Of course any of the arts attracts a host of parasites, pretenders and axe-grinders. There were plenty of them there on Sunday. How furiously and frightenedly they were against Australian national (indigenous) drama. We must be international and universal. Any undue urge to root in environ-ment was decried as narrowing. Only French, Americans, Russians, Scandinavians can achieve universality by being distinctively French, American, Russian or Scandinavian. These people seem to regard any nascent Australianism as a crude taint to be avoided for the sake of culture, thus showing they are sick, through being unrooted. Their idea of being international is to receive humbly and greedily from other national cultures: how can they overlook the urgent, healthy, self-respecting, vivific angle of contributing something to the international pool? Simply because it is too hard, and they are a soft, careless people, till, in the quest for adventure—diversion—they find some fellow threatening them with a bayonet.

Only here and there was there a voice raised for Australia, and unfortunately, though valiant, these had the limited outlook . . . which makes ammunition for the expatriates. Les Rees, surprisingly, spoke for the Australian cause, but haltingly, as if he had only thought of it after catching my eye.

These two samples of the discussion showed a turtle-like lack of a sense of humor: (1) In the reporting of national theatres in the Home land, up rose Jeannie Ranken,[150] who once cultivated me effusively, but who since the 'offensive' 'Pioneers on Parade' pretends not to see me, an action in which she has my co-operation; rose up and said the Glasgow National Theatre had been overlooked. She referred to herself as a Scot (no plebianly rooted Australian she!). This theatre had been started by a Scot with a national (or regional) drama and was now gratefully called after him and subsidized. Ah, ha! Jeannie, I'd have no objection to a theatre here called after Miles Franklin, or Dymphna Cusack, or B. Roland, or anyone else who had written and got produced vigorous native drama, but that would lack universality and be crudely self-conscious. (2) A delegate announcing herself as from the Communist party wound up with a plea for universal drama, not an Australian theatre which would be sure to be narrow and deleterious. This came oddly from an impassioned Russophile. This speaker was vociferously applauded by a group around me,

---

150 Franklin added a note in her diary following Ranken's death later in 1945: 'And now poor Jeannie Ranken has gone off the stage for ever leaving my comedy of life the poorer by one player, if only one with a tiny part & in which we never were on the stage together except for the briefest moments. I remember we had supper together one night after both broadcasting under the unloved Gladys Owen (Mrs Moore). We had begun auspiciously till I offended her pretentious associations with the blimps by my irreverence in "Pioneers on Parade".'

conspicuous among them that middle-aged man with a beard who wears shorts & sandals, sells vegetables at high prices, is loudly opinionated and smells like a goat is reputed to smell.

Well, I am concerned passionately with attempting to develop Australian drama so that we may give as well as take from world drama.

Coming out for luncheon recess I had the luck to run into nice Betty Roland who insisted that I join her lunch party at her flat in Darlinghurst. We went by tram & bought cheese, pie, butter etc. en route. Also there was Parkinson. There were May Hollinworth, an English horror female axe-grinder named Graham, a friend who helped Betty with the lunch & Mr Bissett. I had asked Betty on the tram who Bissett was and it boiled down to 'Oh, everyone knows him as Mr Bissett'. I was an incongruous intrusion. I overheard them scuttling to ask Betty who I was. Bissett is a bug in the British Drama League, & Parkinson has attached himself to Actors' Equity. On the way up I had asked Betty what was C. Duncan's play likely to be, judging by the judges, of which Mr Bissett was one, & May Hollinworth, & that paralysing female Tildesley another. All expatriate-minded & eager for acting exhibitionism but with no understanding that all their gyrations depend on the playwrights, who are basic.

Well, to revert, Betty said that as soon as Mr Bissett read Catherine's play (in the recent three act play competition) he put it aside marked as the probable winner, and all the judges were eventually agreed. 'I'll have to meet Mr Bissett,' said I, 'to be able to judge whether I'd lean on his judgment.' I saw him & I don't, especially plus his colleagues. Now to hear the play. Dear, oh dear, how such people chatter—quite smart in imitated sophistication and established culture, but utterly stumped by Australia, and antagonised by anyone who can create something original from its potentialities.

I had no more standing at this party than a convict in snob society and was uneasily situated because I had submitted a play to M. Hollinworth who had not even acknowledged its receipt and I had put two plays in the recent competition which had probably been discarded at first glance. An uneasy moment like 'getting warm' in hunt-the-thimble was when Mr Bissett looked at me and said, 'Who are you? A playwright, aren't you?'. 'Not if you could help it,' thought I. Betty saved me by calling from the kitchen, 'No. A novelist. "All That Swagger".' 'Oh, yes,' said Mr Bissett, 'I'm ashamed to say I haven't read any of your books: tell me their names.' 'I haven't read any of yours either,' I said, 'tell me some of them?' Somehow that disposed of him.

As I was among aliens, and didn't want to spoil my hostess's party by behaving like an illegitimate child, I jumped into the swim and drew Parkinson out. He must have announced: 'When I was an Undergraduate at Oxford' a dozen times during the session. He said he and the present Arch-Bish of Canterbury were fellow undergrads. I said I had sat on the platform with the late Arch-Bishop Temple. Parkinson is quite human & easily handled so I soon had him telling me that he has written a libretto for an Australian opera. I said I hoped it was not the same old European ballet & operatic theme of a prince or swell seducing an innocent maiden and running about the stage leering & peering till she dies of a broken heart. (Vide Giselle and Rigoletto.) Oh no it is to be full of Australian animals & many imported rabbits which all disappear when a gun is fired. I had no trouble with Bissett as soon as the food came, as he dived voraciously into tinned macaroni—two helpings—plus anything else that came his way. Then we had to hurry back to the Conference & Mr Bissett took us in comfort in a taxi at his own expense—so he was useful for something.

Aftermath. Next day I met Leslie Haylen and Dalziel at the Martha Washington for tea. I told them the conference was as

typical of Australian attitudes as the little restaurant which would
have been the Mrs Curtin if we had any developed Australian
consciousness. I said a lot more, & he took me up eagerly. Said
if I would direct a little theatre & could find one, he could get it
helped at once. He said in parting that if I could still be so
enthusiastic he could not fail in guts to go on in spite of pressure
groups, as to be heard at the Conference. He asked me to write
him a letter with my views so he could show it to Curtin. I did.

7 August 1945   Well, my dears, nothing but a chat with
'aquils'[151] will assuage me for the dud experiences of life. On Sunday
night Will Lawson was advertised to speak at F.A.W. [Fellowship
of Australian Writers] on the ballads. A subject on which he would
have nothing new to tell me, but I knew that Will had been
hunted up to fill a non-appearance, and that I could not desert
him as a Lawsonian, not when we run after strangers, and when
he stands so hardily for Australian literature: so, though I fain
would have sat at home in aise and listened to other duds and
mediocrities on the radio, and have read two books which I have
to get through for the Book Society, I hoisted myself wearily on
to my weary feet and into my coat and set off. Meagre audience,
of course. Will garbled excerpts from the old ballads neither in
old recitative style, with its fluency, nor in the new style, which
seeked to deny chime in verse or poetry, as we once would have
denied illegitimacy, and this is neither here nor there. Camden
[Morrisby] in the chair. He will do all the vice-presidential work now
while the V-P's go abroad earning or seeking better entertainment.

---

151 'Aquils', Franklin's abbreviation of *aquila*, Latin for eagle. Franklin loved word
plays and 'aquils' are equals because eagle rhymes with equal (almost). This is
a typescript of a letter which Franklin has pasted into her diary. It is probably
addressed to Mary Fullerton, Mabel Singleton and Jean Hamilton in London,
to whom a copy may have been sent.

In the front seat was displayed a heavy back topped by a heavy head with a rim of hair around an assertive baldness. He handed up a note. Camden read it and announced that present was Mr Stewart from the Bread and Cheese Club and that he wished to address us. This was in the question time. Well, that man reeking in respectability and Sunday clothes, ponderously arose, with great deliberation faced the audience and proceeded to address us as if he were a Presbyterian with a two-hour sermon to deliver. He posposed in the most barren, irrelevant manner possible, demanding where were the ballads of the gold-digging days? He had written demanding them from some Orange paper and answer came there none. Why Orange more than any other place should have produced ballads predating the balladists that Will L. had rounded up was beyond me. Your friend Mr Leonard was sitting beside me and looked as if he were going to rise to a point of order, but the giggles I was taken with deterred him, and I said that the man was a guest and that any minute he would burrrrrst into Roberrrrrrt Burrrrns. But strange to say he didn't. I don't know why. There is always someone to rise and say Lawson and our balladists could never be Rabbie. Like the one, I think I told you, who rose on another occasion and said that Lawson was all very well for Australia, but Australians would have to get it into their heads that they were a very small unimportant part of the world. As he had been yapping about the grandeur of Burns, at that moment I snorted, 'Australia, a small unimportant place be damned, so is Scotland!' Well, this Mr Stewart went on to the end. I think even Mr Lennard at last was more interested in seeing how long he would last than in his being irrelevant. Such a male pomposo! It gave me an inkling of what life with that kind of father must have meant in the old days. I never till that moment realised the possible horrors, I having had such a different progenitor, who had no more idea of suppression of any sort than he had of taking people down for profit.

Then last night Paul Frolich hatched his egg at last. He was the pa emu sitting on a play by D. Deamer entitled 'Judgment'. He has been producing it for twelve months in July. The event came off last night. Again my humanities involved me. I toiled out to the Maccabean Hall where the mess was perpetrated. To begin, Paul and Dulcie must be liked. There was a big audience, about three times as many as went to Catherine Duncan's 'Sons of the Morning', at Killara. It was certainly a brave, if not a reckless or perhaps merely a foolhardy effort in production.

One of those dreadful town hall stages. Curtains very bravely arranged for scenes and they had attempted all sorts of colored lights with an equipment that reminded me of the old magic lanterns in going wrong—most primitive. No lack of courage and industry.

The play was a fearsome farrago of wornout ideas flung together—no, apart—by the characters. She had assembled a party in a studio just before the outbreak of the next world war. It was supposed to be symbolism. Poor Dulcie, she can't even speak coherently, and when she came on mouthing mouldy half-hatched nothings about love and life and rolling her stomach in her famous hula undulations the audience openly sniggered, though I must say they were very well-behaved on the whole. They were much relieved in the drinking scenes and when bastards and bloodies came to the aid of the text, and cheered vociferously to relieve their feelings. It was so very painful, especially as Paul espied me and tore up to know what I thought, and said, 'Go on, say it is a rotten play! Say it is a rotten production and everything gone wrong.' I countered that with, 'I suppose I would be the most sympathetic and understanding person here about the things you have done without equipment, but in that first scene none of us heard a word—tell the girl to speak up.' Thank God he was called away. The man must have worked to distraction, because they were the amateurist amateurs I have encountered, even in my depths of suffering in pursuit of Australian drama. Difficult scenes to put on with a professional cast and adequate equipment—the attempt was collossical, but nothing could have redeemed that phoney sawdust play.

This party took place in a studio as a big parade of armaments was about to pass. Present were the imitation Noel Coward smart Alecs and a business man, and the artist and his mistress, and his subjects to be painted, and also in comes a drunk and a thief and a traveller meant to be 'Jesus Christ drinking beer'. Then a bomb falls out of the parade—cracker effects without burning the curtains. Now they are all dead and rise up to judgment by the 'Traveller'. They all repent and go lovely and helpful in brotherly love, even the business man manufacturer of armaments. Oh dear, oh dear, oh dear! It was pitiable. I escaped in haste as the easiest way out of a dilemma . . .

I forgot to say there was also a Voice that started behind the scenes in the judgments and brotherly spasms, and all the cast kept joining in intoning. It made me think of our effort. Great highlight when a Jew mother came in with black wrinkles painted on her forehead and began to wail. Then in the dim light of the crackers and catherine wheels in came daddy of same persuasion with a lengthy Santa Claus beard. Buoyant laughter. I couldn't help laughing myself. The actors were certainly courageous to stand up to such swill. What a pity they had not something that would have been a discovery. It made me shiver—that kind of people are so sure of their talent and have the pluck to exhibit it. Am I equally deplorable to try to write either novels or plays? Please regard this as strictly private. I do not wish to ridicule it in public because there was something pathetically courageous in the whole thing. I wish you could have been with me. With all its lunacy it touched me more than 'Positions Vacant'. It might very well be less obstructive of our development than slick trite empty imitative stuff that gets a prize. It was a symbolical play set in any country or place, by which poor Dulcie tried to get out of the hard work of interpreting her own country and actuality. Also, through the amplifier, to start, Dulcie very belligerently announced that it was a strictly private performance by invitation, and if there were any press people present they were not to write anything about it. This, that poor misguided Paul told me, was because of the great anti-war sentiments in it—controversial, he said. That was another evasion because I don't think even Goering or Gabbles could have been frightened by the war sentiments—something about war investments that made everyone go off into glee, not with the author, alas, but merely at her.

c. August 1945   I have kept this little clipping[152]—till it is soiled & yellowing—for old sake's sake—nostalgia. It takes me back to my childhood and my teens. Mother was a regular subscriber to 'Madame Weigel's Fashion Journal'.[153] It was an 'elegancy' to which she clung through the leanest lean years. It was one of the touches of her upbringing that set her above the other women to whose company she was reduced at Stillwater. Mother always dressed herself and us by Madame W's paper patterns, which were renowned for their accuracy and style. Mother was equally capable in executing them and we were always turned out as no others were. I can remember Stella S.

---

152 Newspaper of 12 January 1940 reporting the death in Melbourne on 11 January of Madame Johanna Wilhelmine Weigel, a founder of the Australian paper dress pattern industry.

153 *Weigel's Journal of Fashions* was published in Melbourne from about 1880. It changed its name to *Madame Weigel's Journal of Fashion* in about 1915 and was still publishing under that name in 1950.

trying to deprecate Linda [Franklin] as a fashion plate because she was so lovely in her perfect flounces and dainty laces.

Madame Weigel was to me a figure of legend as Mrs Beeton, or 'The Ingoldsby Legends'[154]—a disembodied but static entity. Now I discover that she was a living being all those years, only one year older than my father, having been born a year before him and living for 9 years after he had gone. Regret saddens me that I could have known Madame Weigel and told her what a figure she was in my young life. Fifty years ago I pasted examples of her fashions in my scrap book.

We used to paper the walls of the pantry, the W.C. and the kitchen with her pages—most interesting to all. I can see some of them still in memory. I can see also the Bulletin illustrated verses that shared the western wall—one about the mother-in-law joke:—when this old joke was new they fought with saurians in the slime, they rode to fight with griffins grey in warrior garb of grime. (Well, the warrior garb of grime is also still with us.) Another Bulletin verse was in the shade behind the door on the north wall—a parody: Oh don't you remember sweet Alice Ben Bolt who if living today would travel about on a bike Ben Bolt and talk in a truculent tone, and sweet Alice who might have been living today is better laid under the stone, and words to that effect.

That was a fine kitchen for our situation. Dear old Father always wanted to give Mother of the best. He had no predatory gifts to aid him so the result was that we were housily and socially above our income—a precarious & trying position. The kitchen had smooth slab walls and a vast hearth with a colonial oven at

---

154 R.H. Barham *The Ingoldsby Legends: Or, Mirth and Marvels*, first published in book form in 1840. Franklin retained in her library an 1855 edition which had belonged to her mother. She also retained an 1869 edition of Mrs Beeton's *Book of Household Management*.

one side, then an advance on the camp ovens of the neighbors.
A high shelf ran above the hearth and the east wall had commodious
shelves running to the ceiling. There was a back & a front door
and another door running into a roomy store room. The ceiling
was carried up in an arch, like a mansard roof, whereas in other
kitchens ceilings were absent, & where often a few sheets of bark
laid on the beams served as store rooms. The four rooms of the
detached kitchen building were all ceiled. Even our big front
verandah was ceiled with grooved pine—a great extravagance
everyone thought. There were also breast-high walls at each end
similarly lined. The house throughout was boarded with soft
white pine all as dainty as a bandbox.

These memories are stirred by Mme. Weigel. In her fashion
journal she also ran a serial, which was devoured greedily by my
romance-hungry adolescent mind. I was not so unintelligent
however as to be satisfied with the stories—they seemed to me
very thin and unfilling. I remember some by Carmen Sylva,
Queen of Roumania.[155] In the Balkans in 1917, the Serbs brought
me a Roumanian poet of sorts. He was an unattractive, conceited,
ugly creature but I did my best with him in scraps of French and
Serbian. I told him of reading the works of Carmen Sylva. The
man was astonished. We had to bring out a map & show him
Australia, of which he had previously never heard. He was
vociferous about our staggering culture to know Carmen Sylva's
works. Why, the people of Roumania did not know them! The
interpreter had to come to make sure that he had heard alright—
the fame of myself and my national culture grew into a legend.
What a lovely story that would have been to tell Madame Weigel,
who would have been only 77 when I returned to Melbourne
after last war.

---

155 Carmen Sylva was the pen-name of Queen Elizabeth of Romania.

7 October 1945　　Professor J.I.M. Stewart (Michael Innes) over the air in 'Spotlight on Literature' session. A record should be made of this man making an address. The old school tie accent is going out of favor. People of later days will not know what it was like, why esteemed, why offensive. He was a perfect example. If reproduced by a mimic the mimic would be accused of caricature. The bored condescension, the haw-hawness of self-superiority, the hollow pomposity—incredible. He was also a good example of the professional policy of spreading a little jam on a wide piece of bread.

In looking at our shelves there is very little to show in the way of the novel for over a hundred years. In a condescending manner he came to short stories & considered Clarke's 'Pretty Dick', Hilarly Fane's 'Tomorrow', Baynton's 'Tramp', H. Lawson's 'Loaded Dog' and Dyson's 'Golden Shanty'.[156] He is off to perpetrate similar wasting-disease pronouncements & obstruction of nascent Australian Literature at Belfast University.

5 March 1946　　Have just read 'Trilby' again after 50 years. It and 'The Story of an African Farm' were the two most exalting novels read in my girlhood. The novels I read between 13 and 20 still remain my favorites: 'Vanity Fair': 'The Newcomes': 'Pendennis':

---

156 *Pretty Dick* by Marcus Clarke was first published April 1869 in *Colonial Monthly* and published in the collected volume *Holiday Peak, and Other Tales*, 1873. Hilary Fane's 'Tomorrow' not identified. Barbara Baynton's 'Tramp' was published separately in the 1890s in Sydney under the title *The Chosen Vessel*. It appeared with the title 'The Tramp' in *The Bulletin Story Book* in 1901 and in Baynton's classic volume *Bush Studies* in 1902. Henry Lawson's short story, 'The Loaded Dog', first appeared in *Joe Wilson and His Mates* in 1901. Edward Dyson's short story 'The Golden Shanty' first appeared in the *Bulletin*'s Christmas issue for 1887 under the title 'A Profitable Pub'. It was published in Dyson's volume of short stories, *Below and On Top* in 1898.

'Dombey and Son': 'Esther Waters'.[157] (I have not re-read 'Esther Waters' but still remember its beginning & end by rote, like a poem, & still hanker for the book.) To this list I have added 'Les Miserables' & 'War & Peace' & 'Under the Greenwood Tree' & 'Far from the Madding Crowd'.[158] What other books, stories did I love of those days: 'The Kentucky Cardinal': 'The Choir Invisible': 'Winslow Plain' (S. Pratt McLean Green): 'The Potter's Thumb' (F. Annie Steel).[159] Of course I enjoy Meredith and Gissing, adore Jane Austen, but their books do not stand out as seductively as the others listed.

I had never since seen 'Trilby'. Miss Gillespie bought the paper-backed cover. It was not considered reading for a young girl but it could not have escaped me once in the house unless kept under lock & key, & I don't remember that Miss G. had anything locked. Twice during the intervening half century I have seen the stage adaptation of it—in New York in 1913 or '14 with Wilton Lackey as Svengali & Ellalaine Terris as a singing Trilby. I saw E.T.'s production again in London during the war; I forget who was the Svengali but Rosina Phillipi again did Mme. Vinard as she did in the original production when Gerald du Maurier was Dodor, Lionel Brough The Laird & H.V. Esmond Little Billee, & of course, Dorothea Baird and Tree[160] the principals.

---

157 George du Maurier *Trilby*, 1894; Olive Schreiner *The Story of an African Farm*, 1883; W.M. Thackeray *Vanity Fair*, 1847–8; W.M. Thackeray *The Newcomes*, 1853–5; W.M. Thackeray *The History of Pendennis*, 1849–50; Charles Dickens *Dombey and Son*, 1847–8; George Moore *Esther Waters*, 1894.

158 Victor Hugo *Les Miserables*, 1865; Leo Tolstoy *War and Peace*, 1865–9; Thomas Hardy *Under the Greenwood Tree*, 1872; Thomas Hardy *Far from the Madding Crowd*, 1874.

159 James Lane Allen *A Kentucky Cardinal*, 1894; James Lane Allen *The Choir Invisible*, 1897; Sarah Pratt McLean *Winslow Plain*, 1902; Flora Annie Steel *Potter's Thumb*, 1901.

160 Sir Herbert Beerbohm Tree, 1852–1917, actor-manager.

Not a page of that book had I forgotten, nor an illustration, though I had never had it as my own to study & familiarise—just one concentrated reading. I used to race along the verandah to the end room, occupied by Miss G., and lap it up, & dote. What intensity, what poignancy of enjoyment, what glamor! And here after all the years it was again—the frontispiece as reproduced in the Daily Telegraph's review—& oh, it is a glamorous story still! It retains its infinite seduction—still no flaw in it.

It reeks with nostalgia, true love, young love's heartbreak & self-immolation, virtue, decency: it moves in the fairy world of princesses & dukes & duchesses, in the success of great musical & other artists—and <u>mateship</u>—in <u>Paris</u>—& youth, youth! I read it in the days when Melba was the delight of every little girl who could play a five finger exercise, & when I had a contralto to make people weep at my will, & could also trill on high C—only once in a lifetime—ah yes—only once, & never again, but this story was the one & the once. And the illustrations were the author's own, no fantasies that ignored the text or disagreed with it. Yes, it was irresistible to youth—the tenderness, the sincerity, the simplicity, the sentimentality, if you will, but so sensitive that it was sentiment. I remember the closing verses, but I disagreed with my mother's delight in the statement about the middle-aged Taffy 'than which there is no better at their time of life and no better time of life than theirs'. Hoh! Old people finding any joy in their time of life! Positively ludicrous!

Ah, as I read those lines in my maturity! I found them in Mother's desk in 1938 after she was dead. She had copied them & kept them over 40 years. I doubt if she had ever re-read the book either!

c. August 1946   Take a gob out of Kylie Tennant's descriptions of the country in almost any of her novels & you see her big vocabulary, vigorous and copious. She and X. Herbert are a pair in this, in other qualities as well. Xavier Herbert lacks spiritual integrity and sociological orientation. They both revel in the unrespectable and riff-raff, but it would seem less out of sympathy than for the sport and <u>pour epater les bourgeoisie</u>. X. Herbert is egotistical in an overwhelming way, he not only exhausts others but winds himself in his search of himself. Kylie's ruthless disregard of other people's feelings protrudes into her characters. One is repelled while one admires. In her considerable ability, which includes a sense of humor, she merely holds people up to ridicule and contempt. She lacks pity. Were she a little more creative than so brilliantly reportorial, or had she pity, she could be great. She doesn't seem to care whether her characters suffer or not, and the result is that after about fifty pages the reader doesn't either.

3 October 1946 On Monday evening George Clune telephoned me to come to lunch. I jibbed a little, then he said it was important. Going to throw over 'Bring the Monkey' I expected. I was to wear my <u>hat</u> mentioned in Buzz's column.[161] 'Fancy, you getting into the social news with a hat!'

(Once I found delight & stimulation in hats. Used to make my own. Could have filled a shop with the prettiest things. Wearing one of my own that had immediate & wide success I was approached one afternoon by a smartly gowned woman coming out of Marshall Field's,[162] who wondered if I'd be so generous as to let her share my milliner. I said I had made it myself. 'That is always the way,' said she. 'If I see something really smart <u>and</u>

---

161 The *Sun*, September 1946, reporting a party at the ABC, stated: 'Miles Franklin, whose classic *All That Swagger* is a bethumbed part of our bookshelves, gazed serenely under a spring hat bright as a Persian garden'.
162 A Chicago department store.

pretty, I can be sure it is not to be duplicated.' This one was a toque of pale pink rosebuds on a navy blue foundation with two tulle wings at a jaunty angle to indicate an aeroplane, then in the hat news. I wore it with a navy blue coat & skirt & net blouse . . . In those days if I were depressed, I'd make myself a new hat and up would go the mercury. I have noted as a sign of gathering age that hats no longer delight me. The struggle is to get anything comfortable & unridiculous, yet not too defiant of the prevailing mode. The one in question is a black sailor made out of one I bought in Melbourne in February 1941. I trimmed it myself. I should have liked roses but none were procurable under pounds, so I compromised with poorer stuff—red, white, ochre, and threw in some blue, like a dash of perfume, to mitigate the primary harshness.)

Thus accoutred I went yesterday to George's restaurant at 61 Macleay Street, Potts Point. To my unease, there was William Dobell.

I never look in the mirror these days without wishing I could end it all as easily as I could have done when in my teens. I don't want to be victimised as a decayed moron corpse as a companion piece to Joshua.[163] The cutting-away of my mastication muscles and gums has made me as exaggeratedly wrinkled as if a Maori Chief's markings were age wrinkles. My face is entirely spoiled.[164] It is hard to bear.

---

163 Dobell's portrait of fellow artist Joshua Smith won the 1943 Archibald Prize. When the award was announced in January 1944 it attracted outrage with allegations that it was a caricature. Smith refused to speak to the artist; Smith's parents begged Dobell to withdraw the portrait from exhibition. A court action was launched to overturn the award. It failed, as did an appeal. The incident traumatised Dobell, who suffered a nervous breakdown and removed himself in 1945 to Wangi Wangi on Lake Macquarie.

164 Franklin had had extensive dental work while in Chicago.

Well, there stood the villain, but I gaily sailed in without a blink, greeting him as an acquaintance, in disregard of George's conventional introduction. This surprised him. I said I too had been at Dora Birtles' party and was near enough to hear his conversation. 'Also, I was standing near your elbow the afternoon you opened the photographic exhibition at Davy Jones'.'[165] He said he didn't like doing that. I said that was obvious, but that his diffidence was endearing, whereas stage fright tunes me up till my funk seems like fierceness.

His presence is gentle and quiet. He is not glib or wordy or self-assertive. I should have enjoyed him except it takes more courage than I have to put up with my collapsed cheeks, & what did he want me for except perhaps that I had been recommended to him as a Joshua ready-made: and if he would do that to his man friend & a fellow painter, whom he knows, what chance had I, an unknown female? However, there was no acid, bounce, or casuistry in his personality as exposed yesterday. He was so quiet & slow that he seemed under—rather than over—articulate. I said he would have to forgive my ignorance of his work and all painting, that I was getting the book on his work.[166] 'Let me give it to you,' he said spontaneously. 'No! No! I would not accept such an expensive thing.' He insisted. I said I had nothing but a very small thing to give him, but he earnestly assured me he'd very much like to have it. George then filled in with condemnation of A. Huxley's 'Time must have a Stop'[167]—of all the unreadable trash! etc. etc. I gathered honey by borrowing it. 'I'll give it to you,' said George. 'I didn't know what to do with it.'

165 David Jones, a Sydney department store.
166 *The Art of William Dobell*, edited by Sydney Ure Smith with an introduction by Brian Penton, 1946.
167 Aldous Huxley *Time Must Have a Stop*, 1945.

Dobell and I walked up the street together as far as the Union Bank where he told me he had a studio and said, 'Come up to see me some day.' He said also that he liked the hat. I said painters were things to keep away from unless one were so chocolate-box beautiful that she could stand the libel.

I felt he wished to paint me but was shy about asking: 1. perhaps he is sensitive at approaching; 2. perhaps he had some scruples about making a Joshua of me, being an Australian & brought up in the prevailing point of view about nothing but epitaphal works being permitted (see my prefatory note to Furphy biography[168]) . . .

The fact of Alice Cooper Stewart's footling effort was also deterrent. One of those stuffy half-cooked followers of the muse of painting or letters, and if Wm Dobell did me she would be crushed & think him the reason, whereas if she is eliminated in the preliminaries, as I should expect, the mistake can stop there.[169]

On the other hand, had I been of the stuff that succeeds I'd have developed W.D.'s tentative overtures regardless of Alice or of Joshuarian dangers to lap up notoriety. Alas, I'm schizophrenic!

---

168 In her prefatory note to *Joseph Furphy: The Legend of a Man and His Book*, 1944, Franklin wrote: 'No matter how unseemly a man's actions, immediately after he is dead de mortuis nil nisi bonum remains the accepted formula for his printed chronicle: practically nothing is allowable beyond eulogy expanded from an epitaphic text. This outmoded reserve can be attributed to neighbourliness, to parochialism, or be dismissed as hypocrisy, but it cannot be flouted by an author who desires publication. Thus, Australian autobiography and biography tend to be unexciting by comparison with the divulgences which spice many American and English memoirs; naturally, if illogically, the circumscribed product is then shunned alike by publishers and readers.'

169 Identity of Alice Cooper Stewart unknown. From letters written by her in 1949 in the Miles Franklin papers, Mitchell Library, it appears she was an amateur artist and collector. She did enter a work for the Archibald Prize around 1949 and this paragraph may refer to an earlier attempt to enter a work which would then compete with the proposed portrait of Franklin by Dobell.

I'd like to live removed, as in a monkery from these blowflies, and at the same time am the most surging realist, and insist on delving into the basic facts. So that was that! I put the prospect of Dobell from me and hope for the best with Alice, that is that she'll be painlessly eliminated without being hung.

Dobell also said in course of conversation that he had heard a great deal of me from Frank Clune and wished to meet me, & then again from John Hoey.[170] Horrors! I thought it showed what a practising nonentity I was if Wm Dobell had to hear of me from Hoey, whom I had met once for a few moments at a lecture by Dymphna [Cusack] to the actors, and who had come out for an evening recently before he sailed on a windjammer. I had sent him papers while he was sitting about the country comfortably in camps. I found out from Dobell that he knew equally little of him, that he had pushed up and introduced himself—on what basis except Khaki; and Khaki fever is now past.

So that was that! I determined to wait till Dobell sent the book, wondering if he'd keep his promise.

Beatrice Davis had been appointed publisher's editor at Angus & Robertson in 1937. It was probably the first such position in Australia and she held it until 1973. She first met Miles Franklin at meetings of the Fellowship of Australian Writers and of the English Association following Miles' return to Australia in 1932. At these meetings, according to Beatrice, Miles 'was always a magnet and a star with her impertinent wit and forthright views, with her generous encouragements of younger writers, her insistence that they should

---

170 John Hoey, a budding Western Australian writer, had written to Franklin in 1946 seeking advice about establishing a literary agency in Australia. He seems later to have worked for Burns Philp in the Pacific.

proclaim their Australianism . . . she enchanted me'.[171] Beatrice worked with Miles on a number of the latter's books and Miles would nominate Beatrice as one of the judges of the Miles Franklin Award, a duty Beatrice fulfilled until her death in 1992.

23 November 1946   Night before last went to annual dinner of the English Association held at University in room presided over by the painting 'Hermione'. Went at invitation of Beatrice Davis, who was in the chair. On arrival in adjoining room Kenneth Giles loomed tall & heavy with another fellow, Felix Barton, & a third, whose name escapes me. I rose remarking I'd need stilts if we met regularly. 'I'm surprised to see you here,' said Giles, condescendingly. 'Why? I'm in my own country & my own residential city.' 'Oh, of course, how stupid of me! Of course you'd be here.' Then he added, 'I was writing a letter to you this afternoon.' 'I hope it was a love letter.' This flabbered him slightly. It was apropos my alterations in the agreement re 'Sydney Royal'.[172] He returned, 'I've met nearly all your points.' 'I hope so,' said I. 'You go and meet them all, like a good fellow, so we can enjoy ourselves when we meet socially and I shan't have to dodge you as a scoundrel who has taken me down.' He was prepared to pursue the matter. Had I any business instincts I should have taken him aside while the iron was warm in my favor; but abashedly I said I could not discuss it there . . .

(I had not been to one of these dinners since dear old Inigo Jones had proposed the toast of Australian Literature & I had responded to it. Pilcher, coadjutor Bishop, and Canon Garnsey thanked me for a most moving & interesting address. Guy Howarth was amiable about it & later put much of it in

---

171 Beatrice Davis 'An enigmatic woman', *Overland* 91, 1983.
172 Miles Franklin *Sydney Royal: Divertissement*, 1947.

'Southerly',[173] & Ernest Harden congratulated me on the 'best speech of the evening'. I said that was not much of a compliment in view of the general quality. Otherwise I was ignored by the 'majestic maggots' as Leisa Gunnell[174] calls them, & went home. Found the gates closed out by the Benevolent Homes route and climbed over them, tearing my net evening frock on one of the spikes. The toast to English language was done there by Dr Mitchell, who took a heavy half-hour to analyse and hypothesize and haggle generally about where the accent fell in priapus. I didn't care a cuss; my interest in the old gent being nil, and my knowledge of him largely contained in the cliché about the priapic gleam that glints from the eyes of elderly bucks on beholding a juicy wench or a well-displayed flapper) . . .

Professor Trendall . . . asked me would I like a glass of cordial. I would. 'As a total illiterate may I ask what you profess?' 'Greek!' said he, with obvious pride. As we progressed, he said something about being distrait when he had to speak. As the toasts were literary, I asked what phase of Australian literature he was going to discuss. 'Is there any?' said he with the quintessence of super-ciliousness, with the further indication that could there be such a spurious commodity it would be unnecessary.

Good lor!

'Then what are you going to speak on?' 'Greek vases.'

Why Greek vases? Why not Phoenician or Etruscan?

He said Australian literature was all nonsense, it should be literature in Australia.

Dear! Dear! How stupid he was. So stupid that I should not accept him as an authority on Greek vases, no matter how much

---

173 *Southerly* 2, 2, July 1941.
174 Leisa Gunnell produced Franklin's play, *Call up your ghosts*, in Adelaide in November 1946.

he may have absorbed on the subject. If there can be Greek vases it is more reasonable that there can be Greek or German or Australian literature, seeing that there are many languages—more languages than vase-making marls—and that a language is more personal to a man or a nation than pottery.

Trendall wasn't worth wasting time on but I was amiable so as not to disgrace Beatrice. She is delightful, like a thoroughbred polo pony, small & slight but with no suggestion of undignified littleness. I like her black hair, and her beauty, especially the way her head's put on, & her high cheek bones in the three-quarter profiles from the back. She has intelligence, fire, courage & perception. And she was generous to me. In describing the gathering as one of the Society's largest & most successful she said it was honored by the presence of so-and-so and so-and-so, and 'two of our most distinguished authors, Miles Franklin and Marjorie Barnard.'

18 December 1946   Last night Dora Birtles came late to the Executive Board meeting of Fellowship of Australian Writers and announced for all to hear that Wm Dobell wants to paint Miles. Enthusiastically received. Someone said, 'Let's ask him to do it cheaply and we could buy it for the Fellowship.' By way of parrying the blow I said, 'The man is mad. The man <u>ith</u> definitely mad.' I said then directly to Dora, 'Why should he want to pull my leg? Let him paint <u>your</u> portrait.' She said, 'He never suggested painting me: I only wish he would.' 'But,' I said, 'he does not know me.' 'Yes he does,' says she. 'He met you at my party.' 'Then why didn't he ask me himself?' 'He's frightened of you,' she said. That is not reassuring. What dragon tales has he been told by the picayune coyotes that yap at the heels of their biggers?

At any rate he is pursuing the idea after meeting me, as he was not aware that I was at that party till I told him. 'He only wants to ridicule me,' I reiterated, whereupon Pixie O'Harris said many kind things. 'Then why don't you paint me?' I remarked. 'Oh, Miles, would you let me! I'd love to.' And there, I'll be in another chocolate-box mess, but Pixie is so kind, and her lines are as pretty as herself—surely I can't come to much harm with her, should she mean it.

10 January 1947   . . . before Christmas, telephoning compliments of season to George Clune, he in passing said Dobell wanted to paint me and said to tell me not to sell the <u>hat</u>. Then why didn't he ask me? 'Oh, Bill said you had no use for painters, said they were good people to keep away from.'

Like a bird with a shiny object luring it to its doom I'll go back to Bill Dobell through the lead I've left through not yet sending the book. He has not sent his yet either.

So, after New Year I telephoned Dobell, saying my name was Franklin, possibly he did not remember me but I had promised him a book and was a person who kept my word. 'I promised you one too,' said he without hesitation and then said he had been very busy on his Magnus Mural and at Church Point where he was buying a bit of land. I said I could drop the book for him some day as I was passing. When would I be in, that day or the next? I said not tomorrow, which was Wednesday. 'Thursday then?' Yes, alright, I have another appointment at Kings X on Thursday. 'What time?' 'What time would suit you? Are you busy with sitters or anything?' 'No, not busy & quite alone, just finished the mural.' I promised to appear some time in the afternoon.

So I wrote in 'My C. goes B.': to Mr Wm Dobell, a resplendent brush from a pale goose quill Miles F.: I put on the black dress in which I had Mother photographed for her 80th birthday, wore the new Roman striped scarf with the pink and blue fringed ends, put on a white hat with big daisies with black middles, and sallied forth yesterday. Arrived at the flat, I knocked softly on the door at the moment Dobell opened it: we confronted each other simultaneously, and laughed. He said he was expecting a friend. I said I was terrified of taking up his time and would stay only two minutes. No, he said, the mural was that minute finished, and he was done work for the day. There it was, the paint, or at any rate the paint droppings still wet.

I know nothing of painting, though I find great delight in certain pictures, nearly always a landscape. I had seen nothing of Dobell's but six portraits (2 Wakehursts, Penton, Joshua, Billy Boy and Thelma Clune)[175] and liked none of them, so what was I to say, first to keep my ignorance from being absurd or of la vache [bovine] kind, and second so as not to be a hypocrite, for I will not applaud novel, drama or picture which I do not esteem from one angle or another.

The carnival hue represented looked to me rather a dark indistinct messy scramble. I could feel Dobell sensitively waiting both on behalf of his work and also as to what I'd exhibit of myself. I have never garnered the idiom with which art hangers-on go squinting at pictures, including twitterings about light and depth and feeling and shade, life and strength, tone, color and good old chiaroscuro, and that solid fact perspective.

'What a lot of work! What a frightful, terrible lot of work!' I rested on that.

'Yes,' he said, it was a lot of work, too much. He was tired of it; had had a struggle to keep from going stale on it. He did not

---

175 Portraits of Baron Wakehurst, Governor of New South Wales, 1937–1945; Brian Penton, writer; Joshua Smith, artist; Thelma Clune, wife of writer Frank Clune. The Billy Boy was a war time portrait of a construction worker.

like these big canvases, he would take no more such commissions but would get back to the small things that he liked.

But it was the crowd of small figures that seemed like niggling work to me. It seemed to me a small canvas, tiny for a mural; my experience being based on the vast wall displays in Los Angeles public buildings and the work of Rivera (?) [Diego Rivera] the Mexican, at that building in New York where Katherine Dreier gave a display of a film and Archipenko held forth in 1931. Painting a large canvas would to me mean swinging in a moving cradle and sparring at a wall like that of a flat building in house-painting style.

He said he had had difficulties with his patron, who was a Jew, and who had thought to suggest what he would have considered suitable, but D. had said that he could not do that, he could paint only as he himself conceived and saw. The mural was designed for a caravanserai where among the patrons would be orthodox and sedate families with birthday, wedding and other family shivoos. I said, such a canvas would draw many patrons simply to see it during years. He said he had not charged nearly enough, it had taken him so much longer than he expected; but at our first meeting he had told me that he was three months painting the Joshua.

I chuckled inwardly thinking that the orthodox mugwump patrons would experience a thrill from it, would think they were enjoying startling scandal, plumbing the depths, as the soggy and inexperienced pretensiosities do when F. Clune admits a bloody cow or a bastard.

'I mustn't take up your time,' was my slogan: he insisted that he had only to put a picture in a frame for a purchaser and then he was really done. So I regarded the mural again and began to like it better as the characters grew to individualised notice. There were three figures in the front row that show inimitable characterisation and a dog at the side ultimately captured. It would take many words and much pondering to get what he has there into writing. Perhaps that is what took up the time. I remarked that he ran to blonde figures. He said that was for light. My mind went to the problem of color as light where I had thought loosely only of color.

Gradually I was at ease and up at the other end of the room, and we discussed all sorts of things. That he wanted money because he desired a nice home and studio away from where he was: too accessible. At Church Point no one would bother him. 'Oh, wouldn't they!' said I. 'The drunks would muster on you there, and miss the last bus, and you'd have to mother them for the night.' I asked him about his family, what he came from. He said his father was a bricklayer and I'd know what that would mean. I said it was a good thing to be 'drug up genteel' and correct, it gave stability and something firm to start from. I asked him had he a wife. He said no, he thought it was better for him to remain lonely. He said he had been engaged twice. I said so had I, several times. 'Were you like me as you saw the noose descending, sniffed the breath of freedom and made a breakaway?' When he was engaged once he got the travelling scholarship and the girl wanted him to give it up and stay at home, so she did not understand, and he knew they would not have been happy.

'Hardly!' I agreed, and retreated with part of my mind into vast archives of data of women who forsake their own prospects to nurture male practitioners like the potato the willow slip.

This girl had married another but now was free and wanted him to take her on again. 'Are you going to?' 'No!' 'Then beware or you may succumb at any moment.'

He has a sister of 63 unmarried, who lives with him, but she is not sympathetic to his friends, won't have snooty people patronising her. We exchanged experiences of the difficulty of our families assimilating. I said I knew it must be very hard on my family, that I had compromised—had ruined myself without comforting them—half-and-half. I told him how Norman, lately dead, had refused to meet my friends, 'those old writing things'. But when I could corral him, they and he had a great time, they revelling in his wonderful gifts as a raconteur; instance the Darks and Gordon Buchanan.[176]

Dobell gave a similar experience. Thelma Scott and a friend came down to his studio impromptu and his sister decamped when she descried them. As she knew them on the wireless, when she came home later & discovered who they were, she was disappointed.

Then he gave me his book and I went through it. He likes the Dupain photograph. Told me Max had tricked him by taking it unawares while he pretended to be taking someone else who was present.

I did not say that I had recently spent the afternoon in Max Dupain's flat with his mother-in-law, who had said she would be wild with excitement if Dobell would ever dream of painting her, and would let him do what he liked, even Joshuarisation.

He asked me if I had brought my book. 'I don't want to hold you up, but . . .'

'Yes, I've brought it & have written in it. You must write in yours.'

He said he didn't know what to write. He was not good at that sort of thing. Now if he were Frank Clune . . .

He wrote in his book and I was bewitched by the flowing freedom of his writing, and realised that it was not writing but

---

176 Gordon Buchanan, born 1865, son of the pastoralist and explorer, Nathaniel Buchanan. Author of *Packhorse and Waterhole: With the First Overlanders to the Kimberleys*, 1933.

the skilled lines of drawing. Very different from mere calligraphy by a hand that is cramped by a cramped position for an extended time, overpushed to keep up with the mind till it degenerates to a tortured scribble.

'I wish I could write,' he said fervently.

I have thought of two writing adventures on which he could embark.

Going through his book we came to the dead landlord.[177] It horrified me. 'Oh, how terrible, how horrible!' I exclaimed, 'what a <u>dreadful</u> thing,' but I added, 'I mean <u>great</u> in its terribleness. It makes me want to cry!' It touched me so that I felt its stark uncompromising penetration of the futility of life. There was that poor old man, defeated, revolting, yet wrapped in an awe inspiring dignity, beyond even the pity of us, who still have to go through with it. I saw in a flash why Dobell has been acclaimed. This looks so French, so old masterish, like things dimly remembered in the Louvre and Luxembourg galleries, from other generations of painters. He said he might have been influenced by was it Renoir? that he liked him. I thought in that moment that he might be intending a compliment instead of a cruelty in requesting to paint me.

He told me about the painting of this picture. He had to help the wife lay out the corpse, when he was dead about five minutes. He had never seen anyone dead before and it was a severe shock to him. The wife is painted beside the bed brushing her hair. He said he supposed it was nervous reaction, but immediately they had finished the job she let her hair down and brushed it vigorously. He wanted to send that landlady the book but feared

---

177 'The Dead Landlord', painted in London from life in 1936. It was the inspiration for Patrick White's play *The Ham Funeral*, 1947.

that that portrait might hurt her, so discussed with me the practicability of cutting out that leaf. I asked where was that picture; he said he had it, that was the picture he had to put in the frame.

Each time I waked-up to the flight of time, in some gentle almost imperceptible way he detained me longer. 'I can make you a cup of tea. I'll wash the cups.' He did, but not sufficiently to my fastidiousness; something like a bit of turnip adhered to the rim. But I had explained my sort of impossible baby-pap tea, & with no commotion or argument he got it right—a miracle— an artist indeed!

In going through the book we came to his self-portrait. I went into the impossibility of an artist or anyone being able to see his own eye because all the life, character and emotion expressed by the eye has to be drawn out by someone. His eyes in this portrait, I insisted, are as if in reverie, there is not the electric response that makes a real eye different from an artistic reproduction.

I wonder if ever that living, pleading, electrified eye could be captured by an artist. He went into the problems of self-portraiture. I noted also that his own portrait was not distorted by the long gander-necked coat hanger effect of so many of his victims.

On the subject of eyes he said how he had been disturbed by finding a spot on one of his, but he hoped it was clearing up. Here again was another problem of the artist and his sight. I recalled Alice Henry, who, when the talk was of a singer, often dwelt upon the strain of having the instrument with her always, which at the time had not made sense to me, & for that reason has hung around for 35 years like a missing piece from a puzzle. If a writer were an undefeatable soul it is conceivable that he could express himself with the aid of a Dictaphone, though robbed of sight and hands. Not so an artist, take his hand or his sight and a Rembrandt would be lost inside his physique.

Then he put the Dead Landlord inside his frame & said he hated parting with it, but he needed the money and this customer would take the picture to Paris where it had a chance of getting into the Salon.

The two minutes having expanded into two hours—two very pleasant hours—I rose really to go and he asked if Dora Birtles had delivered his message. I said yes, she had blurted it out to the full committee, and it was greeted with laughter, which had hurt me, in view of the implications. He said that was because of Joshua and that Joshua had not objected, had thought it fun to be painted like that till his family made the rumpus.

I thought, no wonder!

He had wanted to paint me for the Archibald prize. He said Frank [Clune] had persuaded him to enter the portrait of Thelma [Clune], but he wished he hadn't. They would never give him the Archibald again[178]. I said why? He said he had many enemies. Penton hated him. I said everyone seemed to hate Penton. He said Penton gloried in all the disturbance he stirred up; all the same, he did not think Penton liked to be so disliked. I said, 'Of course he doesn't. We'd all like to be popular, or at least not abhorrent to our fellows.' . . .

Then I told him I was very sensitive about my spoiled face, showed him how you could fold up the cheeks. He said he hadn't noticed, only that it would be a nice flat line to paint. I said I had started life moon-faced & any beauty had been beauté du diable and it was not fair to paint me now when I was old & ruined. He said he was interested only in character and had an ambition to

178 In fact Dobell won the Archibald prize on two further occasions: in 1949 with his portrait of artist Margaret Olley and in 1960 for the portrait of his surgeon, E.G. MacMahon.

paint a writer. He had not time to read much but the radio had been turned on while he was painting & he had heard parts of 'All That Swagger' & he liked it.

I said, 'I wouldn't want you to do a chocolate-box fantasy that would make a fool of you—and of me—but if you could do something that wouldn't wound me and make me an object of ridicule and still would be a credit to you I'd like you to do it.' He said he could. Then I said, 'Alright, but let us keep it a secret adventure till it is done!' He thanked me with apparent sincerity and warmth, 'Thank you, Miss Franklin.' Then he added, 'I do hope I'll be able to do it,' then he added further, 'If you don't like it we can tear it up.'

He couldn't have said more than that, if he was sincere, and there is not some intention of doing one thing for me to see and half-a-dozen other Joshua sketches to show others and have a Roman holiday at my expense. But he doesn't seem like that. He's not facile or voluble—quite the contrary; he is endearingly unstressed and soothing. If he is not cruel I should like him and enjoy his gifts: besides he is an Australian who has had to emerge from and surmount the same rigidly respectable and circumscribing ideas as bound us all. At any rate I am indebted to him for supplying a spark or two to ignite thought in a new dimension of realisation—tremendously stimulating, as I have been segregated for years among people who supply me with no more mental pabulum than parrots.

21 January 1947   It was so nourishing to meet Tom and Peace [Moore] again, the war sunk long since, at least, to latency. I had sat between them at the films on the last night of the long armistice which began in 1918 and endured, if precariously, till 1939. We met at the Australia [Hotel]. It is always warming to have Tom's generous kiss & hug. We had dinner at Cahill's down below.[179] We talked, of course, of many things but principally of the Herald's novel competition, not so long concluded. They had thought 'I Camp Here'[180] first until they came to 'The Harp in the South'[181] at the very end. Perhaps yet it will be a better book. Tom questioned me about the 'Harp' and I brought out all the jocular evasions I have exercised since I've been prodded about it over the 'phone & elsewhere by adulatory or irate readers, who want me to take sides. This formula runs to the effect that the woman has done immense service in stirring up the bugs and exhibiting them in Granny Herald. The storm of letters from the unsophisticated, bigoted, uninformed people to that estimable journal, who otherwise would never have heard of the story, and which show no sign of literary understanding, shows that it has been like a good dose of Epsom salts.

Also by touching, however superficially and sentimentally, on the matter of abortion, 'she is paving the way for (Florence & Dymphna's opus[182]—I thought silently, and said aloud:) 'that novel you had in your head', some material gained as Tom now repeated from the Queen of the Abortionists in Newtown (how did Tom come in contact with her: she is in the University vicinity and Tom is not of monkish temperament), who had said the Chief of Police would not touch her as his wife was indebted to her for 11 abortions.

---

179 Cahill's was a chain of restaurants. The restaurant in Castlereagh Street, Sydney was on two levels.
180 By Esther Roland, pen-name of Mrs Eena Job, published in 1948. It won second prize in the *Sydney Morning Herald's* novel competition, 1946.
181 By Ruth Park. Winner of the *Sydney Morning Herald's* novel competition in 1946, it was serialised in the *Herald* and published in 1948.
182 Dymphna Cusack and Florence James published *Come In Spinner* in 1951. It won the *Daily Telegraph's* novel competition in 1948.

Selah!

Tom said he had been thinking that the 'Harp' had stolen his thunder. I said no, broken the taboo: that when the broaching of a subject makes a stir it can be treated & rehashed for a decade by other writers—better, imitative or supplementary. Tom said the Herald people were very pleased with the way the judges had worked, and managed the competition, but that he has refused to act as a judge again next year. 'I might be a competitor myself,' said he laughingly. Well, 200 pounds is not to be sneezed at, and his story, as outlined to me, if Tom would let himself go, would be as frank and sordid as 'The Harp' and could have more power, if Tom didn't fence-sit.

But Tom came back to what I think of the story. Well, I am attracted neither to the story nor its author. Tom & Peace are, they had been meeting her at the Rees. So the flat tyre and the puffed fluke are revelling in their congeniality and commercial success. Of course I didn't utter this, instead I said, 'I liked the buggy parts much better than the sentimental'.

My private opinion of 'The Harp' is that it entirely lacks architecture, that there is a withering lack of an independent or able intelligence behind it. 'Come on, Miles, what do you think of it?' persisted Tom.

'Where is it placed in time?'

'Immediately post-war-now, I should think.'

'Well then, it is supposed to be realistic, yet it is just floating about. If it is the immediate present, the people are not yet so poor, the war money is sinking, but not all gone. The people's temptations are different than those depicted.'

'But the war is well over.'

'Yes, but not its effects. If not directly, then in her detail she could not have escaped it. From here to Cape York & across to the Leeuwin they're still in jungle green or old khaki & army boots, & wear badges, or go on crutches, so she has dodged reality to babble about the Catholic Church. In fact it is shallow.'

Tom said it was the only story with any humor. That 'the Irish always make humor'.

Ruth Park certainly didn't.

'Now,' I said, 'I've read only two instalments of "I Camp Here", but it is pinned in time by mention of Hinkler; though at present the story is about children I find it much superior.' Tom agreed that the clear style had made him think it, 'I Camp Here', might be Vance [Palmer]. Nonsense, said I, Vance could never be so alive. No, said Tom, he has no life in his work at all.

That's why it's so admired by the dummies.

30 January 1947   And so for another look at the Longstaff Lawson[183] which I saw when it was done. People chivvied it in those days, and it did not infatuate me—not then. It does now. How moving it is, sitting there with the penetrating & beautiful eyes looking out all these years as they looked when I first met him. All his personal beauty, sensitiveness and genius captured in its prime. Lucky Longstaff in his subject, lucky Lawson to be so perpetuated.

4 February 1947   I called on Mary Gilmore. She is increasingly apocryphal in her assertions. Very against the British—an old snake really, seeing the way she touted for a British title—always pandering to Government house and quoting the vice-regals to

---

183 A portrait of Henry Lawson by Sir John Longstaff in the Art Gallery of New South Wales. Painted in Melbourne in 1900 while Lawson was en route to England.

Above: Thelma Clune, Frank Clune and Miles Franklin, Oodnadatta, South Australia, June 1937. (Ref: Mitchell Library PX *D250/1, no. 125)

Left: Joseph Furphy, 1903, the year in which *Such is Life* was published. (Ref: Mitchell Library PX *D250/3, no. 29 (a))

Percy Reginald Stephensen, c. 1934.
(REF: MITCHELL LIBRARY P1/S)

Xavier Herbert, Darwin, 1 April
1938, on receiving news that
Capricornia had won the
Sesquicentenary Literary Prize.
(REF: MITCHELL LIBRARY P1/H)

Marjorie Barnard, c. 1935. (Ref: Mitchell Library P1/B)

Flora Eldershaw and Frank Dalby Davison at the Authors' Ball, Sydney, 14 May 1938. (Ref: Mitchell Library P1/E)

Kate Baker planting the Joseph Furphy centenary tree, Shepparton, Victoria, 2 October 1943. (Ref: Mitchell Library P1/B)

Dymphna Cusack, 1947. (REF: MITCHELL LIBRARY PX *D250/3, NO. 21 (A))

Dame Mary Gilmore, 1948 (REF: P1/G)

orman John (Jack) Franklin with his aunt, Miles Franklin, published in the
ıstralasian, 13 October 1945. Jack Franklin qualified as a pilot in September 1943 and
e photograph may have been taken at this time. (REF: MITCHELL LIBRARY PX *D250/1, NO. 99)

Right: William Dobell, 1940s. (REF: MITCHELL LIBRARY P1/D)

Below: Ion Idriess, c. 1940. (REF: MITCHELL LIBRARY P1/I)

Facing page: Miles Franklin, 1940s, wearing one of her typical floral hats. (REF: MITCHELL LIBRARY PX *D250/1, NO. 154)

Right: Miles Franklin, probably taken in Perth, 1950, when giving Commonwealth Literary Fund lectures. (REF: MITCHELL LIBRARY PX *D250/1, NO. 172)

Below: Jounama Creek, Talbingo. After her death, Miles Franklin's ashes were at her direction scattered in this creek which flowed past Old Talbingo Homestead. (REF: MITCHELL LIBRARY PX *D250/4, NO. 50)

show she has been there. A tit-bit this time was that the Queen
Alexandra Nurses can nurse only royalties (?) and one of M.G.'s
friends was nursing John, 'Queen Mary's idiot son', and when he
was dying one night the door opened and in came a terrible old
hag, stringy neck, withered face, hair in wisps on shoulders,
altogether an apparition. She went to the bed, kissed the boy &
retreated. The nurse wondered if she should raise the alarm but
as the old hag turned at the door she recognised old Queen Mary.
'Pathetic isn't it,' remarked old Dame Mary, 'that she looked like
that with her make-up off.'

This may have been Queen Alexandra, and God knows she
suffered enough to make her look a wreck, it could not have
been Queen Mary who, 30 years ago, I bet, with all her make-up
off was still a fine upstanding lump of a house-frau . . .

Another assertion of Mary's was that all the early school books
used here were Irish. She always assimilates & takes to herself
anything I tell her and on the subject of permissible words I said
in my girlhood a stallion had to be called an entire, and the sweet
little pets of girls would coyly call him a 'big horse' to show their
innocence & purity. Mary immediately went one better: she said
a horse neighed, a mare whinnied, a bull bellowed, a cow lowed.
I said I never heard that distinction before except in regard to
perspiring where vulgar workmen or horses sweated, men
perspired, but young ladies only glowed. She said it was in the
earliest school books here which were all Irish because the Irish
were always ahead of England and in those days there were no
English school books because there was no education at all for
the poor in England.

So I got her on to other matters. She is helping to adulate Ruth
Park, wonderful writer, and related to M. Gilmore in whose lineage
is a Rosina Park of Bally—somewhere. Ruth Park in reply says her
second name is Rosina & her people came from the same Bally.

25 February 1947   Well, Mother, this letter is to you, the only way I can relieve the sense of desolation & aloneness. John [Jack Franklin] accumulates things like a mallee hen. The bathroom cupboard is stuffed with the two trunks he inherited from his father, plus suitcases. There is a large box in the laundry, and more stuff in his father's little room. In addition he is so filling the front bedroom that I can't use it for a friend when he is not here.

Neither he nor I can help it that we have nothing in common but, despite that, my affection would be deep for him and I'd be content with no return at all except decency and good manners. I have never said one critical or sharp word to him since his father's death, no matter how much the provocation, nor the melancholy he affects me with. I think, supposing he crashed,[184] & at my last meeting I had been angry with him I should be wounded to sickness for ever by my own sayings. But I think he really wants pulling up. I am willing to have him here as a home base without any financial compensation but he is deteriorating rapidly & deplorably. He has long been beyond endurance; seeing I am easy he is taking more & more advantage of it. Doesn't treat me even with ordinary courtesy. Never considers me in his comings or goings. It might be his house & I a housekeeper engaged to keep it open for his convenience, only in that case he would have to pay instead of having everything free, even the telephone. I am merely a free place of convenience for him to save money for his vices and wasting—an annex to a pot-house wherein to lie all day and go out to drink & other foolishness at night.

His mates who were going to 'iron him out' have abandoned [the] idea of his reform. Older men say he will stop short & have

---

184 John Franklin had joined the RAAF.

sense any day now. I can see no signs, & feel I should take a stand, but I need your concrete ideas of codes. I am too liberal & speculative to apply my own abstemious codes of behaviour. This generation has discarded them.

However I had to remonstrate with him about the piles of belongings, but then I relented & compromised. I got him to clear the big high shelf in the cupboard off the breakfast room and allowed him to make a new hoard there.

We found a trunk of his father's which by dates in it must have been stowed in the year of Rene's [Irene Franklin] death. Norman must have suffered, but he still had you to help & sustain him, and to maintain a nesting base here: and there was John [Jack Franklin], a dear lovable little boy then, for him to struggle for. (And how he did struggle and pinch & deny himself for that boy till the end!)

We found all the photographs of Norman & Rene and others framed, some whom neither John nor I could name. There was a scrap book kept by Rene in which I (touchingly) was remembered. We took out one or two things: the old Venterman Bible, I had wondered where it had gone. John added some of his own things and returned the trunk to the shelf.

There were other heart-breaking parcels. I thought you had disposed of Linda's [Ida Franklin] wedding shoes. Tiny things of white satin. How could we have walked in them, for in those days we could wear each other's shoes. Lace lyle-thread stockings which we had instead of silk.

There was also Aunt Bertha's [Lampe] letter to you and an uncashed cheque for 2 pounds which she must have sent you in those impoverished days at Stillwater. She also complained of her ill-health & suffering, which a few months later killed her. There was also a worn velvet bag of hers. I suspect it went with her wedding or going-away dress. I remember that dress and the exquisite bonnet that went with it when she came to visit you at Stillwater. It was of velvet trimmed with the most beautiful silk lace. I was somewhere about 10 & with a stupendous memory. You had that lace among your things when I came home nearly forty years later. I had not seen it nor heard of it during the interval. You were astonished when I said, 'Oh, there's the lace off Aunt Bertha's wedding bonnet'. You wanted to know who had told me that, and I said, 'No one told me, I remember it distinctly'. I still have it. It is as fresh & [word indecipherable] as when I first saw it.

There was also a sampler of Aunt Emma's [Lampe], with date 1861. She must have been a tiny girl then—all that remains of her who died in youth and beauty so long ago. There was also Aunt Bertha's crewel work, flowers on dark cloth with pinked scollops to adorn the three-cornered shelves put up in the old slab housed in lieu of whatnots.

You kept these tokens so faithfully all those hard years when I was in USA & you had no home, when Father got really on the rocks. Faithful & tenacious under cruel odds you kept even my trivial things—not one missing—& only in rough cases that you had to construct yourself. Oh, Mother, how you struggled! You never let go, never missed a stitch. You had unrelaxing fortitude. No wonder that when dying, as you looked out into eternity without a quaver or a murmur or an expressed hope or wish or word of farewell, you said several times: 'I have done my best. I have done my best.'

How can I shed the chronic anguish of remembrance?

To set it down in writing is an old cure, perhaps it has some efficacy. Some new shock treatment that would finish me altogether would be the only cure, but would it be the end, or perchance to dream?

I shall make a little pyre of the shoes and stockings and the tiny gloves—were they Laurel's [Franklin]? You remembered them all with unrelaxing tenacity. As I let go there will be no wrack nor wraith of any of us. We shall have faded as all the other countless myriads of nonentities. Sparks for a moment in the dark, but why should I have this terrific power to suffer?—wasted power, surely? Neither the exalted nor outstanding last long either in the bewildering immensity of time. Why are the dead for ever silent?

I would be at ease now if only I could arrest John's deterioration. He could be so lovable if he would turn from following false standards and foolishness and settle into decent useful manhood.

March 1948   My life now is merely a low form of existence and has sunk to a stream of interruptions. Any real life in the sense of innerness, recreation, literary attempt, spiritual or cultural cultivation through reading or repose comes merely in snatched interruptions of the chronic interruptions.

Jean [Devanny]: 'All women artists and writers of any kind are simple and soft about men.'

Me: Very softly, 'All?'

Jean: With finality, 'Yes, all. If they are not, they are homo-sexual.'

'There's one that's not,' thought I, but halted on the realisation that I may not rank as a writer, but I pursued my stand unspoken —'One that was not weak about men carnally yet who is normal and healthy; one who finds incest, lesbianism, onanism, homo-sexuality, sodomy and all such vices and perversions revolting even to mention, one who never knew of such infamies till fully adult, and who remains unacquainted with them in actuality, and is aware of them only in books and gossip.'

Jean, however, knows all. Such megalomaniacal self-assurance! She outdoes men in raucous assertiveness, perhaps because men, like royalty, are more in a position to take themselves for granted.

There is but one true panacea for world salvation, she has espoused it, and Torquemada would be a soft angel compared with what she would decree for infidels—as for heretics!! She was reared she said in the R.C. faith and to her the end—her end—justifies the deed. Imagine power in such hands!

When I said during the evening I was tired, she said she didn't want to go to bed. Half-an-hour later she rose and announced she was tired and would go. While she works, she works, and no matter what happens to others. She wanted me to take 30/- a week and fully board her and leave her entirely free to work, no faintest suspicion that I was disrupted occurred to her. I said no one had enough money to hire me to run a boarding house, but if she wanted to feel comfortable she could pay 5/- a week for the wear and tear on the room and gas and electricity, and supply some of the groceries. She acted on this generously. She is not mean or unlovable despite her ideas and politics. When she rests she must not be disturbed. Good discipline for me.

Jean: 'Poor old Katharine [Prichard]. She can't write about working people. She's a petite bourgeois writer. Her Sally!— a working woman never in her life would act like she did'.[185]

I sailed in here, foolishly squandering my strength. 'Rats! Are none but the communist laborers to be depicted in Australian novels? Sally was a warm, a decent, a generous, a gifted and

185 Sally Gough, central character in Katharine Susannah Prichard's goldfields trilogy: *The Roaring Nineties*, 1946; *Golden Miles*, 1948; and *Winged Seeds*, 1950.

experienced portrait of a pioneer woman, and what many of them endured and overcame. Sally was very like an old friend of mine, and if ever anyone worked—slaved—she did. Nurse in the hard days in a bush town typhoid epidemic. Saved dozens, including Chinese and the surveyor and his brother, scions of a noble house. Married one of them; then as a housewife with no means did double duty. Her aristocratic husband went farming. When he lay down on the job, futile, she with her bare hands and small frail body brought in the hay harvest. I doubt if she had even a rake. You ass! isn't that work? Ten times as hard as the day of any pampered "proletarian" sitting in an office scattering dandruff over the surroundings as she preens against the forty-hour-week closing hour. Sally was a fine picture of the same sort of thing. You must know your period when novel writing, and Katharine shows she does that in Sally. You're as ignorant as Howarth, who says that in "Old Blastus" the fuss over illegitimacy is not warranted—doesn't know his period.'

(And apropos, K.S.P. said she knew an old man who, as late as 1916, when he found his daughter had 'fallen' shut her up and would not let her be seen.)

But Jean was not shifted in her premise.

Jean: 'J.B. Miles says he can't read her, that I am the only Australian writer who depicts the working class as they are.'

Glowry and Glammour be! Ain't it grand that we have this one dear lamb of genius even if she seems to me like a ram done up in ewe's wool. Gor' save! I am unacquainted with J.B. Miles; an A.G.S. [A.G. Stephens] or a Desmond MacCarthy may be wasting in him. Jean speaks of J.B. Miles as if he were Christ. Softens her voice to form his name.

Jean: 'He says to me, Jean, you have your great wisdom.'

This tends to send my opinion of Miles as an ordinary man down instead of up. Jean ranks him the equal of Stalin and Lenin and above any man in Australia or New Zealand in intellect. Jean talked of her childhood as having been bitter, when she ran wild as a rabbit and had to seek people to lift her drunk father into the sulky so she could get him home.

Jean: 'All children should be taken from their parents and reared by the State. All children should be taken away at ten months and properly trained. It doesn't matter a scrap about the mothers. Parents shouldn't be considered at all, only the children.'

Probably she was talking out of the idea <u>absorbed</u> (she doesn't think), that if children are caught young they can be bent to any bigotry. In Jean's dictatorship it would be communism. She talked of Clara, an Italian mother with a mentally deficient child, which should be sent to an institution.

Jean: 'I told her she should have put him in a home where he could have been taught basket-weaving and been happy with mates. "It's your duty to get rid of him," I said. A young woman's life swallowed up looking after that child—had to empty his bowels and feed him.'

Me (in small voice): 'You said the mother did not matter, it was only the child.'

Jean: 'This is a different case!'

Quite! but all the same, are mothers of worthy children to be used merely to give them birth? Jean and old blood and guts Paton would have been twin souls. Their creeds have different labels but equal ruthlessness. She almost makes me revert to type sufficiently to fear that a person with such politics must be infected with bugs . . .

P.R. Stephensen used to say, quite unoffensively, that she looked like a splendid virago. She was a handsome woman in those days. She had height, strength, zest, a good profile, and with her hair driven back with a comb and held in a distinctive mop she would have been in place as a ship's figurehead. Like a valkyr or some fury she would have urged men on to slaughter and revenge . . .

The Fellowship of Australian Writers. Adverting, as business 'gents' put it, to Jean's arrival, she had been here no more than an hour or two when she began on the Fellowship, a subject I was desirous of discussing with her in view of the need for reorganization and getting in fresh workers, and more writers known to the public. Never was the organization more needed with so many of the English-speaking publishers from UK and USA arriving to exploit our unorganized field to the service of big business and the production of more and more books, a trade in which the new writer of literature is as likely as not to be neglected and lost, and the intrinsically Australian contribution in danger of being swamped.

Some of us have long been disturbed by the inadequacy of Camden Morrisby. He is timid, conservative, and would be incapable of initiating policy. He has many good qualities as a sort of host and caretaker and would be valuable if balanced by able assistants and a dominating and active President. But with Les Haylen, no more than a figurehead absentee, the organization depends on a rousing secretary, which poor old Camden could never be. He is deadly afraid of Reds: his idea of following literature is to delve into the past for odd scraps of gossip or curiosities, which he retails in trivial detail and ceaseless repetition like a puppy chasing its tail. His weakness is to fiddle-faddle on details and to miss main issues. In addition, of late—for a long time now—he has been neglecting committee instructions. Does not reply to letters, and when a statement of policy is outlined changes it because of his timidity and conservatism. Then the poor fellow has been too often indisposed—giddy and generally off-color, some of us suspect because he has no stable job and, as he says, has to 'scratch around for a living', and has a diet almost exclusively of tea and bread. The standard jokes of standard old maids' fears of burglars under their beds is outdone by Cam's timidity concerning subversiveness in politics or any social question unless dehydrated. The young reds want to oust him, so does B.A. [Bartlett Adamson]. That would be cruel, as he has been so generous and faithful and gains an office and prestige from the job as well as the honorarium. He has confessed to me he wishes to retain it. I want him to have as assistant an energetic young rebel like Marjorie Pizer to outbalance his lacks. He would be an instructive break on her bumptiousness and new-panacea fervour—the two to represent the opposed prejudices among the writers. I also want a vice-president who will be capable of acting deputy when Les Haylen—if re-elected— is constantly absent. The F.A.W. dwindles. Judy Brown left, insulted by Marjorie P. Glen [Fox] won't work with Cam, Camden fears the radicals and is sickened by 'all those horrible, disgusting old women'— 'I hate them, I hate them, Miss Franklin'—brought in by Dulcie Deamer. George Farwell has said openly to me that B.A. is the obstructing factor in reorganization, etc. or, Mavis Mallison is revolted by D.D.'s drunken antics.

Several I have invited to join and help conditions for writers are firm in refusal on the grounds that the F.A.W. is now nothing but a sub-committee of the Communist Party. I have pled with them to help me maintain it as a fighting organization to better conditions and maintain royalties, etc., for all writers irrespective of their politics or religions. But alas, sectarianism is becoming more and more schismatic here. The successful writers are so pleased with themselves that they are above the F.A.W., or are too busy grabbing their harvest. Many are also journalists and guard themselves through the A.J.A. [Australian Journalists' Association], and look upon really literary writing as a mere genteel hobby, and so it goes.

So I tried to put the situation to Jean, but she bore me away on a torrent. At first I was doubtful of her, then resistant, then dismayed, so I requested her to halt so that we could discuss it with Glen that evening without repetition.

In the evening (March 6, 1948) when Glen, Jean and I were in the sitting-room, Jean broke like a released torrent from a spillway and expressed herself somewhat thus. I made notes:

She recognised what I had brought forward. She knows the F.A.W. is now merely a sub-committee of the Communist Party, and that is because Camden has sabotaged it. He is the cleverest, the subtlest man in town and is specially employed by Catholic Action to destroy the F.A.W. because the R.C.s know that writers are dangerous. The Communists know that writers are the most important people in the world and want them to be strong.

Me: 'Nonsense! Camden Morrisby is a Protestant.'

Jean: 'It's not nonsense. Do you think the R.C.s would employ a Protestant on 2SM for years? Cam's a Catholic, and his nephew is a Trotskyite . . . '

Even in days before he became Secretary—at my instigation, by the way—I never suspected him of machiavellian genius, and said so. Jean contended it is the R.C.s who have the genius to use seemingly harmless fools.

According to Jean, Camden has shown the F.B.I. that the F.A.W. is the said sub-committee by telephoning Marjorie P[izer] or George Farwell continually at communistic headquarters, because the F.B.I., which registers every call from and to there, will thus connect the F.A.W. with the Commos inextricably. I still contended that Cam had to call George F. & M.P. at Communist Headquarters because they had no other telephones.

Jean said we must work more subtly for the <u>party</u> than this. I resented this by snorting that I was not concerned with benefiting that <u>Party</u>, nor with F.A.W. members' religions or politics so long as they practised them privately or elsewhere. In F.A.W. I wanted the equivalent of a trade union, a fighting organization for all writers whether blimps, tories, socialists or commos: that writing literature is not the endowment nor prerogative of wearers of shirts of any one color; that all writers apart from their creeds and social situations, as all women, whether the daughters of duchesses or charwomen, have issues in common pertaining to their state of being women, so have writers.

Jean roared on, ignoring my brief for the claims of writers per se—sweeping me aside in her fervor to save the F.A.W. for the good of Communism by purging it of the Communist Party. She outlined her plans.

I said that for months past at every meeting I have brought forward the need to have some plan for the approaching annual election: Bart Adamson always disregards this, says it would be undemocratic to have a ticket to be voted for. I said I was democratic, and did not suggest a ticket, but, seeing that we had no important people left on the Executive, and that often we did not muster even a quorum, I thought it would be common-sense to see that there was a good roll-up of members to provide desirable people for nomination. I left with A.B. [Alex Bookluck] and Camden certain names of writers to be invited, and who, if they came in, would balance the communists in the membership, but never had any response either from A.B., Bart or Camden. What happens is that a few mediocrities attend, who feel important to belong to a fellowship of writers, and they have a spree voting in other nonentities, who do not attend, who have no power, and then I am left to take the chair and be worried by Cam about every detail. (I am firm that I shall this year retreat from this waste of time & undignified footling situation.)

On some lines Jean and I agreed, only that I want the Fellowship for the good of Australian writers to aid Australian writing for the interpretation of my beloved Australia. Jean wants it to further communism—that's where we go separate roads.

Towards the end of one evening she [Jean Devanny] asked rather challengingly 'Have you any religion?' 'Yes, I'm firmly religious, though nebulously too, that means I'm truly agnostic as far as any surmises of what happens to us after death. For the present I believe in honesty of purpose and decency in practice and could no more live comfortably without them than without cleanliness and warmth.'

Jean (dismissingly): 'All people believe in decency & honesty.'

Me: 'Quite! I should like to add that in application of decency I would not betray a dog and have him in fear for his life or freedom. The strongest tenet of my religion perhaps is to allow freedom of thought, to allow the human mind to probe, to imagine, to discover; and sympathy: to realise that each human being is a frail mortal prone to suffer, to be defeated, to be full of fears and longings: to share and to help where ever possible.'

Jean (herself again): 'Everyone should be allowed freedom of speech so long as it doesn't mean any harm to others: then they should be stopped and controlled.'

Me: 'But you wail that you daren't go against the commos or you'd never sell another book—they evidently don't believe in freedom to think.'

Jean: 'We must seize power first and then we can let writers be free.'

Simple, ain't it!

12 March 1948   Went to Ada's [Holman] cocktail party to celebrate the appearance of her memoirs. Poor old dear, she looks as if pulled out of a rag bag for a final appearance, still gallantly attempting to be the woman of the world and of letters with the

few remnants she can scrape around her. Even Evatt and Farrar
missing this time. Old age in Australia, where there is no help to
maintain any comfort or cultural grace, is a bleak prospect. Not
a bad evening gown, but a soiled singlet obtruded well up her
bare back. Una [Ada's sister], in attendance, never pushed it down;
perhaps did not wish to risk Ada catching pneumonia again. Her
hair was as usual, many teeth missing, and her make-up so
haphazard as to make her look positively dissolute, but I don't
care, I love her and she has always been my friend, all through
her heyday, since she came to see me at Miss Scott's. The people
present seemed nonentities and no more cultural than those of
Jones Streets, but in a slightly higher income and residential
bracket—had been abroad. Bridge partners evidently, and bridge
addicts will stoop out of snobbery to collect the necessary partners.
One woman, with nothing that I could discover in her head, was
regretting what she called an intellectual party instead of 'calling
trumps'.

c. April 1948   Ego 8—continuing the Autobiography of
James Agate. Harrap. London 1948.
   Page 221. Sept. 1. Saturday.
   (In a letter from Neville Cardus):
   I am sick of Australia; compared with Sydney or Melbourne,
as far as culture or common sense go, Rochdale is as Athens under
Pericles. I have not heard ONE witty remark from an Australian
in five and a half years. Dein bin ich, Vater!—rette mich!
   Ever,
   Neville.
   Well, the smart-alec retort to the above is that Neville never
met me, as I am one of the poor, and do not enter the successful,

blimp, circles in which Neville operated. Australian society is poor fare, but Australia was a safe place of escape from the culture and society of England and the Continent during the first half of this decade, and to which Neville could have returned at any time.

It was typical of Agate and his success that he published what was doubtless meant to be a private remark. What a fine hunting ground and preserve these old Blastuses of journalism have in London! They get into the society of mostly everyone by force of their press position and sheer hide. Their gossip is about people known to 'the furthest extremity of the globe' so they are presented with an interested ready-made audience, and if they make notes have a bank to draw on for years; and the greater their ruthlessness, this side of libel, the greater their success. No woman would be encouraged in this field. In a woman such ruthlessness in betraying confidences and exposing privacies would be censured as <u>cattiness</u>, but it is accepted from men. Is it part of their nature, the nature by which they rule the roost and then strut and crow without self-consciousness, and with such financial and social success?

1948   This entry goes back to July 5, 1947 for which I scribbled a note or two, & so of course, left it at that. Was bidden to Dora Birtles' party—good heavens, it's nearly a year ago! At her last party I was one of very few women in evening dress & felt unnecessarily 'got-up'. This year ('47) I could not stand the cold so got myself into new royal blue house dress with plenty of woollens underneath, and this time the small minority were those similarly suburban. A clear nippy night, the house was wide open and on Balmoral Heights breezes from the ocean as keen as knives chased each other through the open doors—one gas fire in an oblique corner of the double room, not lighted till well after 9 o'clock. Heaps of food, jorums of drink, but heat very scarce.

A charming house for parties (in warm weather) with that attic room across the top with a dignified entrance corridor to it, is a rarity. Talking downstairs, dancing up. A great basket of kronpiks and a tray of savouries were available all the time till the substantial, but not recherché hot meal about 10.30, of various minces and stews and spaghetti. I have no gout for spaghetti, but there were chocs and stuffed eggs, radishes too, laid out in a freezing verandah. There may have been cakes.

No celebrities of the tonnage of Harry Watt and William Dobell present this year. The belle of the party was a Mrs Hairs (?)—a one-time Canadian, tall, beautiful, grey-haired, professionally coiffed in Edwardian style with orchids in her tresses, black evening gown and pearls. After Canadian houses, the poor thing perished. She hugged the fire, so, shivering, I cultivated her. She was charming, but ordinary and very dull; rumoured to write sonnets. The sonnet form is not a favorite with me so I doubted her ability to conquer its difficulties sufficiently to stir me, but one never knows.

Around us collected the Adamsons, a Mrs Fleming, a Mrs Cheadle, the I.K. Sampsons and others. Kenneth Giles wandered in and out and assiduously circulated the kronpiks and savouries—his leading interest, I'll bet. A cat came in and received attention. I platitudinously asked Giles if he were fond of cats, he whimsically replied, 'I pretend to be'.

A Josephine O'Neill was introduced to me and pretended (falsely, I'll bet) that it was a great honor. Clarrie Martin came up and spoke. Thelma Scott. Other members of the 'Sons of Matthew' cast, with their natural beards, made the place look like an old-time Sunday afternoon of dads on the verandah, while the young men, shaven except for moustaches, flirted or rode elsewhere. Wilfred Thomas introduced himself to me. Very pleasant. Said that in the Northern Territory he had inquired of the bushmen what was the best novel of the area and was unequivocally assured that it was 'All That Swagger' (which is, surprisingly, set at the other end of the continent in the snow country). I noted Tom Challon, a bit sprung. Max Afford & a script clique gathered near-by and talked shop. Max's voice was happy about his success and how someone had spoken of his 'distinguished grey hair'. I did not recall myself to him, he being distinguished to me as a merely commercial writer whose <u>Australian</u> play set in Hampstead, London, had to be translated back to Melbourne by American purchasers to make it coincide with its description: 'an Australian play'.[186] It was in any case imitative and feeble. My standards may be silly, unavailing, but I have to make my own, and they serve me. They are the pole I swing to.

A wholesome, sturdy-looking pair of young doctors, named Rutherford, accompanied me upstairs to see the dancing, when I had wearied of the charming but inane Mrs Hairs. She had asked me if I ever tried to write anything. I said, sometimes, but I was not very successful, and introduced some other subject lest some dunce might intrude with disclosures embarrassing to me. The noise of the dancing was too much for even the boogie-woogie dopedees. A disc of raucous jazz, swing, or whatever the trade name of cacophony is at present, was exaggerated by a loudspeaker. Two girls were the stars among the dancers. They had short dresses. One had nothing on above the waist but a shred of 'soft filmy stuff'. Her mate also had a bandage around her breasts and a naked canal around the midriff. One was a poor trivial little

---

186 Max Afford's *Lady in Danger* was performed on Broadway in 1944.

figure, a thin brain evidently. They both had more power of heel than personality, and needed it in the frost, but one did not perform so expeditiously or exhibitionistically as the other. Judy Brown observed that they had only to show a bit of flesh above the knee and let it be seen they were brainless for all the men to come dithering and buzzing like bees.

I returned to the fire and dullness and Connie Robertson, very handsome in a pillar box red velvet floor-length gown, but no nakedness, who embraced me and sat on the hearthrug at my feet. A Mrs Fleming seemed a good sort. She told how arduous and disappointing she had found Australia—the way the women had to slave without domestic help was unbelievable to the women from Home. She retreated to England and told her mother of what she had to endure, and that it was beyond her. The mother listened attentively and then said, 'You say all Australian women have to live under these conditions—do all their own work, etc?' 'Yes,' said Mrs Fleming. Then the mother said, 'If they can live under these conditions you must go back and learn to do likewise'.

When I grew tired of the folk around the fire again I joined the Rutherfords at the far end of room as they were to leave early and show me the quickest way to transport. Sitting in the seat nearest to me was a smartly-dressed, rather good-looking woman, talking to the one man present in white shirt and black dinner coat, who looked like a waiter taking a spell between serving a round of drinks, and as though he despised the low-class people on whom he had to wait. The Rutherfords made introductions, in which no name was mentioned but that of Dr Emery Barcs, the misplaced waiter. I graciously said I listened to his words of wisdom over the air 'and pictured you as a vast man distinguished by a beard'. He replied condescendingly, 'I am distinguished, but I haven't the beard'. 'That's a pity!' said I, without knowing what

I meant, except that I found his personality offensive. He did not ask for any explanation, but relapsed into that coma distinctive of Middle-European men when they are not expounding their own egos to nubile females. Their only notice of women of any other age would be if they (the women) could be useful.

Barcs presently said to his companion couldn't they go home, that he was cold. Little wonder! It was patent he was bored to the back teeth and had no training nor amiable desire to make the best of it, as I had. The woman replied irritably: 'Unfortunately I can't go yet. There's a woman here named Miles Franklin I must see. They are all talking about her'.

Barcs: 'What has she done?'

Woman: (dismissingly) It was clear that she was playing up to this man's 'sophistication' by showing she was as above and contemptuous of native pretensions to culture as he. 'Oh, years ago she wrote some bit of a book about her career.'

Barcs: 'Was it any good?'

Woman: 'I don't know. I never read the thing.'

Barcs: 'Then let us go home. I'm cold.'

Woman: 'Now, she's written another about her career blowing up.'[187]

Barcs: 'Is it any good?'

Woman: 'No.'

Barcs: 'What's in the books?'

Woman: 'Nothing, only their names.'

Barcs: 'Then why must you see her?'

Woman (irritably): 'Oh, when she says anything they all sit at her feet and worship her.'

---

187 *My Career Goes Bung* was first published in 1946.

I put my hand on the woman's arm and said very softly, 'My dear, don't sit about in the cold any longer. I am Miles Franklin; so now you can go home'.

She was utterly disturbed. What curs we all are to dismember our acquaintances behind their backs and feel such utter confusion if it comes to their ears.

Woman (gushingly): 'Oh, isn't that a nice thing of you to do. Very nice! Very kind of you indeed! . . . Did you hear what I was saying?'

Me: 'I heard my name.'

Woman: 'I was saying the loveliest things about you, and you heard me, wasn't that wonderful . . . (all flustered). Did you really hear what I said?'

Me: 'I have very good hearing.'

Woman: 'Then it was really nice, wasn't it?'

The eminent Dr Barcs meanwhile looked even more strangulated with self-superiority and indifference.

Me: 'Thank you. May I have your name?'

Woman: 'Iris Dexter.'

I said, 'That is a very pretty name', and escaped, to relieve her confusion . . . I had boobed the situation through not being so quick on trigger as in my alerter days (I'm inclined to go off into own thoughts nowadays). I should have set Iris Dexter completely at ease by (1) going away without disclosing my identity, or (2) by feigning I had heard my name only and asking her to tell me what she had said, for after all, she was paying me obliquely a high compliment.

Judy Brown is very much herself always. She kept expressing her surprise at the charm of Dora's home and congratulating her somewhat in the tenor of a Laird's Lady commending a crofter on the upkeep of her but and ben. I left the home with the Rutherfords and Judy, and when we parted from the Rutherfords,

Judy gave her report. She had not been in my clot around the fire. She was disgusted with Clarrie Martin for his profuse 'bloodies' and other foul language, which she considered unbecoming in an Attorney-General. Judy continued that the grog was just beginning to work, the party would now warm up and the girls would go home to sleep with their men friends: <u>that</u> she could understand, if she loved a man, but baulked at it as mere routine the first time they met.

(I suppose if you earn your living by the flesh in a man-made society the routine has to be accepted to gain success. My tastes being utterly different my success is nil.)

Caught the midnight train from St James, home before 1 a.m.

Went to sleep easily so the evening had been neither stimulating nor painful, and, I suspect, that my comfortable weariness came not alone from the boredom of husks but that I had walked around and around the headland in the keen winter winds for thirty-five minutes and let the party grow before entering because the ferry Dora told me to catch got me there before I could see any other guests through the windows and open door. Selah!

And that takes me back to March 13, 1905.

So the Suttors did originate as market gardeners![188] F.B., afterwards Sir Francis, Suttor was in politics in my young days, and one of the most charming, lovable and good-looking men in Australia. Overseas visitors admitted that he at least among colonials was a gentleman, and used to inquire after him affectionately. The Suttors were boss squatters of Bathurst as the Faithfulls, Gibsons and Chisholms used to lord it around Goulburn— very County indeed, in those days of the ascendancy of the squattocracy.

188 Franklin had been reading of George Suttor in Eleanor Dark's *Storm of Time*, 1948.

Sir Francis was delightfully hospitable & had a Sydney house. He used to give theatre or other parties to all the little bright eyes of any prominence and he indulged me to a private dinner and the theatre afterwards. On the evening in question I had to come from Penrith and stay the night with Rose Scott. She welcomed me as lovingly as ever. Her home to me was like that of a favorite aunt's, and something more. She used to call me her spirit child and say that she wished I were her daughter: I adored her. I dressed in my bridesmaid dress, and as time drew on wondered that Miss Scott remained in day clothes. The fat was in the fire! Sir Francis had not invited her. In those days girls were not invited by gentlemen without their hostesses: you didn't treat your hostess's house as an hotel for bed and breakfast only. I said I would telephone Sir Francis that I could not go to his dinner. Miss Scott said that would merely evade the issue. Sir Francis had treated me lightly and insulted her, and he must be rebuked.

It was the only time I ever saw Rose Scott disturb her reputation as an angel—purring, seductive, soft, lovable— the ideal for ladies of her day. She was adamant, and really angry. She said with fire that such conduct was to be expected of a parvenu, that his people a generation ago were only market gardeners while hers for centuries had been of the nobility, bishops, generals, etc.

I was so sensitive that I can vividly recall my anguish, though I can see it as a trifle today, & can't understand why Miss Scott should have held to her attitude so unrelaxingly. I was so aghast at committing or being the object of such a gross social faux pas that I collapsed into a suffering, sobbing, jellied mass of shame. The passion of my upset startled Miss Scott, and she set about retrieving me from myself and her displeasure with Sir Francis. She telephoned Sir Francis that I would be a little late—telephoned herself to him. He was all charm, said they would wait for me as I had come so far, but he did not repair the damage & invite Miss Scott, even at that hour.

I baulked again. A night in jail would now have been preferable, but Miss Scott insisted that I must go and also that I must bring home to Sir Francis the enormity of his omission. I had to pull myself together & bathe my eyes. There was no paint in those days: I was unacquainted with even powder till well over forty. Mrs Suttor, I remember, in my Mary-Anning days[189] was censured by the servant fraternity because the very same day as the title was gazetted she was in the servants wanted columns advertising as Lady Suttor. If only I could have taken a train for Penrith instead of a cab to Darling Point!

I remember that flat failure of an evening. Lady Suttor was in Melbourne, but all was correct, Mrs Langloh Parker was the chaperone. I remember Barty 'Banjo' Paterson and Consett Stephen were there and some young woman in a green dress, of whom only that recollection remains. I must have been a bore to my host if in that character satisfactory to the other women. I could not come out of my shell. I was so unsophisticated that I had wilted like a pumpkin vine in a frost, and besides, was weighed down as with leg-irons by the ordeal of having to pass on Miss Scott's displeasure—the only unpleasant thing she ever made me do. I was expected to sparkle. Barty Paterson had trumpeted my parts abroad. At first everyone listened when I was asked a question. Lord Tennyson was then trying to be my patron, if only I had known how to profit by such an unprecedented opportunity, and I was asked did I not find him very dull and uninteresting. (H.H. Champion spoke of him as 'a hopelessly grocer-like individual'.) Lord Tennyson was as kind and indulgent of my ideas as a father and I can never snap at the hand that tries to help me, so I said he was not spectacular but he had the cool, negative charm of a cucumber, and, I added,

189 When Franklin was in domestic service, 1903–4.

'and you know there are times when a cucumber is most delicious'. When I come to think of it this was rather penetrating and was received as in character—my character.

Mrs Langloh Parker was the belle of the occasion. Her book, 'Australian Legendary Tales', was a pioneer in the field, gathered in far New South Wales—primitive in those days—and had won a preface from Andrew Lang. She was a widow, and while she went for her wraps the men discussed her financial state and the need to get her re-married. She was in Sydney prior to departure to England, first class per first class liner, a first class hunting ground for marriage then. Women went armed with a trousseau of 'feminine' furbelows and exposive frocks, and aided by segregation of males in idleness—no wireless, no radios to interrupt—and long warm days accelerated romance.

Consett Stephen talked politics and said of George Reid that men of his class had no right to be wasting their time in Parliament unless they could help the landed and professional classes and feather their own nests. We set off for the theatre, a pair to a cab. Barty Paterson seized my wrap, but Sir Francis put him with the unremembered girl while he dedicated himself to Mrs L-P and I fell to C-S. Barty murmured in my ear as he relinquished my shawl (my lovely thin Indian one that was eaten by the moths last year) 'What I've got against these affairs is that the wrong man always gets the right woman.'

I certainly felt that C-S was the wrong man to my taste, as his politics and his person were both alienating to me. I, no doubt, was a horror to him. He asked me to smoke a cigarette, which made me uneasy as an affront approaching Sir Francis' to Miss Scott. He said his wife smoked, that the women in the best society did. I said yes, when I went slumming with the Salvation Army (to which I had been instigated by Mrs Edgeworth David [Caroline David], who had done likewise) I noticed the ladies I met there all smoked. At the theatre Sir Francis put me beside him, and Barty took my other side. It was 'The Orchid' and bored me to shreds. Paterson said that the American star was so 'sprung' that she could hardly carry on. Sir Francis kept saying it was a splendid show and that he could enjoy it again and again.

But the evening, joyless though it was, drew to its worse conclusion. Sir Francis took me back to Miss Scott and I had to carry out her instructions. If only I had had the ability of more normal girls to evade or lie I could have saved myself the ordeal of being unpleasant to dear Sir Francis, my kindly indulgent friend, who had petted me in his rooms at Parliament House. He took a pride in pouring cafe-au-lait and let me loose upon the upper house to sit beside Sir Normand MacLaurin and all sorts of privileges.

I stumbled out some sort of tale, did not convey, evidently, that the affront was to Miss Scott, not to me. He called me a dear little girl, bade me not worry, was sure I was mistaken in thinking Miss Scott gave a thought to her omission from the party. 'We are old, old friends,' he said, and that he had not wished to sink me among too many elders. He was sure Miss Scott would not enjoy 'The Orchid', that he invited her to different evenings when serious political moves were in the wind. That was that!

To this day I don't know why Miss Scott was so needlessly huffed. I'm sure it was as Sir Francis said, exactly. He was then 66—9 years older than my father, but he did not look it. Genial, kindly, happy, there was no suggestion of age in his manner, and I'm sure that that manner was the same to all whether young girls, mature widows or cabinet ministers. I had met him casually around Parliament house, he had congratulated me, so when he was knighted, I returned the compliment and said with the temerity of sincerity and unsophistication that he was like a real knight. What it is to be silly and young, better however, than to

be old & silly, but Sir Francis, by his response, was delighted with my effusion. He was, despite his years, as unsophisticated as I, or more truly, unspoiled and unspoilable and unsophisticatable, in the spurious sense of the term. We continued to write to each other but I never saw him again. I was little in Sydney, we were harassed by that beastly failing farm and soon to be scattered— Mother and Father to Queensland, Norman had already left home and I away to America. When I came back, many years later, Sir Francis was dead, and B. Paterson was an old wrinkled man nearly 70.

A set of questions regarding neurosis, heard on the air:
  Are you afraid of the dark? No.
  Of Solitude? No.
  Of Falling? No.
  Of People? No.
  Water? No.
  Of Thunder? No, I enjoy it.
  Lightning? No. (I add) Fire? No.
  Of Disease? Yes, of cancer and paralysis.
  Of Ridicule? Yes and no.
  Of Poverty? Yes. Not to be able to pay my way would flatten me.
  Of the Future? Yes, of the chore of death.
  Of Failure? I am used to it.

'The Story of an African Farm'.
  When I visited Uriarra[190] in 1901 I was delighted to find there this story, which I had longed for but, of course, could not afford.

---

190 In c.1837, Alexander and John McDonald settled on Urayarra station, later known as Uriarra. It is on a tributary of the Murrumbidgee River, close to the present day Canberra.

It was astonishing to see it there, where never a book was read or seen, except the Bible, and the old man, evident aristocrat though he was, was reputedly illiterate. The old lady was able to read the newspaper to him haltingly . . . Uncle Thomas once asked Mrs McD. cynically what she did about the long words, and she, without guile, and not expecting any, replied matter-of-factly, 'I jump 'em'. Alec classed poetry & drunkenness as synonymous, and reading novels on the same level. To see that book there was equivalent to riding along a dull parched track and suddenly espying some gem accidentally dropped. I inquired how it came there. Morton at that date was ardent about me, and I wondered. The young men of that date had been inflamed by the adventure of the Boer War and had ideas of migrating to S.A. Morton had bought the book for its title and found the agricultural label false to his practical necessities. It had been a waste of money: he couldn't make much out of it as a story, though it was so talked about. That news of it had reached him at all is the measure of its fame. I wished that I could have it. He thought it so little interesting that he did not offer it. What a treasure! I plunged into it with rapture. Morton said not to waste my time on it while there: I could take it home with me, and he did not want it returned.

I found that book recently, in a perfect state of preservation, kept all these years by Mother—Hutchinson's Colonial Library paper-backed edition . . . Mother had pencilled her name on the title page & noted 2 pages among the ads. at the end. She had here and there marked some passages faintly in pencil. This is evidence of how deeply the book must have interested her because she reared me to regard books as <u>objets d'art per se</u>. It was vandalage—worse, vulgarity, to mark a book. To dog-ear it, turn it on its face, soil it or to leave any other clues of ill-treatment was dirtiness and illbreeding. So strictly implanted in me is this attitude towards books that it is only of comparatively recent years that I have felt at liberty to grangerise and annotate my own books.

In 'The Story of an African Farm' I have put my mother's initials (S.M.E.F.) against her marks to separate them from some of mine, added during re-reading. The essence and much of the contents of the story had remained in my mind. I remembered the opening and close as vividly as poems. I had retained for nearly half a century the poignancy and depth, the sense of fellow-feeling, the release and comfort the book gave me, but was surprised to find I had quite forgotten the love-making part when Gregory goes away and pretends to be a woman to nurse Lyndall. That had been intoxicating in my young days, but it seems unreal and novelettish now, and reminds me that A.G.S. [A.G. Stephens] dismissed the love-making in 'M.B.C.' [*My Brilliant Career*] as untrue and a failure because I knew nothing of love, and my girlish imagination had gone astray.[191] That's what must have been the case with Olive, but the remainder of the novel was reality illuminated by genius, and a feast to her attuned readers.

I used to think of Olive Schreiner as a girl of my own age until years after I saw a photo of her in a dress of the same pattern as my mother's wedding frock. Mrs Lucy Spence Morice said it was the wonder book of her generation, as it was of mine. I wonder would young women today care for it. Had I taken the interest in title pages and prefaces then that I do now I should have seen it was dated June 1883 and probably had been written some time before that. When I read it 'M.B.C.' had gone overseas and was in print. I had seen a letter written to Hebblewhite by Chapman,

---

191 Stephens wrote in his review in the *Bulletin*, 28 September 1901: 'There is a little that is false where "Miles Franklin" has to supplement her diary from imagination, in the love episodes; but she has imagined so sincerely that the relation remains true in relation to herself, and is false only as regards things external to her'.

to whom he had evidently written of my efforts, in which was: 'Have you heard anything more from your Olive Schreiner?' So, it was intoxicating to discover the nature of Olive's book.

When I visited A.G.S. later he showed me some pressed violets sent to him by Olive in response to a letter from him, and he gave me a reproduction of her photo, evidently from a frontispiece. I exclaimed breathlessly, 'Isn't she lovely!' He replied, 'No lovelier than yourself! She has a better nose than yours, but your eyes are better than hers.' The above photo was signed and I observed that 'faithfuly' had only one 'l', whereupon A.G.S. said in his deflating way that if I had Olive Schreiner's genius I could spell as I wished. Long after, in London, when I pointed Olive out to my dear Nell Malone, she said, 'She looks like you'd expect Olive Schreiner to look!' . . .

Eventually I met my idol in London during the war of 1914–18, at a very select luncheon, given by Misses Newcomb and Hodge in the name of their League, through which they struggled bravely to extend woman's suffrage and democracy to all the peoples within the Empire. They and their faithful band kept on and on through the days when to mention matters so sane and advanced was almost treasonable, and would have been violently suppressed in any country but England. Olive wouldn't say a public word at all, was worse than I, and would never overcome her panic for any cause whatever. I had nothing that I could say to her in the hearing of others, especially reformers to whom reform came a long way ahead of literature, and to whom only genius that could help to grind their own axe was of account. It was too late for the raptures I might once have felt in meeting her.

'Drums Under the Windows' by Sean O'Casey (Macmillan & Co, New York, 1946), third in his autobiographical series of (1) 'I Knock on the Door'; (2) 'Pictures in the Hallway'; (4) 'Irishfallen Fare Thee Well'.

Here we have the man who wrote those gloriously moving plays 'Juno & the Paycock', 'The Plough & the Stars', 'The Star turns Red'. This is a turbulent performance, a rush of Irish cantankerousness, emotion with all stops out, and the inherent Irish genius. Such a degradation of poverty, such a cruelty of deprivation, but nevertheless it burns like a torch with the hilarity and illumination, the perception and the rage of Irish humour. O'Casey worshipped J. Joyce's work and this book is in many parts a fond imitation of Joyce's style. In places it sinks into the twilight insanity of Anna Livia Plurabelle in sheer pastiche. The fantasy sometimes becomes tedious, too out-of-bounds to be unravelled without an application and attention that I can no longer afford: in other places it is made a devastating criticism of human society as known to O'Casey. The book is written as parochially as a deaconess's letter, but such parochialness! The poverty is shocking, and no rage and rebellion against those responsible for upholding such a state of affairs could be unjustified or excessive. Dublin poverty is renowned for its depths: it filled my head with lice on the only day I made contact with it in a R.C. church congregation. The book is a scalding commentary on Ireland's subservience to Rome, though she would destroy herself in her fanatical hatred of Westminster. To know what would become of freedom, of all artistic expression, when the Vatican can impose full dictatorship is trenchantly revealed in the way Synge's play was attacked without its contents being known. It is to be seen in the fact that most of the Irish great have been and are Protestants, Shaw, Synge, Yeats, O'Casey, Parnell; and Moore left the church & J. Joyce never got over his quarrel with it. What dire blight does Rome impose on the soul that this should be so?

The Irish would be happy completely under Rome with all light blocked out because centuries of domination from that quarter have already bigotized, twisted and almost blinded the Irish soul. O'Casey knows their bigotedness, backwardness and benightedness. We are tainted here as shown by the way anything stronger than pap is banned or attacked.

It is a book you want to read with a congenial friend at hand with whom to savor the impish twists (often overdone), the richness of illumination, the overwhelming, irrepressible humour as when the Viceroy asked were the police alert against disorder, the sergeant replied, 'Ready to dive on disordher, sir, the way a dhrone would dive on a queen bee!'

'Storm of Time' by Eleanor Dark (Collins: London and Sydney, 1948).

What does the title mean? especially as Time seems to stagnate rather than storm, even today, in this far quarter of the globe. Nice map on inside cover. At a snap estimate based on two pages, about 342,200 words. Follows on the 'Timeless Land', which was a tour de force. This is a monumental achievement; time will test its success and/or art. In the matter of zeal, integrity and forcefulness it shows 'Tomorrow and Tomorrow'[192] as artificial and transient, imitative and synthetic.

Of course I have a strong pull to treat it tenderly out of love of Australia and interest in a fellow writer for whom I have an inherited affection. Nevertheless it did not seduce me: I could put it down any minute. I skipped the history layers, and the story parts, though painstakingly done out of sparse, stiff material, are very humdrum. The dialogue is not witty or touching— merely utilitarian. It has required immense and patient research, unwavering purpose, intelligence and industry to marshal the people and incidents on such a crowded canvas, but I think it will receive more lip service than it will awaken delight. I did not find it as warm and moving as Ellis' biography of Macquarie.[193] That

192 M. Barnard Eldershaw, *Tomorrow and Tomorrow*, 1947.
193 M.H. Ellis *Lachlan Macquarie: His Life, Adventures and Times*, 1947.

had more spontaneous infatuation: this is an equally painstaking, comprehensive compilation, but it does not glow. One trusts Eleanor's integrity in research and presentation, and this with 'Timeless Land' puts her in a high classification by herself. Clever little thing: good luck to her!

She has brought home to readers what our early governors must have endured, first the heroic Phillip, and, in this, Hunter, King and Bligh, who had no easy exile. As for the convicts— one is sickened and saddened always to recall them. Eleanor also shows as no one else has thought of doing what a tragedy it was to the real owners of the land, who, to begin, were so gentle and friendly; and she gives the woman's point of view always, another chain upon adventure and excitement in a story.

Am I not carried away by the books as I long to be (1) because I am too near to Australian history & subconsciously debauched by the legends, pageantry, tradition of English history, still living and glamorised by its fairy tale re-enacted daily by the royal puppetry? (2) because even I have come to accept only men's struttings and posturings, breakings and makings, bullyings and boastings as colorful and important, and women's prescribed place as trivial and unworthy of consideration?

'The Gallery' by John Horne Burns (Secker and Warburg, London, 1948).

A brilliant book, a high talent. This is a series of vivid and interesting short stories, termed a novel because the writer makes them radiate from the hub of the Galeria Umberto in Naples. In some ways it is less, and in others more truly entitled to come within the classification of a novel than is 'Such is Life'. Furphy's story is a real novel intricately interwoven from first to last but torn apart by the philosophical, political and other digressions. 'The Gallery' is a sheaf of short stories claiming to nail itself together as a novel by the device of bringing the Gallery into each tale. Burns shows the Americans in Naples after the conquest and depicts it as we know it must be. The United States are improving to welcome such agitated and outspoken self-criticism as herein. The author has a lively vocabulary, an inhibited awareness, more wide than deep or penetrating.

The book is a sex manual; one can see here how the Yanks held up the ill-fed Neapolitan women for food, the V.D. that ensued and the inside workings of a detention hospital for its treatment. A prime exhibition of the male sex, sexually rampant. The writer is evidently a typical, clever American who has had luxurious opportunities of schooling and living— no inhibitions. He knows all the answers, and none. The emancipation of women doesn't seem to have occurred to him. He would have no sympathy with or understanding of that kind of liberty and 'demahcracy'. Females in this book satisfy the males' overcharged lust and incidentally serve as incubators for more soldiers and their molls. Seems to believe that any woman who doesn't welcome coition in the first or second round is abnormally below normal.

The Americans have taken to sex totalitarianly to an Oriental degree. They have retrogressed appallingly from Puritanism despite their advanced prophylactics and quick chemical cures, their high-pressure treatments administered by highly-trained young women chosen for their beauty and cheerful dispositions to make the time pass pleasantly for the miscreants. 'These men are sick not sinners.' (See a digest article.) A new 'high' in the duties of vestal virgins!!! A very phallic book. Its ultra virility is not dimmed by any suggestion that any female should have the right to repudiate or eschew concupiscence through fastidiousness or a sense of self-respect, or simple personal cleanliness. Of his fellow-countrywomen, sent with the Army as nurses, etc., he revealingly observes that they were so busy, often tired, and too few to carry out this extra service. He doesn't mention that any withheld themselves. A repellent exposure of total preoccupation with sex. It would be interesting to see what Burns could do in a genuine novel set in the United States.

The sentimentalising of 'love' as found on the sidewalks from women, priest-ridden and bartering sex for food, was nauseating to me.

'Letty Fox—her Luck' by Christina Stead (Harcourt Brace, New York, 1946). 517 pp. Between 225 & 250 thousand words.

Bogging into this after 'Kitty Foyle' [by Christopher Morley] was like having to appraise a full length portrait of a draught horse after a pencil sketch of a light saddle hack. This Australian girl has gone abroad and brought her production up to international standards by writing a handbook on whores. Such a gallery of bitches (the mot just in this case) makes one wonder is chastity among women entirely out of demand in America. There were plenty such as Letty's colleagues forty years ago, but they were the exceptions not the mass, as they would seem to be by the novels of today. I knew of them through the Floyd Dell, Theo. Dreiser, Cram Cook, Ben Hecht, Susan Glaspell, Maurice Browne and the Little Theatre, and the Little Review crowd. Margery Currey Dell and I became warm friends and still are to this day. They were urgent that I should participate in their fevers and experiments in living. They were revolting to me. I expressed what I thought to Charlotte P. Gilman. She said they were 'a thimbleful of maggots squirming in their own juice'.

I remember Floyd and Margery wrestling with me. I was invited to weekends where husbands were exchanged and virgins were 'taught to live'. I never accepted and did not entirely hide my scorn and disgust. They tried to proselytize me through Margery, who was then accepting the doctrine of promiscuity as a part of freedom for women.

I remember an afternoon I went to once, away out on the North Side. The boss woman present was Edna Kenton's sister (I disliked Edna and the sister was nobody but the sister of Edna), who was a coarse advocate of the new sexual freedom—as ancient as Babylon and Sodom and Gomorrah. I recall that Louis Untermeyer's daughter & I were the two youngest and I believe the only two uninitiated females present. She and I expressed our revulsion to each other in a few words at the bottom of the table, where we sat together. We were disgusted, not amused. The meeting was expressly 'to talk frankly about sex', and Margery, who had had me invited, impressed upon me what a chance I was given. I did not like the women nor what they promulgated. I said no word other than the whisper between the young Untermeyer & I: I never saw her before nor since.

Questioned as to my 'reactions' by Floyd and Margery subsequently, I said what I thought. Floyd said I was denying life. I said I was not denying life, but what was offered me here would be death to me. 'But you'll become an old maid!' exclaimed Floyd. 'I'd rather be an old maid than an old harridan,' I replied. This silenced Floyd. 'What do you want?' inquired Margery later when we were alone. She had been deputed to talk to me intimately out of our evident friendship.

'You can't give me back my voice,' I said passionately. 'What I want is an income that would free me to study music and to try some method that might mend my voice, & free me to write as a second interest.'

The loss of my singing voice was still an agonising tragedy that I never mentioned. I could have had money with a man attached several times but death was preferable to 'living in sin' to one of my codes and sensitiveness. As for enjoyment, 'thrilling experience', I looked the men over and shuddered. Floyd—my friend's husband—was too talky-talky and effeminate, I loathed

Dreiser and others, besides, they were all pre-empted, and anything they could offer me carnally was more horrific than the dentist's chair, in which I was then undergoing such torture that one day I fainted in it . . .

I found 'Letty' as repellent as this writer's other books, but not so boring as 'Salzburg Tales' and 'House of all Nations'.

Her men are pathologically chary of marriage—very different from my experience, but I being only a working girl and inviolably chaste, attracted the rich and stable elements.

C. Stead seems to suffer from neurasthenia of the soul and depicts characters in tune with her state. Not a decent person in her gallery, if one abstracts Jacqueline & the mother—who is merely a poor conventional creature—and Lili Spontini, a fool and hanger-on. I read the book firmly to see if it corroborates anything that is going on here as divulged by Jean Devanny. Jean has said nothing that is not to be found in Christina's fictional cases. Christina does not mention diseases contracted. In a state of lecherous catch-as-catch-can without any regard to decency or fair play, driven by nymphomania and satyriasis, infections must occur. One point is that they seem to be 'amateurs' in the sense that this term applies in the snobbery of sports like golf, tennis and cricket: they don't boldly ply for hire. Girls are willing to support men in return for relief of their perverted fleshly appetites. And this takes me back to Floyd Dell again and Charlie Hallinan, Llewellyn Jones and others. I can see Floyd clearly in memory with his black stock and walking-stick, on Dearborn Street,[194] as he and Charlie announced to me the glad tidings that they were feminists. I was so uninstructed that distaste awakened

---

194 Dearborn Street, Chicago, where the National Women's Trade Union League was located when Franklin worked for it, 1908–15.

in me. It seemed to me that the word was related to feminine, and for a man to be feminine was to be effeminate, and utterly obnoxious to me, reared where men were men. (I remember my disgust once when a tall splendid specimen, Mr Ketchman, a prof at some college, whom I was admiring confessed without apology that he was 'afraid of horses!') They expected me to whoop approval of their adoption of the doctrine of feminism, I, so outspoken in my opinions of how women were handicapped, and coming from Australia where women had the vote, and where social improvements, undreamed of elsewhere at that date, were enjoyed by the population.

I listened while they extolled the liberties that 'feminism' would extend to women. It seemed to me that the most striking of these were some of the vices of men—smoking for instance— a mild one—and whoring—which they were to enjoy as men did without losing their respectability. It did not seem to me that such indulgences would make women any more free or happy, but merely that it would relieve men from any sense of responsibility or social disapproval in debauching them. At that time, some men sometimes had to suffer social disapproval for ruining some girls, but this feminism would free men from any sense of regret, responsibility or remorse to any girl. That was far from what I considered freedom or fair play for women.

In short, women were striving to do away with the moral monstrosity of the double standard in sexual behaviour by making men abstain equally with women, which, worked out, is mere arithmetical logic, but men in feminism would escape restraint through dialectics and remove old protections for the subject sex, and thus, with so-called freedoms, put upon them even worse disabilities. This was before 1914. When I returned to New York in 1923 Freud had swept the field. The Puritan dams were broken. Floyd's brand of feminism was operating. Abortions were the order of the day. Margery Currey (long since divorced from Floyd) said all the numerous office girls with whom she was in contact had 'been through it'. The lid was right off virtue, men told me.

Men, terrified at the growing demands by women for equality in sex, panicking at the prospect of obligatory self-restraint, preferred that all women as well as all men should indulge in extra-marital, pre-marital or any other sexual affairs. C.P. Gilman replied to this result of Freud's postulates by a book called 'His Religion and Hers'.

Today, far away at the 'furthest extremity of the globe', among stuffy domestic women of small mental capacity and less experience, where old conventions in behaviour still operate to an extensive degree, I wonder how many approximate in real life in New York to these fictional females, without shame or pride. It agrees with what the girls I know have reported on the approaches the American soldiery made to them during the Occupation. The G.I.s said they liked the fresh vigor of Australian women, and also said that they were the only cheap commodity in Australia!!!!!!

I am glad I am not young now, I don't desire life to stagnate inside outworn customs, and the monogamous marriage, so far, has been monogamous for women only: a new experiment or an extension of the pre-1914–18 one is due. Also, if men will not set themselves against the basic madnesses which end in war, it doesn't matter how each generation is produced for the slaughter, but I deplore the mad waste and degradation of the great power of life-giving in doubtful pleasure which inevitably ends in disease, disillusion, pain and poverty of soul and body.

Christina Stead's style is heavy and dull, it has no charm: only once in all that mess of words did I catch a thought that gleamed such as sex and immorality. Her vocabulary is unexciting: I did not have to look up any word. Her style, though neutral, is adequate because it never gets in the way of lucidity in the case notes. There is no idiom or dialect in it, so it should be easy to translate in these days of internationalism-cum-standardisation. She knows all the passwords and code of whoring. The women all seem shameless and the men without grit. They boast of their 'parts' like the men in 'Le Livre d'Amour de l'Orient', the Cheikh Nefzaoui's 'Manuel d'Erotologie Arabe de la XVIe Siecle (Deuxieme Partie)'[195]— The USA catching up with ancient Middle-Eastern Culture!

*April 1949*____ So poor old Ada Holman has gone! The notice of her death jumped at me without warning from the S.M. Herald. One of my girlhood's company from the Rose Scott days, who called me Stella. On Sunday 10th, I spoke in memory of her with E. Farrar, M.L.A. at the Fellowship of Australian Writers. She was a courageous and warmhearted woman, and always a loyal and affectionate friend to me. She had many illnesses during her last years and grew bedraggled in appearance and inconsequent in utterance, but remained valiant. Farrar told me she was found unconscious alone in the flat on Ocean Street, Edgecliff, from whence she was taken to hospital but never regained consciousness. They did not know how long she had lain.

The last time I saw her was on Saturday evening, January first, when I had dinner with her and her two sisters. She was a splendid cook, and this dinner had become our yearly custom since we had been bereft, she of her husband and I of my family. I contributed a fruit cake and flowers and lemons, and latterly a bottle of wine.

---

195 Franklin had a copy of this book, published in Paris in 1912, in her library. It is inscribed 'from H.R. Aldridge's library'.

Another leaf turned over, another leading player gone from the drama of my life.

I recall going to the Houses of Parliament with Miss Scott and being astounded to find the lawmakers were all so old, unpolished, unimposing and generally 'common'. They had no impressive wit, erudition, appearance or tailoring. (A year or two ago in the same premises the lawmakers impressed me even less favourably as I overheard their touting and 'go-getting' machinations while waiting to have lunch with Dan Clyne.)

So Miss Scott in her dulcet murmur supposed that the dear members of Parliament weren't very impressive to the imagination of a young girl. She sent for Mr Holman, probably as the nearest to the being who might infest my knightly day-dreams. I remember W.A. Holman as he stood before us. I was impressed, not by his rich thick hair, his lineaments, comparative youthfulness, nor by anything only the elegance of a white muffler, which adorned him. And that's all I remember of the Holmans in those days, plus Miss Scott's murmur that she must have Mrs Holman to see us, as she was young and lovely too: and Ada always maintained that she duly appeared at Miss Scott's salon evenings and, like countless folk of that decade, regarded me as a comet of wonder— God knows why. At any rate Ada & Will always retained that attitude.

. . . my next recollected contact with Ada was in Chicago in 1914. She and Mrs Hugh McIntosh [Marion McIntosh] set out for a trip and heard of the outbreak of war en route, but decided to continue. Ada arrived without my address, but lacking an understanding of my <u>non</u>entity outside my native bailiwick, and on the theory that the American drug store had amazingly comprehensive functions, she went into one on State St. and asked for me & Alice Henry. The deity that presides over miracles took her to the only shop in that vast river of population that knew us. Alice H. & I were staggered by the chance, but Ada was never convinced that it was a fluke that we were known.

Margery Currey (then Mrs Floyd Dell), then doing newspaper work, made me promise to let her have a scoop on this premier's wife from a country where women had long had the vote. However, what seemed most striking to Margery in the two women was that their dresses were crumpled. At the cost of $1.50 (6/-) each outfit they had not had themselves 'pressed' immediately on arrival. The American women were still being ridiculed and decried as 'unsexed' to demand a vote.

My next contact with the Holmans was in London during World War I. In 1917 I was off to the Serbian front. Ada & Stella Kidgell [sister of Ada] were at the Rubenstein Hotel near Victoria. Ada gave me a farewell lunch there, at which Mrs H.G. Wells and Agnes Platt or Pratt (?) were two of the guests.

W.A. [Holman] had some big business on that day with Cabinet Ministers and war cocks, and apologised for his absence, and sent me his photograph. I was packed up & had to put it in my shoulder haversack with my passport etc. and said that if I was killed at the Front clasping W.A.'s photo, Ada must publish the circumstances and not have W.A. credited as the secret passion of my life, like Louis Parensell and the Brontes . . .

Returning to London on April 28, 1924, after six months leave of absence without pay to visit my family, I found the office in a turmoil, with a world conference of women on housing called by Henry R. Aldridge for six weeks hence, not a thing done, and my name attached to it as Secretary. Edith Wood, a shallow clerkly card-catalogue type, told me of the lunacies of the Chief.

I had to run desperately around to the offices of the Dominions High Commissioners to scrape up delegates, who might be among the summer hegira of such peoples to London. I had willing co-operation from the Canadian, South African and New Zealand offices. Very different was Australia House.

I started by telephone, and requested Sir Jos. Cook or his Secretary. The person I got sounded like a returned soldier with all the limitations of the R. Soldiers' League's politics and policies in outstanding measure. I got nothing but parrot-robot 'reactions', no matter how I framed my business or stated my reception by other dominion representatives. All I wanted was names of women then in England to whom I could send invitations, and perhaps get a makeshift delegate for that mad-hatter-conceived-on-the-spur-of-the-moment footling conference. Aldridge by this time was very far gone on the way to final debacle.

The moronic parrot at Australia House had a formula which he repeated to every approach. Circumstances were such that he regretted that he could not grant my request: Sir Jos. Cook was not available. No doubt this was a legacy from soldiering days when army cocks sought by such wooden precautions to keep from the enemy what the enemy already knew.

So I went round to Australia House in person, as I did not wish my own State to be the only one unrepresented, even though the congress would be merely façade, and poor at that. I had no better luck in person—was not allowed beyond the waiting room. The returned-soldier element was likewise in control like sentinels keeping everyone out & nothing more. So I sought the Librarian, poor gentle old Mr Stafford. I wanted to look over the visitors' book for likely names. Oh no, he could not let me do that. I said surely I was well known & he could trust me with the names for such a simple worthy purpose. He trembled, but stood firm. 'I'm only a poor old official here, I have no authority.' 'Who else would you approach at the Commonwealth offices but officials?',

I contended, but if I could get nothing from the High Commissioner's office or the Agent General, it was clear that he felt that to help me would be equal to treason in war time. (I recalled Sir Francis Suttor once said that the Agent General should be called General Agent for the State and then he could do anything & everything needed without entanglement in red tape.)

I had to retreat. The only woman I could lay my hands on was Ada Holman, who toed the line as usual without baulking.

Then one morning in the rushed scrum in a hurrah's nest, typical of Aldridge's methods of <u>dis</u>-organization, Mr Aldridge rushed out of the front office cleaning the bit of the dirt from under one uncut fingernail with another equally ragged, his eyes dilating with consternation because Australia House was on the telephone wanting to know why every other dominion was to be represented at the World Conference and his office had received no intimation of it. 'What on earth had happened? Miss Franklin can you explain?' Let me handle this, I said with glee.

Mr Aldridge trembled in my wake. 'Miss Franklin, be very diplomatic, explain in any way you like; smooth him down, don't do anything to endanger dominion relations.'

'This,' said I, 'is a private tow-row, nothing to do with you or dominion relations or the National Housing Council, or boosting or busting the Empiah, it's simply me springing to the aid of my own, my native country.'

Sir Joseph Cook himself was on the telephone and pointed out the grave omission, why was every dominion right out to the Bahamas represented, & Australia alone ignored?

It is indeed a grave omission, I agreed, and proceeded to lay out the facts. I had of course sent the preliminary announcements and requests for delegates by mail, then I had telephoned and got nothing but a stupid parrot reply, over and over; then, busy

& rushed though I was, I had gone to Australia House myself and
had been unable to penetrate further than an ante-room. Neither
my personal credentials nor those of the National Housing Council
had been sufficient to get me any further. I had then tried the
Librarian & so on. I enlarged upon the courtesy & helpfulness of
the other Offices. In the New Zealand, South African & Canadian
offices the great men themselves were not present, but there
were able deputies, & when the head panjandrums came in they
insisted on additions. I said I agreed with him that indeed it was
a grave omission; I said I was not an Englishwoman, overlooking
some [un]important or inconsequential colony, I was one of the
most dyed-in-the-wool Australians alive, always jealous of and
eager for the development & recognition of my country and I
had been appalled by the inadequacy of its London office, the
crudity, the sheer wooden parrot returned-soldier unintelligence
I had encountered. However, I had personally secured my friend
Ada Holman, and as she was our Premier's wife, though an
unofficial delegate, she would be accepted . . . & save my face.

On finding out who I was, Sir Joseph relinquished his contend-
ing and said in a mild & conciliatory tone (he was always the
blue-eyed non-inflammable English type that turns away wrath)
that all he could do was to apologise. 'I wonder if you'd forgive
me so far as to send me two full copies of all the papers and
proceedings of the conference.'

I had never heard Ada speak in public, & doubted her ability.
I asked Lute Drummond, who knew her. Lute, dear Lute, said
she was wonderful, she was a woman who kept her mind tidied
& was brilliant etc. etc.

That was wide of the mark & showed me that Lute and I had
not the same standards in public speakers. Fresh from years of
tarific platform people in the USA I found Ada scrappy &

inconsequential in her remarks. Her utterances were always rather fly-away, and were not consistently based, but as a Dominion Premier's wife she got by and helped to save the day for Aldridge . . .

As early as possible we had asked the Marchioness of Aberdeen to be president & to preside at the opening session. As trained by efficient people in Chicago, I put her name on a list & instructed Edith Wood to see that every notice was sent to these people as reminders. Mr Aldridge had the national religion of royalty & nobility worship—messing around and undoing any bit of routine order, as was his wont, he came upon the envelopes awaiting posting and extracted that of Lady Aberdeen; she was so exalted, so important that he would write to her personally. As usual in numerous other cases, he never got around to the long-winded, devious, palavering letter. Result, on the opening morning at Caxton Hall, I was told that a lady wished to see me personally and privately. It was Lady Aberdeen. 'My dear, I wondered if you still wanted me to open your conference. I promised to do so but have had no final word from you.' I was dumbfounded. I explained, very plausibly (because truly) that Mr Aldridge had wished to inform her personally etc. etc., the Conference called at such short notice, etc. etc. She was most good- tempered and motherly. She 'knew how busy Mr Aldridge was. It was quite understandable.' So long as she knew, she would be there at the right time. 'So long as you are sure you want me, my dear. I don't mind if you don't.' 'You are a dear!' burst from me. 'Without you it would be a meat pie without the meat.' At that she laughed, and said that while her maid had been dressing her hair that morning she had pulled the expired day from the calendar she kept on her dressing table, and saw the Conference on her list of engagements.

This was one of the most gracious and good-tempered examples of good manners illuminated by the golden rule I have ever encountered. It cured me for ever of any impatience I might justly feel towards people for their lacks in keeping me informed as a speaker, I, so infinitesimal compared with that personage . . .

Lady Aberdeen cured me of impatience with one kind of omission; Dr Allan Johnston cured me for ever of any fret about loss of dignity through being kept waiting at a tryst etc.[196] This, however, does not prevent my deploring the years of time that must have been wasted by my own punctuality and the selfishness, muddledness or lack of self-control of others who have failed to keep time. It was this way. He used to companion me sometimes, but frequently there would be a typhoid haemorrhage, a bone to set, a pneumonia victim or other urgent case to keep him away at the last minute. It was so discommoding, especially as it was seldom that I was free of the slavery of committees or other engagements connected with an organization. Once I said teasingly to him I'd rather have a [word indecipherable] peddler as an escort: surely I could be more sure of the tinker's company. He was amused—if ruefully—and said, 'I tell you what, let's make a bargain. I shan't have any sure <u>free</u> evenings for some time, so if you'll telephone me when you want me I'll see if I can get away. If I can't it will be more my loss than yours.' I was not easy about this, having been strictly reared to leave the advances to men, but one evening I screwed myself up to ask him would he escort me to a party at Mary McDowell's. It was a snow laden night, but that did not worry me, & it was his native part of the continent. He enquired where was the party. It was at the University Settlement, I was near the University on the Illinois train line. 'If you don't mind,' said he in a tone which I took to be indifference, 'I'd

---

196 Biographic details on Dr Allan Johnston unavailable. Elsewhere, Franklin spells the name 'Johnson'.

rather not go tonight. I'm very tired, and it's a long way.' He was somewhere not far from the Loop. I hung up the receiver without another word, feeling utterly humiliated. Served me right for making an advance to a young man!

Less than a week later one of my fellow boarders remarked at dinner, 'Sad about Dr Allan, wasn't it?'

'What is the matter with him?'

'I was at his funeral today.'

Pneumonia contracted from a slum patient.

Other doctors told me it was a weakness on his part to act nurse to his poor patients who had no one to care for them.

I had come to know him at the Passavant Hospital [Jackonsville, Illinois] where he was senior interne at the time & where I had been <u>mis</u>-placed for a rest by Dr Young, with whom I was living, and who said she could not see me getting whiter & whiter and thinner and thinner and never having any rest or recreation. The basic reason was that I had no training and no sense of proportion, no realisation of what the human machine could get through in a day. It was a case of a temperamental blood horse doing all that she was suited for and every stodgy chore to boot, but that is another story.

I hadn't a pain or ache, really was an example of a thoroughly sound clean body—if only the tension could have been loosened, if only I could have acquired the habit of sleep and a saving realisation that something was due to myself as well as to my colleagues and the unfortunate! If only!

Allan Johnson used to take me to the theatre to see him do the unusual dressings, particularly the girl who had lost her scalp. She extolled his gentleness. I was captivated by his deft skill.

He once asked me to allow the students to put their stethoscopes on my chest and examine my throat. 'There,' said he, 'is a beautiful example of a well-developed chest.' He said that with such lungs and heart as mine a person would be possessed of tremendous energy and ability to throw off any pulmonary attacks, that I really had too much engine power for my physique, that my mental activity drove me to wear out my body. He said he was the opposite, that he had small lung power, that, for instance, pneumonia or such attacks would be serious.

It was all so very chastely & delicately done, the students blushed & were so worshipful, though my chest was less exposed than in evening dresses today. As a quid pro quo I had some fun stethoscoping the students—all males, and was tremendously interested in the bell-like sound of the chest works under the instrument. It was all so long ago—so many are dead, but I had a letter from Dr Young (now high in her 80s) for Christmas.

12 June 1949   Cold clear day again. After some chores & the cooking got out Merlin[197] & began on the typescript to be ready for B. Davis. Totally alone all day—not even a wrong number on the telephone to break my solitary confinement.

13 June 1949   Not so fine—made fire in kitchen, first one since last year. A wrong number broke my solitude so then I telephoned May and Beatty Bridle and F. Earle Hooper & in the evening Glen [Fox] telephoned me. Worked on Merlin. Also telephoned Renee Mudie & asked her to meet me at F.A.W. [Fellowship of Australian Writers] tomorrow night.

25 June 1949   Felt the cold again. Read 'Ten Creeks', was scarcely warm in the sun at back. Lit fire at noon. No gas till 5.30

---

197 'Merlin of the Empiah' was an earlier title for what eventually became *Prelude to Waking*, 1950.

so cooked evening meal in my new pot on the fire. Chopped down another limb of loquat and the buddleia & pruned red rose & cut result into small pieces for the fire. Solitary confinement as usual, not even a wrong number.

Gas on late in evening so had a good plunge bath.

17 July 1949   Grey day but mild. Worked on 'Ten C.' & dug a bit in garden, but have not the strength for it—everything began to swim so I lay down till time to get evening meal.

Usual solitary confinement.

7 August 1949   Fine day again. I was so washed out and distressed with wheeze & cough so I stayed in bed—or rather ran in and out all day in my pyjamas & coat. Felt too frail for work and it is so desolate to be alone on Sunday—all dead & gone but me. So I finished reading 'Cockatoos'. It is a tragic story but will not be accepted as such because it is not embedded in vices, perversions and crimes—sexual and civic.

September 1949   Was invited by the organizing committee to attend the Ells'[198] dinner, and the Lord Mayor's opening of the book festival week beginning in the City Hall [Newcastle] on Monday September 19, 1949 . . .

I saw in press clippings that Idriess and Timms were to be present, and, for once, thought I'd take courage to gate-crash into an A & R [Angus & Robertson] car. I find that carrying even a normal satchel is too much for me nowadays, and makes travel a misery when no porters are around, and beyond my means when they are.

---

198 Newcastle booksellers.

Beatrice [Davis] was very kind & charming about it, and George Ferguson resigned himself quite disguisedly.

Got up at 8, did chores, ran errands, had a scrap breakfast, lunch at 11.30 and set forth to be ready to start from 89 Castlereagh Street[199] at 1 p.m. The men got back from lunch at 1 p.m. Got away by 1.15, George driving, Timms in front seat, Idriess in back & poor little Iliffe crushed in the middle. The chief blot on the adventure was that I felt my presence cramped that worried little man.

It was lovely driving into the beautiful day in the lush spring greenery. The men halted at Gosford for drinks; I insisted on breasting the bar with them for experience. (Only other similar experience at Jindabyne, where I got a bottle of lemonade, but I was alone there & no alcohol was being served.) Idriess paid, though Timms invited, with flourish. Idriess began to show signs of life under gin, and plagued me to have some. No alcohol for me!

When we were within 50 or 60 miles of Newcastle a furious smoke & rank smell of burning rubber in the front drove us all from the car & a man came running to know did we need a bucket of water. It looked serious.

Iliffe hailed a big car in which was one man. He agreed to take two. They got rid of the female, and Iliffe, as the worker in the exhibition, went too. The man (V.O.T. Reeves) said he was in a hurry to get to Maitland by a short cut before dark. No telephone was within miles so that we could summon a taxi, so he said he would take us as far as the buses. Said he travelled all the time & likes a mate, but is careful whom he picks. He sounded as if I had been a thrust instead of a pick. But probing discovered the son of a Moree pioneer & I wooed him on that line, told him we were on the way to the opening of the book festival. Iliffe then

---

199 89 Castlereagh Street, Sydney, address of Angus & Robertson.

said yes, there were authors left in the car behind, he named Idriess, and Timms—very much second. Mr Reeves had heard of Idriess, & no other Australian writer, I take it, unless it might be Lawson. I had to make my own way without a name. I did so, happily enough, so that Mr Reeves forgot his hurry, took us right into town, found Iliffe's hotel and took us from there to the Great Northern. He generously said he would like my company all the way to Bourke, & we parted blood brothers of the Egbo.

I could get no booking so found my way to the women's lavatory: no towels, of course, however, I washed my hands without soap and dried them on my underclothes, put on my posh white buckskin gauntlets, carefully preserved since London, but never otherwise fixed a hair, and had to make my way to the dinner in the building. Ran into Dr Mackaness on landing. In the lack of amenities & desert of inner life and higher things, 'pon me sowl, I was glad to see him. He is always friendly—no sting—she biting & often malicious.

About thirty booksellers, publishers, members of committee, wifely attachments, with a few authors as exhibits, sat down. The Lord Mayor presided over the toasts. Looks like Bendix when quiescent from hairy-aping, one of those broad, squat, heavy figures suggestive of Tammany politics, but not ungenial. Said to be an ex-journalist: enquiry elicited that he sat in a newspaper office & checked the dog racing lists, when he was chosen for L.M. was called a journalist. But how does he work for a living? I insisted, in the way which so amused Paterson long ago: 'You mean <u>who</u> does he work for a living,' was the reply.

Ells, the bookshop people, gave a lavish meal. Lovely flowers. Started with oysters & the Lord Mayor performed a useful function by eating my share. Then tomato soup, then fowl—<u>much</u> fowl. I had enough for two, and the vegetables were on the same scale, there were no two-peas-to-a-plate as actually happened to Mother at a lunch . . . The sweet was ice cream on a tinned peach—each separate would have been better. Coffee & drinks. I had the pop again for the toasts.

The Lord Mayor drove to get through by eight, no meandering or frills in a book festival, which undoubtedly was out of his order. He drave too heavily, the speakers were deflated and short-circuited. The youth at the head of the writing society said that the whole show rested on authors—only for authors there would be no book festival. Idriess, so inconspicuous & quiet a figure as to pass without notice, here rose with a bushman yell, un-premeditated, and unmodulated, and threw up his arms as if going down in a weedy waterhole, so surprised was he by this rash contention on behalf of authors.

Needless to say it was repudiated, and authors put in proper perspective by the manufacturers of books. Dr Mackaness paid a tribute to A.G. Stephens and stressed the need of a first-rate literary critic among us. Dora [Birtles] was asked to speak, which she did in her graceful unstressed way. She was wearing a long evening gown, the only bird of paradise present. It was a return to her home town so I am glad she was asked to speak: it was a pity none of her books were on show. Timms replied for authors in a very few but well-chosen words. The Lord Mayor shut off Mr Smith—the one on whom the show depended—on dit—in the middle of his speech, after twice interrupting him without apology, said he could speak in the Lord Mayor's Parlour, to which we were bidden at ten minutes to ten.

Thence to the City Hall for the Book Festival. The firms concerned certainly had spared no trouble—no wonder Iliffe was tired & anxious for some return for labor & expense. As soon as I knew Metcalfe was to make the address of the evening I resigned myself to sheer mediocrity of a boring degree. It remained for others to be disappointed.

There was a dainty little platform in a corner to which the author exhibits were called by Mr Smith by mike: Mackaness, Idriess, Timms, Dora Birtles and I. Lord Mayor did opening in five or six sentences, all ungraceful, and disappeared to another function. Then the field was Met's. Many of us know and deplore Metcalfe, and the legend of how he happens to be a chief cockalorum librarian is significant of our biological & cultural backwardness and our political imitativeness. He had a music rack on which to place his address, which was printed, & from which he read steadily at a dead level for an hour, a steady droning hour without gesture, joke, zip, geniality, emphases or inflections, chiefly on Mexican bullfighting. He has been to Mexico to Unesco and purported to tell of his trip. I listened because I had just read 'The Brave Bulls' by Tom Lea, am interested in Prescott's 'Conquest of Mexico' and in Met's seeming fluency in those delightful Mexican words like Ixtlilxochitt, Iztapalapan, Xilotepic, Quetzalcoatl, Iztalapan & the lovely and familiar Yucatan—endearing, stirring assemblages of our alphabet.

But I soon sank into the coma which I learnt to escape in through having spent in my youth too much of my love time & play time in listening to male oratory. I noted the large audience, a few elders but mostly young. Then school boys & girls. They were patently waiting to 'hear the word', eager and expectant. Even I, tortured by stage fright & a feeling of inadequateness, could quickly have had that audience interested in Australian books, and the need for such; fine move of Newcastle's book week, etc. I noted the interest on the faces fade to puzzlement and die to disappointment & naked boredom. They drifted away behind the book ramparts and their talking at times almost swamped Met's drone, but he did not seem to notice, or to mend his pace. I returned from coma sufficiently to realize that his discourse had no connection with the function which he was expected to bless, but which he blighted. He said incidentally that there was country around Mexico City as barren and uninviting as that on the way to Newcastle, and that the Mexicans, despite the backwardness of bullfighting, were immeasurably ahead of us in grants for libraries and education. In two lines at the end he said that we needed Australian books. I thought the times were pushing even him along as it is commonly said that he was hostile to Australian attempts and even does not understand nor appreciate the Mitchell [Library]—is as obstructing as all these fellows who say that Australian literature has not yet started. Poor lout, he can't help having no personality, no artistic or philosophical content, in his peculiar make-up—sort of robot, who works by reflex action or something—must have enough ability to pass set examinations.

A flock of eager children besieged me for autographs and the boys took me to the exhibit of book jackets by those of their own ages. I glanced around surprised to see 'Swagger' among the exhibits, but of course Idriess & Timms had all the limelight, advertisement & a big display.

At the appointed moment we reached the Lord Mayor's den where he sat behind a table. A man brought in chairs. An ice box, disguised as a roomy closet, disgorged endless drinks. How Idriess swills! I had to take another glass of pop—one per day would be too many. The Lord Mayor conversed on about the same intellectual level as Met's, but the old rooster has a better personality and no doubt when free from reputable females & culture could become a boon companion among ward heelers, exploiters & such. He gave us each a book of Newcastle's Centenary. I said it was the first time I had met a Lord Mayor in his own skin and I'd like to have him write with his own pen in my copy. He complied with the alacrity of one commanded, but no familiarity encouraged—oh no! Wonder if he has a missus or is he a Mayor Busse of Chicago.

From this we went to a supper room where there was an immense amount of food including a few stuffed olives, and jellies, trifles & fruit salads. Again no end of drinks . . .

[Next day] When we were out of the main street & properly on our way the men all fell upon Metcalfe—bullcalf—and his Mexican bulls.

Metcalfe, narrow, limited, <u>mere</u> male of the cold constricted order—none of the warm, flamboyant, outstanding mad-bull male. The story goes that Ida Leeson was the top-notch candidate for librarian honors and should have been in line for chief librarian: but she was a woman. The powers hedged by making her mere Mitchell Skipper when that institution had not assumed its present importance. Even so the Fathers of Wisdom were afraid; what if the Chief Librarian fell ill and a female had to deputise—think of the unthinkability of that! So Ida was appointed at less salary for higher gifts, and male transcendence was further guarded by appointing a male deputy librarian. No doubt Metcalfe was the insect at hand and had passed standard examinations. In time he succeeded Ifould, a perfect illustration of Editha's [Phelps] quip.

One day she was leaving the John Crerar library with me without putting in full hours. She pointed to a big, frowsy old man with a beard, who looked like a Domain derelict. 'He's not nearly so competent as I am, but gets paid more for doing less, so I'll leave him some work to do,' she said.

I unsophisticatedly asked why he was paid more.

'Oh,' said she airily, 'he has the genital organs of the male; they're not used in library work but men are paid more for having them.'

As the men continued to rage about Metcalfe I said, it serves you right in view of why he holds his position. They demanded why, I gave them Editha's story for the impishness of seeing it explode on Timms. It ripped 'em all up. Little Iliffe shouted, Idriess yelled, George stuck to his wheel & I could see only the back of his head, but it gruelled Timms. Idriess yelped something about men getting two pounds a week more & that men needed it for the said possessions, & I said you mean they need compensation for such a handicap? Iliffe & Idriess at that simply rolled as well as roared. Timms was not amused. With challenging bullishness he rapped out, 'They're no weight to carry.' Evidently he will hereafter be reconciled to Met's lacks, seeing that his biological characteristics have saved us from a woman librarian.

The men went in for drinks again at Gosford. I refused on the ground of monotony.

George was crisp and clear in his driving. He holds himself in reserve. I don't know if he will ever allow me to know him. Idriess had a nap after the gin & waked up refreshed to ask me was I knocking out another book or was I resting on my laurels. I said I had no laurels to rest on. Idriess said, 'Oh, I wouldn't say that. "All That Swagger" is a good book in parts.' . . .

The men were deadly tired, especially Timms and Iliffe, so I insisted that George should drop us at Pymble & go home to his wife, as I overheard him say that he had to take her somewhere that evening. I arrived home a little after 8 and had some very dry bread & butter and a cup of my swash tea & was as fresh as the morning before. Not a scrap fatigued. It was a grand change from desolation and moping in solitary confinement. I wasn't even hungry, as the fowl the night before & the egg for breakfast stood to me all day. I no longer have the strength or urge to be a continual self-starter, but if I could be relieved of the charing and the garden I could plunge into a rich kind of life, such as a stay in Greta among the immigrants.

What interest I could have, what rich material as a basis for novels I could experience, if I could go about as the women who belong to men do. Like Mrs Mackaness or the other housewomen attached to the conveners and exploiters of conventions, the politicians and businessmen. Like the wives of the architects, builders, civic authorities & others who used to be carted all over the continent on housing jaunts in Aldridge's shows. They were a dull sodden lot of females, with few exceptions, but the property of men, and as such got chocs & souvenirs and preferential treatment, enjoyed luxurious transport and deference, met monarchs & presidents from Spain to Czecho-Slovakia—women who were not young, never had been beauties, weren't even linguists. Be a stupid woman owned by a male is the way to get the cream of life in a man's world.

I was able to note that booksellers, or representatives of publishers know little of the contents of the books they vend. They have not the taste, the ear or the capacity. Take the case under observation, A & R boosted Idriess, an old steady, & Timms, who is a thruster and insister & whom a person with Dr Mackaness's literary standards considers an important Australian writer. But they did not bother about my books. I was there because invited by the cultural committee of Newcastle. My book continues to sell steadily though I've never had a Christmastide sale, was denied editions during the war boom in favor of E. Hill, who has powerful boosters behind her. I've never had a window or even a counter display. These sellers think of books as any other manufacturable commodity such as shirts or pipes or ornaments, whereas each book is a separate entity. These [word indecipherable] sellers are very elementary. I remember when a fur merchant in 1913 in Chicago was palming off our possum furs as chinchilla, I objected, but what I said he considered was a better selling angle than the one he had been trying, so he offered me a picked set of the furs and a sum to sell till the consignment was exhausted. I, of course, refused, was too busy with that beastly reform. The Smiths were always after me as a seller, offered me 10% bonus whereas 2½% was the usual for the run of their salesmen. They said my personality was worth the extra. Others, including the typewriter people in Chicago, said I gave them half a dozen new selling points in a few moments' talk, and the Passenger Manager of the Wabash wanted me to take charge of their complaints bureau. I turned all down because I thought it would take me from writing: inexperienced ass, I stayed in the soul-destroying reform, which was a worse obstruction than business in relation to art, and which reduces art to mediocrity by trying to use it as direct propaganda, instead of respecting it as an ageless challenge and a measuring stick as well as a flowering of the inner life of man.

25 September 1949   Sunday. With Beatrice [Davis] and friends.
A nourishing, opulent day; to be cherished. For months Beatrice & her old friend [Dick Jeune] have intended a bush picnic to give me a whiff of the spring flowers—ever since August 1949, but it was postponed because of a painful and wearing accident to Beatrice's ankle.

The weather turned into a downpour, for days, and Sunday morning continued the deluge. However, Beatrice was not deterred, and the rain perhaps inconvenienced only poor Mr Jeune, who collected F. T. Macartney en route, and came for me about 11.45, and took us to Folly Point.[200] A glowing fire of gorgeous logs—like one of Uncle Theo's [John Theodore Lampe] fires—added beauty and comfort to the comfort and elegance of the drawing room, with its grand piano, wealth of end windows and the round westward window with a rose vine trained to wreathe it with roses, like a Victorian Christmas card. A spacious, gracefully proportioned room, so uncluttered, yet with an amplitude of

---

200 Folly Point, Cammeray, Sydney, where Beatrice Davis lived.

comfortable and gracious chairs. So refreshingly empty so that people could move about with grace, and look out the windows at the trees and Harbor inlet. This is a modernised room in its fireplace but also with many established graces, & some antique, such as the huge brass fender, a complete protection against the fire threatening safety, though gone are the work-marred fingers that used to keep such ornaments gleaming like gold. A rich meal of steak, grilled by Mr Jeune, who seemed to be a dabster with drinks, which I did not taste though I should have liked a teaspoon of the brandy in which muscat grapes had been steeped for a year, just out of curiosity, my curiosity not the grapes'. Vegetables and dessert were in keeping with the steak, including the, to the poor, unprocurable cream.

A sudden post-noon clearance in the downpour and off we went to French's Forest and found a creek swollen to Jounama proportions, and many spring flowers including a waratah or two, surviving like a flame amid the dark greenery. It took me back to childhood and poignant nostalgia for things and relatives long gone, and at the same time so fleeting, so ephemeral that now I sit alone in the silence they have left, with the Australian way of life they strove so laboriously and unrewardedly to establish, now ready for swamping by fecund hordes, who will leave as little remaining record of us as we left of the Aborigines.

A Devonshire tea with ample clotted cream at 'The Windmill' and back to the splendid fire and more rich hot food and talk with F. T. Macartney, refreshing and interesting, he is so concise, so sure, so clear but not very succulent as a steady diet. No uncharted heights or depths, no unexplored back paddocks for discoveries and adventures. One therefore gives him the floor, or merely gossips & exposes no 'soul' to be discredited. You must have <u>form</u>, be perfect in form or literary work cannot be accepted nor last. But literary form in English is as amorphous as the language and always bursting its bounds and re-forming. He and I were driven right home by Mr Jeune.

How delightful life can be, surrounded by comfort and plenty. All this beauty & plenty rests on Beatrice's slight shoulders and sensitive taste, supported by publishing and a foundation of medicine—another lucrative vocation. She is running three lives, with little help such as sheltered women used to have—career, home & social—and gets no time for her music, for which she must long as I once longed, but got no time in my day. Now I am near the end and have had nothing, which would not matter had I had a day worth having instead of an impoverished struggle. However, I shall be just as dead when dead as those who have been served imperially by Life.

27 September 1949   Tuesday. Cocktail party for Robert Morley and wife at Lyceum, tried to ask him a thing or two but rational chat was ruined by G.M. Spencer's affectation & servility at the feet of London culture, though she is a dear kind thing.

c. October 1949   That took me back many years to Chicago and that Professor Hoxie [on being complimented on a speech she made at the launching of the Australian Book Club]. He was one of the first to have a course in public speaking regularised as part of the University's classes. Mrs Robins always had sound ideas about the need for training and to have the best teachers and got him to hold a series of classes for the women's trade union group. One more enterprise to fatigue me and overlay my attempts towards music and writing! I did not join the class because the thought of being a public speaker was abhorrent to me, and in addition to feeling that public speakers were old, boring and dowdy my stage fright amounted to delirium. Its extent can be proven by the fact that to be in my position was to be a platform speaker automatically, where reformers, propagandists, could not be kept off the platform and I must have been pretty useful otherwise to have escaped giving any speeches but two or three short words of greeting. The pressure on me to speak was heavy but I said I would resign & earn my living otherwise in preference, and they always said they would rather have me dumb than not at all. I always wrote their articles for them & many of their speeches. I remember writing Mary Anderson's speech for her the first time she went to Washington, & she practised it on me.

The Prof's class was rushed. Not alone by beginners but by all our established stars—by Mrs Robins herself, who was a justly famous spell-binder from coast to coast because of her verve, her information, her earnestness, her beauty, courage & many other qualities; by Agnes Nestor, who could move Congresses & business men & trade union committees and was a prodigy because of her winning mild reasonableness and her appearance, and despite her lack of grammar; by Alice Henry, so lucid and academic with unimpeachable information; by Emma Steghagen, an old trade union warrior veteran of strikes, by Mary Anderson, Mary McInerney, Agnes Johnson, E.M. Galvin, Olive Sullivan, even Florence Sherwood—all the gang. The Mellin sisters.

I thought I could attend occasionally and look on because of being Secretary-Treasurer of the National Shebang. Prof would not allow that. He allowed no unparticipating visitors. We were each called upon to make a two-minutes' contribution on the speech of some speechifying pupil. Amy Walker (Field) made her speech on the decline of the old style of oratory. People today repudiated it and demanded short pithy speeches that did not waste time. I was commanded to comment. I had lately been submitted to big conferences where male oratory had flapped its wings and crowed regardless of cost & time or the chairman's gavel. I said the more sentimental, irrelevant and out-of-date the speeches were the more they were admired, that had they brought in the pies that mother used to make & the virtue of women & that sort of thing, they would never have been stopped.

Despite my sickening fright this brought loud applause & gales of laughter.

The Prof ruled that on my next attendance I must essay a speech of five minutes, on any subject I chose. The speakers always chose some point of their doctrine that they wished to put over. Mrs Robins, Agnes & Miss Henry were all pulled to pieces by the professor. I was astonished but not so deeply astonished as the speakers themselves. It was felt to be a kind of lese-majesty by the faithful, that we never discussed, yet the Prof. was a very mild and encouraging man. Had he been an acidulous martinet it would have been different.

My time came. I was too sated and too nervous to attempt any exposition of the trade union demands, which were hundreds of years behind the times and more than a generation behind Australian freedoms, such as an Arbitration Court, eight-hour day, woman's political enfranchisement. My real interests were deep in my heart, so I threw away from beaten tracks and did five minutes recommending colored wigs for men. At that date there were some displayed in shop windows, and fashion notes had contained remarks about their decorative & other advantages.

The laughter & applause was so spontaneous and excessive that it bewildered me. Prof waited till it stopped and said, 'Yes, that's all very well. She can make you laugh, but can she be serious; can she move you . . . ?'

I remember a chorus of assurance broke out, led by Mary Anderson, who was always more weighty than glib: 'She can make us laugh & cry any time she wants.' Others upheld this, including Mrs Robins, who said she always thought I could be a truly great speaker. Then the Prof said, 'Miss Franklin is very gifted. I cannot do anything but advise and encourage her. She has everything—voice, appearance, wit, intelligence, youth and above all God's great gift, the power to entertain. She can do as she likes with her audience. All she needs is practice—to overcome diffidence—and experience in presenting her material. We can tell her nothing she doesn't know in herself. She will find her own way with audiences.'

Had he been a gusher this would not have been so unbelievable, but though kindly & tolerant & without any sting he nevertheless had pulled all the stars to pieces . . .

Upon returning to Australia I was called upon by many groups to make addresses. I was supposed to be a veteran speaker who had given hundreds of talks all over America. It was, of course, abnormal that I could have been in the USA as Secretary-Treasurer of such an organization as the N.W.T.U. League for over four years, and editor of its magazine, without having spoken from a platform more than four times and never for more than five minutes. I was compelled in Sydney by pleas to make occasional addresses, always short but always successful, always with the preliminary suffering. I grew worse instead of better and became so lost on the platform that I had to resort to reading what I had to say. I tried to extirpate my sick fright by thinking of the poor boys driven over the top in war to face bayonets and bombs or gas. I used to recite to myself Mary's 'Risings Up' about Tom Duggan having to face the gallows, but nothing allayed that internal physical torment.

Now, by the passing of time, I have lost my rich voice in coughing & my extraordinary clarity of enunciation in the loss of my natural teeth, my appearance has been ruined by age plus the operation on my jaws, which makes me abnormally wrinkled, yet strange to say, the fright has almost gone too. I am no longer self-conscious to a paralysing extent, though I remain nervous so that I cannot remember on my feet. I remain unpractised as a speaker, and the effort deters me. I can't be bothered. Once I overflowed with ideas, now I am bored by having to fashion what I want to say, and have to be plagued hard to speak. Another of my talents left in its napkin to atrophy. Peu importe!

The last years of Miles Franklin's life, and those immediately following her death, saw a number of publications. The fourth Brent of Bin Bin novel, Prelude to Waking, *actually the first novel in the series and written in 1925, appeared in 1950 and the fifth,* Cockatoos, *just a few weeks before her death in 1954. Angus & Robertson reprinted* Up the Country *in 1951 and* Ten Creeks Run *in 1952. In July 1950, Miles delivered the Commonwealth Literary Fund lectures, on the novel in Australia, at the University of Western Australia. They were published after her death as* Laughter, Not for a Cage *(1956). The last Brent of Bin Bin novel,* Gentlemen at Gyang Gyang, *appeared posthumously in 1956. In 1963 Angus & Robertson, which two generations before had rejected* My Brilliant Career, *published* Childhood at Brindabella, *Miles' reminiscences of her first ten years.*

31 January 1950 Feeling terribly discouraged & as if I had better give it all up & die! I've struggled so long for nothing— long enough to prove over & over again that I have no talent for writing. Could have made a success & helped my family had I set to something else. There's not a soul alive to whom I'm of any consequence, none to care a pin how soon I die. Failure & desolation indeed. Took Mrs Morgan figs and in evening went to local cinema with her to see 'A Song is Born'—an awful racket of boogie-woogie jive, jazz etc. interlarded with gangsters. And other trash in 2 shorter films . . .

5 April 1950 Sunny day for a wonder with only one little shower at 5. Met Persia at 1 & went to John [Jack Franklin]. Saw Dr Kirkwood, Assistant Superintendent [of Rozelle Hospital], old & deaf, could not hear what I said. He says John's outlook not good—schizophrenic—depressed. Will give him shock treatment . . . More & more anguish—If I had only one friend to comfort me. That poor boy—he feels abandoned. God help him. God help me. I wish I could control my anguish. It doesn't help John—it is only hell to me—for why?

3 September 1950 Fine chilly day. Struggled with article on theatre again. Did a tiny bit more in garden. Totally alone all day, not even a wrong number call on telephone.

24 September 1950 Fine day. Alone all day, no telephone call, no one spoke to me. Tried a bit of clearing in garden but I'm not strong enough. Read the end of 'Earth Abides', very dull.

13 May 1951 Grey mildish day. Tried the essay. It has gone from me again. Feel really ill—and I think the abject loneliness is a factor—nothing bright or pleasant anywhere, nothing except complete solitude—It takes more fortitude than I am strong enough to muster at present. Ruby Brydon telephoned about John's air boots.

Temperature up again—very little but persistent every evening.

10 June 1951 Fine day—morning sun. Came on to rain again at 10 p.m. No telephone call, the usual solitary confinement all day. Temperature still erratic—sometimes a little below or a little above 98.4°.

13 June 1951 Early morning temperature still 2 points below normal. Grey, drizzling mild day again. I telephoned May—Leslie still in bed, poor girl. I began to go over 'Ten Creeks' finally for the printer. Solitary confinement—it takes willpower to suffer it without depression.

1 July 1951 Showery day again. Big fire all day. Returned to essay but the discomfort of cold and chilblains kept me from accomplishing any but a page or two. Solitary confinement all day, not even a telephone call in or out.

22 July 1951 Cold day—soon greyed over. I stuck close to essay—didn't even read paper. At 4 p.m. washed my head, then washed floor & lavatory. Must have been too much. I suddenly had to feel sick so lay on bed till 7. Took no tea. Listened to radio & went to bed. Lit fire at 9.30 a.m. Solitary confinement all day. One telephone call—did not answer it.

12 September 1951 Fine day again, didn't even take Mrs Morgan's chicks the greens. Went to butcher, so fatigued I find my stuff is full of repetition & disjointed—a rough draft really and I ache so I can't straighten my shoulders. Wanted to get to bed by 9 but Mrs Fogden came in & wasted 40 minutes, then Jean telephoned & now it is 9.30. Too tired to go for bread so took some of that Mrs A threw over for the chooks.

8 October 1951 Cold cloudy day. Very tired. Pottered. Cut down another limb off the loquat tree, etc. etc. Totally alone all day, not even a wrong number on the telephone. Read some more of 'Kon-Tiki'. Such a decent book. Perishing—had the heater again in the evening.

5 May 1952   Fine early but soon clouded over, though it remained mild: did not turn on heater since Thursday. No human contact all day not even a telephone call.

16 August 1952   Fine day again—some clouds—not cold enough for a fire. Did a bit of pruning and chopping: result distressing fatigue. No human contact all day. Called Nell Jordan on the phone. Wrote another 2,000 words of rough-draft reminiscence. Geo. Clune telephoned to say he has been a fortnight in bed with a coronary attack. Was allowed up today for ten minutes.

1 November 1952   Fine but cool day. Alone all day—felt the weight of loneliness sickeningly. Returned to making note for Pixie's [O'Harris] demand.

2 November 1952   Perfect cloudless day. Went in to see Mrs A. & found her weepy. Had a nice lot of work laid out & wanted to listen to an Australian play & Phyllis & Jack came at 3.30 & stayed till 6. Another futile day. I will not answer the door. How am I to get a moment. Vance [Palmer] gave a lovely review of 'Ten Creeks Run'.

20 January 1953   Saw a Fairy penguin on Pitt St. with a man. It must have been a stray. It infatuated me.

31 March 1953   . . . a lovely day, we [with Jean Devanny] set out gaily [for the Royal Easter Show] in a spirit of enjoyment. Our abounding gaiety was so evident, & Jean, like old platform horses, cannot resist playing to the gallery, so our fellow travellers on the train said they wished they were going with us.

I swallowed one of Dr Anderson's pep pills, the effect of which is so releasing on my limbs that I use them only rarely, suspecting they could so string up my nerves as to entirely banish sleep. Jean settled to my guidance like a free horse that has accepted the rein after a long spell. I always enter at the same gate where there are trees and an open space and one of the big halls of industry on the right which are merely a repetition of the ballyhoo and wastefulness of business methods in advertising.

'Come on, Jean, I'll drag you through or someone will say, "What a pity you missed that: the best part of the Show!"'

'There's Angus & Robertson's display.'

It was mostly dictionaries and standard works: a vast bookstore could not be reproduced in its entirety, but on a shelf above the heads of the crowd, two novelists had a spotlight position— Idriess & Timms. A row of each stood out like film stars, no others encroaching upon their eminence. Jean to the attack! The man in evidence was a stout bull-like figure, handsome in Eric Baume's way, aggressive as a jumping ant.

'It's disgraceful, a great firm like A & R's displaying the work of no novelists but trash like that!'

'What nonsense you talk, Madam! It's the opinion of all the editors & critics for twenty years that those are the two greatest Australian writers.'

'You ought to be ashamed to talk such rubbish!' said Jean.

Not recognising my position as Jean's man Friday, the man attempted to enlist me: 'Did you ever hear the like of that!'

He was so belligerent that I merely squawked, 'Unbelievable, deplorable!' and escaped, leaving the man to apply the adjectives as he listed. He was as strident in drive as Heinemann's Capt. Gyde or Jyde when promulgating H.H.R. [Henry Handel Richardson]. I saw him in action at the Book Exhibition at Australia House in London in 1932. It must build reputation to be so supported & displayed . . .

'I mustn't miss the cattle,' Jean began to insist.

'Don't you fear! The very smell of them is assuagement to my nostalgia for the sights, sounds and aroma of the life I was born to.'

Through the leather products and needlework, the cakes and flowers. Between each dive we glanced at the ring, but on this early day the activities there were mere notes such as a painter makes to compile the full mural. We sat on the little hillock near the dairy pavilion on a newspaper with clear space to view the lady riders for the sake of the side saddle, which was the star of the competitors. But Sarah, when led by the Master of the Ring, could not canter slowly enough for the ring-master's old flea-bitten nag, so she had to keep up a slow trot, an awkward pace little better than the running jog of an unpaced bush horse, and Mrs Pope did it in the English posting style, bump, bump, bump, which my skeleton was always too delicate to endure. On the other hand I rejoiced in a swift trot on either the high stepper or the pacer, or single-footer. I could put my toe in the stirrup, grasp a lock of the mane and let the horse run under me for miles without ever touching the seat of the saddle. At such a pace the galloper cannot keep up on a road of hills.

The poultry gave out an exciting orchestral performance— grand opera—the geese screeching dramatic soprano, the cocks brilliant & indomitable trumpeters, the gobblers providing tuba, the bantams coloratura, the quack-quack of the ducks like the boards that are clapped among the percussion instruments— how entrancing it all is!

'Can't you let me in with the geese where I belong,' I pled at the bars.

'Sorry, Madam, but the judging is not finished.' . . .

At three o'clock Jean had had enough. Without any realisation of inconsistency she said she hoped I wasn't one of those who had to stay till closing time. Dr A's drug had kept me much spryer than she was.

'What about the side-shows?'

'I hate them!'

'I abominate them! But we have not called on the horses in their stalls.'

'Oh, Miles, you don't want to do that, do you?'

'No, not so long as you won't say later that I dragged you away before you had seen half the Show.' So home after a happy and absorbing day to a rich meal of chops and fresh fruit, etc. etc.

24 April 1953   Lovely day. Went to Carlton to shop, also to butcher. Prepared for Beatrice [Davis]. She came at 6.30 with 'Cockatoos' which we discussed very little & other things till 12.30. I kept awake till 5.30 & waked just before it struck 7 a.m. Got up shortly after & moved about. Heard B. sleeping. Crept about & did the chores.

25 April 1953   Lovely, perfect day. Arose at 7.30 after 2 hrs sleep and sneaked about at chores. Beatrice tired, lugging heavy parcels & I kept her up talking. Fortunately she slept till nearly nine. Then I gave her breakfast in bed. She had a shower & went home—carrying heavy parcels again. She is a spirited, intelligent soul—few like her to be found. I tidied up a bit & finished a letter to Magdalen Dalloz but was so fatigued that my stomach turned & I had to have a sleep during afternoon. B. likes 'Cockatoos' and

thinks it needs little to be done to it. I am dubious & nervous about it, but everyone is dead so it doesn't matter.[201]

10 May 1953   Fine day but cloudy & therefore cold . . . I telephoned the Fogdens twice & called on Mrs Morgan. In afternoon started to pot my plants again but Dal [Stivens] called & sat an hour talking on the verandah. Another entirely wasted day & I have so few left. My will has become derelict. Lit the radiator for a few minutes before going to bed.

7 June 1953   Cold day. Sun in morning. Shower at 4 p.m. Did a few finishing touches on essay. Then finished cleaning cupboard & found borers in a box on board & the bath slat. So cleaned bathroom and put on some of Williams' borer exterminator. No human contact all day.

17 June 1953   Cold grey day—coldest this winter. I prepared midday dinner for Tom Mutch who came to look at my MSS & to drink from the Waratah Cup. He would not come into the sitting room so we stayed in the kitchen & I lighted the fire there. Not successful because it smoked. He told me how Roderick, Ellis and Mackaness used his research discoveries without a word of

---

201 The manuscript which became *Cockatoos* was a heavily revised version of a much earlier manuscript titled 'On the Outside Track'. It had been completed in 1902 but Franklin was not able to have it published. Several thinly disguised Sydney identities make their appearance, hence Franklin's remark that they are now dead so cannot take offence.

acknowledgement. Poor man should have teeth. He stayed till after 5 p.m. I gave him corned beef, mashed potatoes, carrots, parsnip, swede and choko, coffee, quince pie with cream, plum pudding & sweet sauce.

15 September 1953   Warmed up a bit but in afternoon thunder showers froze us off again. Planted seeds of double sunflower and of thyme. The wisteria my mother planted for me has blown its ecstasy again. A piece from the old Talbingo vine that bloomed when I was born. No bees so there will be no plums though the trees were white with bloom. A storm must come to rend the wisteria: it always does.

If Miles Franklin kept a diary for 1954, it has not survived. She made her last known diary entry, for 1 January 1954, at the back of her pocket diary for 1953.

1 January 1954   Awaked to a grey day. Must have had quite 7 hrs sleep!!! so I felt very well. Left at 10.45 for Killara & walked from station to 36 Springdale Rd, gardens very pleasant. Lena [Lampe] had already arrived, Stanley & family also there but S. rushed off to work & we were left to a great feast. Beautifully roasted turkey & vegs. & 4 sweets. Nuts & chocolates. S. rushed back again & collected his family: Nan, Peter, Margaret & Susan about 4. Ruth, Lena & I with Mrs Waring had more feasting. Then Ruth drove Lena home to Hunter's Hill. I went with them & returned with R. as far as Chatswood to take the train & got home by 8.15. Such a nice warm soft day, grey almost all the time but no rain.

GLOSSARY
OF NAMES

Abrahams, Ivy, employed by Miles Franklin as a companion for her mother.

Adamson, Bartlett, 1884–1951, writer and journalist. Three times president of the Fellowship of Australian Writers; member of the Communist Party of Australia.

Addams, Jane, 1860–1935, American social reformer. Founded in 1889 Hull House, Chicago, a pioneer neighbourhood centre providing advice and practical help to the disadvantaged.

Afford, Max, 1906–1954, playwright. *Lady in Danger*, his best known play, was first performed in Sydney in 1942 and on Broadway in 1944.

Aldridge, Henry Richard, 1868–1953, secretary, National Housing and Town Planning Council, London.

Amadio, John, 1884–1964, flautist, born in New Zealand, moved to Australia about 1900. Married Florence Austral with whom he made a number of concert tours.

Archibald, Jules François, 1856–1919, founding editor of the *Bulletin*, 1880. His estate financed the annual Archibald Prize for portraiture.

Archipenko, Alexander, 1887–1964, artist, resident in the US from 1923.

Austral, Florence, 1894–1968, Australian opera singer. She married the flautist, John Amadio, with whom she made a number of concert tours.

Baker, Kate, 1861–1953, teacher, friendly with Joseph Furphy and promoted his work. She published Furphy's poems at her expense in 1916, and arranged for the reissue of *Such Is Life* in 1917. With Franklin, she won the 1939 S.H. Prior Memorial Prize for a biography of Furphy. This was revised and published in 1944. OBE, 1937.

Baker, Richard Thomas, 1854–1941, botanist and museum curator, known in his time for controversial views on the oil of eucalypts and for his publications on Australian timbers. In his 1915 publication, *The Australian Flora in Applied Arts*, he advocated the waratah as Australia's national flower.

Barcs, Emery, died 1990, Hungarian born journalist who migrated to Australia in 1939. He published *Backyard of Mars: Memoirs of the 'Reffo' Period in Australia*, 1980.

Barnard, Marjorie Faith, 1897–1987, published five novels and three historical works with Flora Eldershaw under the pseudonym M. Barnard Eldershaw, and a number of short stories and historical works independently. Her critical study of Miles Franklin was published in 1967. AO, 1980; the Patrick White Award, 1983.

Batchelor, Denzil Stanley, born 1906 in Bombay, educated at Oxford, journalist, lecturer in English. Published a volume of poetry, 1927.

Baume, Frederick Ehrenfried (Eric), 1900–1967, journalist, editor, broadcaster and writer. His most significant book was *Five Graves at Nijmegen*, 1945. OBE, 1966.

Baylebridge, William, 1883–1942, poet and writer, adopted name of Charles William Blocksidge. A volume of prose, *An Anzac Muster*, was published in 1921 and a volume of sonnets, *Love Redeemed*, in 1934.

Besant, Sir Walter, 1836–1901, one of the founders of the Society of Authors in the UK in 1884.

Birch, Florence, 1873–1957, companion to Ida Leeson from c. 1920s. Took part in plays produced by Marion Mahony Griffin at the Haven Scenic Amphitheatre, Castlecrag, in the 1930s. Senior Vice-President, Kirribilli Branch of the Red Cross for many years.

Birkett, Winifred Gertrude, 1897–1966, writer. *Edelweiss and Other Poems*, 1932; *Three Goats on a Bender*, 1934; *Earth's Quality*, 1935; *Portrait of Lucy*, 1938.

Birtles, Dora, née Toll, 1904–1994, writer, best known for her children's books. Wrote the book of the film *The Overlanders* in 1946.

Blyth, Charles A., tutor at Brindabella.

Bookluck, Alex, died 1967, treasurer of the Fellowship of Australian Writers from 1938.

Booth, Mary, 1869–1956, physician and welfare worker. Founded the Anzac Fellowship of Women in 1921 to promote the Anzac tradition and remained its president until her death. In 1931, the Fellowship established the Anzac Festival Committee, with Dr Booth as chairman, to encourage the arts. In 1936 she founded the Memorial College of Household Arts and Science next door to her home in Kirribilli, Sydney.

Bracegirdle, Leighton Seymour, born 1881, Military and Official Secretary to the Governor-General, 1931–47.

Bread and Cheese Club, founded in Melbourne in 1938 to foster a love of Australian literature, art and music. J.K. Moir was co-founder and first president. It was an all male club.

Brennan, Christopher John, 1870–1932, scholar and poet. His poetry was widely considered to be obscure. Described by journalist Reg Moses as 'an Encyclopaedia Titanica without an index or binding'.

Bridle, Edwin, 1874–1953, Miles Franklin's cousin and one time suitor. Son of Thomas Bridle, 1840–1913, and Mary Ann, née Nutthall, 1845–1914.

Bridle, Ethel Ruby, 1875–1956, cousin of Miles Franklin.

Brookes, Ivy, née Deakin, 1883–1970, eldest daughter of Alfred Deakin, Australia's second prime minister.

Bryant, Beryl, 1893–1973, actor, director, manager. Co-founded, with her father, Bryant's Playhouse, Sydney, 1932. In 1942, the Playhouse moved to larger premises in Phillip Street, previously housing the Little Theatre.

Brydon, Ruby, cousin of Miles Franklin.

Burgmann, Ernest Henry, 1885–1967, Anglican Bishop of Goulburn from 1934; Canberra-Goulburn, 1950–60.

Butt, Dame Clara, 1872–1936, British singer, hugely popular on the concert platform. DBE, 1920.

Cassidy, Lucy, née Sullivan, publicity officer and treasurer, Fellowship of Australian Writers. Married the poet and journalist Robert John Cassidy in 1926.

Cayley, Neville William, 1887–1950, author of the classic *What Bird is That?*, first published in 1931.

Champion, Henry Hyde, 1859–1928, journalist. Founded the *Book Lover* in 1899 and formed the Australasian Authors' Agency in 1906.

Chauvel, Charles Edward, 1897–1959, film director, responsible for *In the Wake of the Bounty*, 1933; *Forty Thousand Horsemen*, 1940; *The Rats of Tobruk*, 1944; *Sons of Matthew*, 1949 and *Jedda*, 1955. In 1935 his film *Heritage* won the Commonwealth Government's film competition.

Clewlow, Frank Dawson, Director of Drama, Australian Broadcasting Commission, from 1936.

Clune, Frank, 1893–1971, accountant who published over 60 popular books, many of which were ghost-written by P.R. Stephensen, based on Clune's research. He married Thelma Smith in 1923. OBE, 1967.

Clune, George, wrote *Why Gather Moss?: Travel and Adventure in Five Continents*, 1940 and a novel, *Easy Come—Easy Go*, 1944, with J.F. Power.

Clune, Thelma, née Smith, 1902–1992, wife of Frank Clune.

Clyne, Dan, 1879–1965, New South Wales politician, 1929–56; Speaker of Legislative Assembly, 1941–47. John Maurice Franklin was in partnership with Clyne in a real estate agency c. 1903.

Collins, Tom, pseudonym of Joseph Furphy.

Cottrell, Dorothy, 1902–1957, expatriate Australian novelist and children's writer living in the US.

Cousins, Walter, died 1949, publisher, Angus & Robertson, 1933–49.

Cowling, George Herbert, 1881–1946, Professor of English, University of Melbourne, 1928–43. When asked why he did not include Australian literature in his courses, he is alleged to have replied 'Australian literature? Is there any?'

Crocker, Arthur, active in the Fellowship of Australian Writers, published *South Sea Sinners*, 1914; *The Great Turon Mystery*, 1923 and *Australia Hops In*, 1935.

Crockett, Vivian, born 1893, published the novels *Messalina*, 1925, and *Mezzomorto*, 1934.

Cronin, Bernard Charles, 1884–1968, journalist and writer, best known for *Bracken*, 1931 and *The Sow's Ear*, 1933. His play *Stampede* is included together with Miles Franklin's *No Family* in *Best Australian One-Act Plays*, 1937, edited by T.I. Moore and William Moore.

Currey, Margery, previously married to Floyd Dell, member of literary circles, Chicago.

Curtin, John, 1885–1945, Prime Minister of Australia, 1941–45.

Cusack, Dymphna, 1902–1981, writer. Best known for the novels *Jungfrau*, 1936; *Come in Spinner* (with Florence James), 1951; *Say No to Death*, 1951; and *Picnic Races*, 1962, and for the play *Red Sky at Morning*, 1942. She collaborated with Miles Franklin on *Pioneers on Parade*, 1939.

Dalley, John Bede, 1876–1935, journalist, editor and novelist. His novel *Max Flambard* was published in 1928.

Dalloz, Magdalen, born 1887, at one time stenographer, Women's Trade Union League, Chicago. Later lived in Florida.

Dalziel, Allan, 1908–1969, political secretary to H.V. Evatt.

D'Arcy, Dame Constance, 1879–1950, obstetrician and gynaecologist. President, Medical Women's Society of New South Wales, 1933–34; Deputy Chancellor, University of Sydney, 1943–46. DBE, 1935.

Dark, Eleanor, 1901–1985, writer. Best known for her historical trilogy *The Timeless Land*, 1941, *Storm of Time*, 1948, and *No Barrier*, 1953. Her first published novel was *Slow Dawning*, 1932, followed by *Prelude to Christopher*, 1934, and *Return to Coolami*, 1936. AO, 1977.

David, Caroline Martha (Cara), née Mallett, 1856–1951. Married, 1885, Tannatt William Edgeworth David, Professor of Geology, University of Sydney, 1891–1924. She published *Funafuti: Or, Three Months on a Coral Island*, 1899.

Davis, Beatrice, 1909–1992, legendary publisher's editor at Angus & Robertson, 1937–73. She was named in Miles Franklin's will as one of the judges of the Miles Franklin Award and was the only judge to continue in this capacity until death. Married Frederick Bridges (died 1945), medical practitioner, in 1937. MBE, 1965; AM, 1981.

Davison, Frank Dalby, 1893–1970, writer. Best known for *Man-shy*, 1931, and *Dusty*, 1946. The former won the Gold Medal of the Australian Literature Society; the latter won the *Argus* novel competition. President, Fellowship of Australian Writers, 1936 and 1937. MBE, 1938.

Deamer, Dulcie, 1890–1972, actor, journalist and writer, and a member of Sydney Bohemia in the 1920s and 1930s. A founder in 1928 of the Fellowship of Australian Writers. Her play *Easter* is represented together with Miles Franklin's play *No Family* in *Best Australian One-Act Plays*, 1937, edited by T.I. Moore and William Moore. She was famous for her appearances in leopard skin in the 1920s and for dancing the hula-hula. She was crowned 'Queen of Bohemia' in 1925.

Dell, Margery Currey, *see* Currey, Margery.

Devanny, Jean, née Crook, 1894–1962, feminist and writer, born in New Zealand, migrated to Australia in 1929, member of the Communist Party of Australia from 1929 until 1950 though expelled between 1940 and 1944.

Dixson, Sir William, 1870–1952, book collector. Bequeathed his collection to the Public (now State) Library of New South Wales.

Dobbie, Alice M., President of The Tuesday Club, 1935–37, which met fortnightly for 'discussion of literary and topical subjects' at The Women's Club, Elizabeth Street, Sydney.

Dobell, Sir William, 1899–1970, artist. His portrait of Joshua Smith won the Archibald Prize in 1943. He also won the Archibald Prize in 1948 and 1949. Knighted in 1966.

Drake-Brockman, Henrietta, 1901–1968, novelist and playwright. Her play *Men Without Wives* won the New South Wales Sesquicentenary Competition, 1938.

Draper, Ruth, 1884–1956, British actor famous for her one-woman shows.

Dreiser, Theodore, 1871–1945, realist writer, Chicago.

Drummond, David Henry, 1890–1965, politician. New South Wales Minister for Education, 1927–30, 1932–41.

Drummond, Jean, died 1935. Opera singer, younger sister of Lute Drummond.

Drummond, Ruth Janet (Lute), 1879–1949, operatic coach. Joan Hammond was one of her pupils.

Duncan, Catherine, born 1915, Australian actor and playwright. Lived in Paris from the early 1950s and worked in film and television. Her play *Sons of the Morning* won the 1945 Playwrights' Advisory Board Competition.

Dupain, Max, 1911–1992, photographer.

Eldershaw, Flora Sydney Patricia, 1897–1956, teacher, public servant and writer. Collaborated on five novels and three historical works with

Marjorie Barnard under the pseudonym M. Barnard Eldershaw. President of the Fellowship of Australian Writers, 1935 and 1943. In 1938 she edited *The Peaceful Army: A Memorial to the Pioneer Women of Australia, 1788–1938* which included a chapter by Miles Franklin on Rose Scott.

Eldershaw, M. Barnard, pen-name used by Marjorie Barnard and Flora Eldershaw.

Ellis, Malcolm Henry, 1890–1969, *Bulletin* journalist and author. His biography of Lachlan Macquarie was published in 1947. He also published biographies of Francis Greenway, 1949, and John Macarthur, 1955.

Esson, Louis, 1879–1943, journalist and playwright. Wrote a play on Eureka, *The Southern Cross*, first published in 1946.

Evatt, Clive Raleigh, 1900–1984, politician. Member of the New South Wales Legislative Assembly for Hurstville from 1939. Miles Franklin's local member in the New South Wales Parliament. Brother of H.V. Evatt.

Evatt, Herbert Vere, 1894–1965, politician and judge. Justice of High Court, 1930- 40; Member of the House of Representatives for Barton, 1940–58; Leader of the Federal Opposition, 1951–60. President, Trustees, Public (now State) Library of New South Wales, 1937–63. Married Mary Alice Sheffer in 1920. Miles Franklin's local member in the Commonwealth Parliament. Brother of Clive Evatt.

Fairfax, Ruth, née Dowling. Married, in 1899, John Hubert Fraser Fairfax, born 1872, sheep breeder and director, John Fairfax & Sons Pty Ltd.

Farrar, Ernest Henry, 1879–1952, trade unionist and politician. President, Legislative Council of New South Wales from 1946.

Farwell, George, 1911–1976, writer. Editor of *Australian Book News*, 1946–48.

Fellowship of Australian Writers, founded in Sydney in November 1928 to promote the interests of writers. It organised the now abandoned annual pilgrimage to the Henry Lawson statue in the Domain, Sydney. Branches were established in other states. Inaugurated Australian Authors' Week in 1935.

Ferguson, George Adie, 1910–1998, Managing Director, Angus & Robertson, publishers, 1930–69. CBE.

FitzHenry, William Ernest (Bill), 1903–1957. Joined the staff of the *Bulletin* in 1917 and remained there in various capacities until his death.

Secretary of *Bulletin* novel competitions, 1928 and 1929; S.H. Prior Memorial Prize; and Fellowship of Australian Writers.

Fogden, Mary, presumably the wife of James Fogden who lived at 22 Grey Street, Carlton; a neighbour of Miles Franklin.

Fogden, May, presumably the daughter of James Fogden who lived at 22 Grey Street, Carlton; a neighbour of Miles Franklin. She married Bert Swales in 1940.

Fox, Glennie Millicent (prev. Mills), 1906–1976, journalist. Active in the Fellowship of Australian Writers, married Len Fox in 1943.

Franklin, Annie, née McKinnon, Miles Franklin's aunt. Married Thomas Franklin, 1873.

Franklin, George, born 1842, Miles Franklin's uncle. Married Margaret Connell in June 1884 and took up residence at Oakvale.

Franklin, Hume Talmage, 1889–1925, brother of Miles Franklin. He married Elizabeth Eva Wilks, died 1932, in 1915.

Franklin, Ida Lampe (known as Linda), 1881–1907, sister of Miles Franklin. Married, 23 November 1904, Charles Graham. Their son was Edward John Mervyn, born 1906.

Franklin, Irene Caroline, née Crossing, died 30 December 1925, wife of Norman John Franklin, married 22 November 1919.

Franklin, John Maurice, 1848–1931, father of Miles Franklin.

Franklin, Laurel Susannah, 1892–1903, sister of Miles Franklin.

Franklin, Linda *see* Franklin, Ida Lampe

Franklin, Margaret Susannah Helena, née Lampe, 1850–1938, mother of Miles Franklin.

Franklin, Norman John (Jack), 1921–1956, nephew of Miles Franklin. He was killed in a car accident at the age of 35.

Franklin, Norman Rankin, 1886–1942, brother of Miles Franklin. He married Irene Caroline Crossing, died 1925, in November 1919. Their only child was Norman John, 1921–1956.

Fullerton, Emily, 1875–1958, sister of Mary Fullerton.

Fullerton, Mary Eliza, 1868–1946, poet. Left Australia in 1922 and lived in England. Franklin became a close friend in London in the 1920s and edited and arranged publication of her poetry under the pseudonym 'E'.

Furphy, Joseph, 1843–1912, wrote under the pseudonym Tom Collins. Miles Franklin had met Furphy in Melbourne in 1904 after the publication of his best known work, *Such Is life*. She became an admirer and supporter of his work and a correspondent. Franklin wrote his biography, *Joseph Furphy: The Legend of a Man and His Book*, 1944.

Garnsey, Arthur Henry, 1872–1944, Anglican clergyman. Warden of St Paul's College, University of Sydney, 1916–44; Canon of St Andrew's Cathedral, Sydney, 1916–1944.

Garran, Sir Robert Randolph, 1867–1957. Active in the Federation movement, became a foundation member of the Commonwealth public service and from 1916 was Commonwealth Solicitor-General until his retirement in 1932. His *Annotated Constitution of the Commonwealth of Australia*, published with J. Quick in 1901, is a standard work. He was interested in the arts and published a translation of Heine's *Book of Songs*, 1924, and *Schubert and Schumann: Songs and Translations*, 1946.

Gibson, Robert A., lived at 50 Grey Street, Carlton, a neighbour of Miles Franklin.

Gillespie, Mary Anne (Mae), 1856–1938. Miles Franklin's school teacher at Thornford Public School, near Goulburn. She lived at Hurstville, Sydney, in later life.

Gilman, Charlotte Perkins, 1860–1935, American feminist and writer. Franklin retained a number of her books, some personally inscribed, in her collection.

Gilmore, Dame Mary, 1865–1962, poet, journalist and literary legend. She edited the Women's Page of *The Worker*, 1908–31, and published nine volumes of poetry, the first in 1910 and the last in 1954, as well as two volumes of reminiscences. She dominated literary Sydney at this time much to the chagrin of Miles Franklin, who detested her though it seems that this was not reciprocated.

Gordon, James William, 1874–1947, poet who wrote under the pen-name Jim Grahame. Published three volumes of verse: *Call of the Bush*, 1940; *Home Leave and Departing*, 1944; *Under Wide Skies: Collected Verses*, 1947.

Gowrie, Zara Eileen, 1879–1965, wife of Baron, later Earl, Gowrie who was Governor of South Australia, 1928–34; Governor of New South Wales, 1935–36; and Governor-General, 1936–44.

Grattan, Clinton Hartley, 1902–1980, American journalist, writer and academic with an interest in Australia. Miles Franklin helped organise his 1937–38 visit as a Carnegie Fellow which resulted in *Introducing Australia*, 1942. Published an American edition of Joseph Furphy's *Such Is Life*, 1948. Professor of History, University of Texas, 1964–74. His collection of Australiana housed at the University of Texas is important.

Green, Henry Mackenzie, 1881–1962, journalist, librarian, writer, critic and lecturer. Librarian, Fisher Library, University of Sydney, 1921–46. His most important and lasting work is *A History of Australian Literature*, 1961.

Grey, Zane, 1872–1939, popular American writer of westerns. Visited Australia several times for big-game fishing.

Griffin, Walter Burley, 1876–1937, and Marion Mahony, 1871–1961, American architects who had married in 1911. Miles Franklin first met them in Chicago. Walter's ideas illustrated by Marion's drawings in 1912 won the international competition for the design of Australia's capital city at Canberra. From 1921 Walter worked on his plans for houses at Castlecrag, Sydney, which were designed to blend into the natural landscape. Marion organised a number of cultural activities at Castlecrag staged in a natural amphitheatre. In 1935 they left for India; Walter died there and Marion returned to Castlecrag in 1937 and soon afterwards returned to practise architecture in America.

Hall, Charlotte, employed as a companion for Susannah Franklin from 1936.

Hall, Ken G., 1901–1994, film producer, founder of Cinesound Productions Ltd, 1931. Responsible for *On Our Selection*, 1932, *The Silence of Dean Maitland*, 1934, *Tall Timbers*, 1937, and *Smithy*, 1946.

Hamilton, Jean, c. 1890–1961, expatriate, lived in London, associate of Mary Fullerton and Mabel Singleton.

Hammond, Dame Joan, 1912–1996, opera singer. New Zealand born; educated in Sydney. DBE, 1974.

Hartigan, Patrick Joseph, 1878–1952, Catholic priest who wrote verse under the name John O'Brien. His best known book is *Around the Boree Log and Other Verses*, 1921.

Hatfield, William, 1892–1969, writer. Emigrated to Australia in 1911 in order to write of outback life. Books include *Sheepmates*, 1931, *Desert Saga*, 1933, *Australia Through the Windscreen*, 1936, and *I Find Australia*, 1937.

Haylen, Leslie Clement, 1899–1977, politician, journalist and writer. His maiden speech in the Federal Parliament, 1943, advocated the establishment of a national theatre. President, Fellowship of Australian Writers, 1946–47 and 1957–58.

Hebblewhite, Thomas John, 1858–1923, Goulburn journalist who gave early literary advice to Miles Franklin. He wrote to Franklin in September 1898: 'I should strongly advise you to leave the unfamiliar world of lords and ladies and strive to worthily interpret the soul and meaning of things which are at hand.'

Henry, Alice, 1857–1943. Melbourne journalist and, from 1906, office secretary, National Women's Trade Union League, Chicago. She edited the League's journal, *Life and Labor*, 1910–19. Returned to Australia in 1933.

Herbert, Xavier, 1901–1984, writer. Best known for his first novel, *Capricornia*, 1938, and his last novel, *Poor Fellow My Country*, 1975, which won the Miles Franklin Award. He married Sadie Norden.

Heysen, Sir Hans, 1877–1968, artist associated with Hahndorf, South Australia, living in the same house there from 1912 until his death. He was married to Selma Bartels.

Hill, Ernestine, 1899–1972, writer. Best known for *The Great Australian Loneliness*, 1937, *My Love Must Wait*, 1941, *Flying Doctor Calling*, 1947, and *The Territory*, 1951.

Hinkler, Herbert John Louis, 1892–1933, aviator.

Hollinworth, May, producer associated with Metropolitan Theatre, Sydney.

Holman, Ada, née Kidgell, 1869–1949, writer and wife of W.A. Holman, Premier of New South Wales, 1913–20. Her *Memoirs of a Premier's Wife* was published in 1947 and a new edition appeared in 1948.

Holman, William Arthur, 1871–1934, Premier of New South Wales, 1913–20; member of Federal Parliament, 1932–34.

Hooper, Florence Earle, published *The Story of the Women's Club: The First Fifty Years*, 1964.

Howarth, Robert Guy, 1906–1974, lecturer in English, Sydney University, 1933–55; foundation editor of the literary journal *Southerly*, 1939–56; Professor of English, University of Cape Town, 1956–71.

Huntingfield, Margaret Eleanor, wife of Baron Huntingfield, who was Governor of Victoria, 1934–39. A scholarship in Lady Huntingfield's name at the University of Melbourne commemorates her social work.

Idriess, Ion Llewellyn, 1889–1979, popular writer of over 40 books, publishing at least one book each year from 1931 to 1964. OBE, 1968.

Ifould, William Herbert, 1877–1969, Principal Librarian, Public (now State) Library of New South Wales, 1912–42.

Iliffe, B.E., born 1906, employee of Angus & Robertson from September 1920.

Illingworth, Ruby, died 1977, Social Secretary and later Treasurer, Fellowship of Australian Writers.

Jenkins, Mrs, perhaps the wife of Albert Jenkins who lived at 7 Grey Street, Carlton.

Jenner, Dorothy Gordon, 1891–1985, actor, journalist and radio personality. Used 'Andrea' as a professional name.

Jones, Inigo Owen, 1872–1954, meteorologist, artist and musician. Vice-president, Queensland Authors' and Artists' Association. Pioneered the technique of long-range weather forecasting.

Lambert, George Washington Thomas, 1873–1930, artist and sculptor, was responsible for the statue of Henry Lawson near Mrs Macquarie's Chair, Sydney, 1930. He was assisted in this statue by Arthur Murch, painter and sculptor, 1902–1989.

Lampe, Alice Helena (Lena), 1868–1964, Miles Franklin's maternal aunt.

Lampe, Emma Elizabeth, Miles Franklin's maternal aunt.

Lampe, Henry Frederick, 1868–1945, Miles Franklin's maternal uncle. Married Eliza Ann Wilkinson, 1867–1935.

Lampe, John Theodore, 1857–1931, Miles Franklin's maternal uncle. Married Margaret Elizabeth Bridle, 1884.

Lampe, Mary Martha Bertha, Miles Franklin's maternal aunt.

Lampe, Sara Metta, Miles Franklin's maternal aunt.

Lampe, Sarah, née Bridle, 1831–1912, Miles Franklin's grandmother. On 12 February 1850 married Oltmann Lampe, 1816–1875, at Gundagai, New South Wales.

Lampe, William Augustus (Gus), 1862–1959, Miles Franklin's maternal uncle.

Lancaster, G.B., 1874–1945, pen-name of Edith Joan Lyttleton. Friend of Miles Franklin in London. Her novel *Pageant* was published in London in 1933 and, on the recommendation of Franklin, published in Sydney in 1933 by Endeavour Press. It won the Gold Medal of the Australian Literature Society.

Lang, Andrew, 1844–1912, Scottish-born scholar, folklorist, poet and London man of letters.

Lawson, Bertha Marie Louise, née Bredt, 1876–1957, widow of poet Henry Lawson who had died in 1922. She had married him in 1896 and separated from him in 1903. In 1943 she published *My Henry Lawson*.

Lawson, Henry, 1867–1922, Australia's most famous writer. His first book was published in 1894. First writer in Australia to be given a state funeral.

Lawson, Jim, born 1898, son of Henry Lawson.

Lawson, Will, 1876–1957, writer. Best known for *When Cobb & Co Was King*, 1936. Friend of Bertha Lawson and helped write her reminiscences, *My Henry Lawson*, 1943.

Leeson, Ida Emily, 1885–1964, Mitchell Librarian, 1932–46.

Lindsay, Jack, 1900–1990, expatriate Australian writer who by 1938 had published 13 novels as well as short stories, history books, plays and a number of translations and edited works for the Fanfrolico Press which he helped to found.

Lindsay, Norman, 1879–1969, artist, writer, critic.

Lindsay, Philip, 1906–1958, writer. Left for England in 1929 and by 1938 had published nine historical novels as well as a number of works of non-fiction.

Linklater, William (Billy Miller), 1867–1959, writer associated with the Northern Territory.

Lloyd, Demarest, 1883–1937, businessman, American suitor of Miles Franklin, c. 1907–c. 1914.

Lofting, Hilary, 1881–1939, civil engineer. Wrote short stories and a book on Ned Kelly; edited the unabridged version of Marcus Clarke's *For the Term of His Natural Life*, 1929.

Lowe, Eric, 1889–1963, writer. Author of a trilogy dealing with station life: *Salute to Freedom*, 1938; *Beyond the Nineteen Counties*, 1948; and *O Wilting Hearts*, 1951. Another novel, *Framed in Hardwood*, was published in 1940.

Lyons, Dame Enid Muriel, 1897–1981. Wife of Joseph Lyons, Prime Minister of Australia, 1932–39. In 1949 she was elected to the House of

Representatives, one of its first two women members. She remained in Parliament until 1951. GBE, 1937.

McCarthy, Mrs, presumably wife of James P. McCarthy who lived at 28 Grey Street, Carlton, a next door neighbour of Miles Franklin.

McCarthy, Sir Desmond, 1877–1952, British journalist, theatre critic and literary editor.

Macartney, Frederick Thomas, 1887–1980, best known for his abridgement and rearrangement of Morris Miller's 1940 bibliography of Australian literature which was published in 1956.

McCrae, Hugh, 1876–1958. Published several volumes of poetry—such as *Satyrs and Sunlight*, 1909, *Colombine*, 1920, and *Idyllia*, 1922—and was for a time highly regarded by a few.

MacDougall, Duncan, 1878–1953, actor, director, manager. Founder Playbox Society, Sydney, later Playbox Theatre Circle, 1923 (ceased productions 1931).

McFadyen, Ella May, poet and children's author.

McIntosh, Marion Catherine, née Backhouse, died 1959, married Hugh Donald McIntosh, 1876–1942, sporting and theatrical entrepreneur and newspaper proprietor, in 1897.

Mackaness, Dr George, 1882–1968, educationist, historian, bibliographer. Head of English, Sydney Teachers' College, 1924–46. He published major biographies of William Bligh, 1931, and Arthur Phillip, 1937, and edited the much-used poetry anthology *The Wide Brown Land*, 1928. OBE, 1938.

McKell, Sir William John, 1891–1985. New South Wales Premier and Treasurer, 1941–47; Governor-General of Australia, 1947–53.

MacLaurin, Sir Henry Normand, 1835–1914, physician. From 1889 Member of the Legislative Council of New South Wales and from 1896 Chancellor, University of Sydney. Knighted 1902.

Mann, Cecil, 1896–1967, journalist, editor of the 'Red Page', the *Bulletin*'s literary pages. He wrote fiction and edited Henry Lawson's works.

Martin, Clarence Edward, 1900–1953, New South Wales Attorney-General, 1941–53.

Martin, David, born 1915, poet and prose writer. Hungarian born, arrived in Australia in 1949. AO, 1988; Patrick White Award, 1991.

Maurice, Furnley, 1881–1942, pen-name of Frank Wilmot, poet, bookseller and manager of Melbourne University Press.

Metcalfe, John Wallace, Principal Librarian, Public (now State) Library of New South Wales, 1942–59.

Miles, John Bramwell, 1888–1969, general secretary, Communist Party of Australia, 1931–48.

Mitchell, David Scott, 1836–1907, book collector, bequeathed his collection to the Public (now State) Library of New South Wales to form the Mitchell Library which opened in 1910. Cousin of Rose Scott.

Moll, Ernest George, born 1900, Australian born Professor of English at University of Oregon, 1928–66. Published a number of volumes of poetry.

Monypenny, Kathleen, 1894–1971, librarian, Mitchell Library. Wrote youth fiction and poetry.

Moore, George, 1852–1933, Irish writer. Settled in London, 1911. His book *Esther Waters*, 1894, was a favourite of Miles Franklin's.

Moore, Tom Inglis, 1901–1978, writer, critic and editor. Leader-writer and literary reviewer for *Sydney Morning Herald*, 1934–40. President, Fellowship of Australian Writers, December 1934 to June 1935. In 1954 he introduced at the Australian National University the first full-year university course in Australian literature. He married Peace Little in 1927. OBE, 1958.

Morgan, Mrs, presumably the wife of William Morgan who lived at 25 Grey Street, Carlton; a neighbour of Miles Franklin.

Morice, Lucy Spence, 1859–1951, South Australian kindergarten worker, niece of Catherine Helen Spence.

Morrisby, Camden Risby, 1893–1973, secretary, Fellowship of Australian Writers.

Moss, Alice Frances Mabel, 1869–1948, president, National Council of Women of Australia, 1931–36.

Mudie, Renee, née Doble, married Ian Mudie, 1911–1976, poet, in 1935.

Muscio, Florence Mildred, 1882–1964, president, National Council of Women of New South Wales, 1927–38, and federal president, 1927–1931. Chairman, Women's Executive Committee and Advisory Council, Australia's 150th Anniversary Celebrations Council, 1938. OBE, 1938.

Mutch, Thomas Davies, 1885–1958, journalist, unionist, parliamentarian. New South Wales Minister for Education, 1920–22 and 1925–27, friend to Henry Lawson, indexer of historical records and Trustee of the Public (now State) Library of New South Wales for nearly 40 years, 1916–53.

Napier, Sydney Elliott, journalist, chairman of the Literary Committee, Australia's 150th Anniversary Celebrations Council, 1938. President, P.E.N. Club.

Neilson, John Shaw, 1872–1942, poet. His *Collected Poems,* edited by R.H. Croll, was published in 1934 and another volume of poetry, *Beauty Imposes*, was published in 1938.

Ogilvie-Gordon, Dame Maria Matilda, 1864–1939, Scottish geologist; published over 30 original works. President and Vice-President of the English National Council of Women and Vice-President of the International Council of Women.

O'Harris, Pixie, 1903–1991, pen-name of Rhona Olive Harris, née Pratt, children's author and illustrator. She inspired Miles Franklin to write the posthumously published *Childhood at Brindabella*, 1963.

O'Sullivan, Evelyn Inez (Eva), 1880–1957, public servant. Daughter of Edward William O'Sullivan, 1846–1910, politician, Minister for Public Works, 1899–1904, and Agnes Ann O'Sullivan. E.W. O'Sullivan had been the local member when the Franklins lived at Stillwater.

Palmer, Nettie, née Higgins, 1885–1964, literary critic, published essays and poetry. Wife of Vance Palmer.

Palmer, Vance, 1885–1959, writer and reviewer. Best known for *The Passage*, 1930, which won the 1929 *Bulletin* novel prize, and *The Swayne Family*, 1934. Husband of Nettie Palmer.

Pankhurst, Adela, 1888–1961, daughter of Emmeline Pankhurst. Migrated to Australia and organised the Women's Peace Army. Founding member of the Communist Party of Australia; subsequently she became anti-communist. She wrote plays and political pamphlets.

Park, Ruth, born 1923, writer. Born in New Zealand, arrived in Australia in 1942. Won the *Sydney Morning Herald* Prize for *Harp in the South*, 1946. Won the Miles Franklin Award for *Swords and Crowns and Rings*, 1977. AM, 1987.

Parker, Catherine Langloh, 1856–1940, published *Australian Legendary Tales*, 1896. It was the first substantial collection of Aboriginal legends and tales. Her husband, Langloh Parker, who she had married in 1875, died in 1903. She met her second husband, Percival Randolph Stow, in London in 1905 where they married before returning to Australia.

Paterson, Andrew Barton ('Banjo'), 1864–1941, poet. Best known for *The Man from Snowy River* and *Waltzing Matilda*.

Paton, John, 1867–1943, merchant and soldier.

Penton, Brian, 1904–1951, journalist and editor of the Sydney *Daily Telegraph*, 1941–51. He wrote two novels, *Landtakers*, 1934, and *Inheritors*, 1936. Instigated the *Daily Telegraph* £1,000 Prize Novel Competition, 1946.

Phelps, Editha, died 1931, worked at the National Women's Trade Union League in Chicago with Miles Franklin. She went with Miles Franklin on a short holiday to London and Paris in July 1911.

Pizer, Marjorie, born 1920, poet. Established Pinchgut Press with her husband, Muir Holburn, 1947.

Praed, Rosa, née Murray-Prior, 1851–1935, married Arthur Campbell Praed, 1872. Prolific writer of over 40 popular novels.

Pratt, Ambrose, 1874–1944, Australian writer.

Prichard, Katharine Susannah, 1883–1969, journalist, writer and founding member of the Communist Party of Australia. Best known for *Black Opal*, 1921, *Working Bullocks*, 1926, *Coonardoo*, 1929 (it shared the 1928 *Bulletin* novel prize), *Haxby's Circus*, 1930, and *Intimate Strangers*, 1937. With Jean Devanny she established the Writers' League, 1935, amalgamated with the Fellowship of Australian Writers, 1938.

Prior, Kenneth S., chairman and managing director, the *Bulletin*.

Propeller Young Writers' League, formed in 1930 under the auspices of *The Propeller*, the local newspaper of the St George district of Sydney which includes Carlton where Franklin lived. Franklin was at various times vice-president and patron.

Quinn, Roderic, 1867–1949, journalist. Published a novel, *Mostyn Stayne*, 1897, and three books of verse.

Quirk, Mary Lily May, 1881–1952, member for Balmain, New South Wales Legislative Assembly, 1939–50. Her late husband, John Quirk, 1870–1938, had previously held the seat.

Ranken, Jean Logan, published *Dream Horses, and Other Verses*, 1912; a novel, *Tzane*, 1926; and co-edited and contributed to *Murder Pie*, 1936, a mystery in 16 chapters each written by a different author.

Rees, Coralie, née Clarke, 1909–1972. Married Leslie Rees in 1931. She wrote for radio and collaborated with her husband on four travel books, published from 1953 to 1970.

Rees, Leslie, 1905–2000, writer and drama critic. Federal drama editor for the ABC, 1936–66. His play, *Sub-Editor's Room*, later the first Australian play to be televised, was included, together with Miles Franklin's play, *No Family*, in *Best Australian One-Act Plays*, 1937, edited by T.I. Moore and William Moore. He married Coralie Clarke, 1909–1972, in 1931. Miles Franklin sometimes refers to him as Leslie Clarke Rees or L.C. Rees. AM, 1981.

Reid, Sir George Houstoun, 1845–1918. Premier of New South Wales, 1894–1901; Prime Minister of Australia, 1904–05.

Richardson, Henry Handel, 1870–1946, pen-name of Ethel Florence Lindesay Robertson, writer. Best known for *The Fortunes of Richard Mahony* trilogy: *Australia Felix*, 1917; *The Way Home*, 1925, and *Ultima Thule*, 1929. A one volume edition appeared in 1930.

Robertson, Constance, née Stephens, 1895–1964, journalist. The daughter of literary critic A.G. Stephens, she was appointed editor of the women's supplement of the *Sydney Morning Herald* in 1936.

Robertson, George, 1860–1933, publisher, joint founder of Angus & Robertson and developer of its Australian publishing program.

Robins, Margaret Dreier, 1868–1945, President, National Women's Trade Union League, Chicago, 1907–1913.

Roderick, Colin, 1911–2000, editor, Angus & Robertson, 1945–65. Named in Miles Franklin's will as one of the judges of the Miles Franklin Award.

Roland, Betty, 1903–1996, writer. Best known for the play *A Touch of Silk*, 1928, and for her three volumes of autobiography: *The Eye of the Beholder*, 1984, *An Improbable Life*, 1989, and *The Devious Being*, 1990. Scripted the first full-length talking feature film made in Australia, *The Spur of the Moment*, 1931.

Rosman, Alice Grant, 1887–1961, Australian born popular novelist who from 1911 lived in England. Her novel *The Window*, 1928, was a bestseller.

Ross, Lloyd, 1901–1987, secretary, New South Wales Branch, Australian Railways Union, 1938–43 and 1952–69. Author of *William Lane and the*

Australian Labor Movement, 1937, and a biography of John Curtin, 1977. His play *The Rustling of Voices* is represented together with Franklin's *No Family* in *Best Australian One-Act Plays*, 1937, edited by T.I. Moore and William Moore.

Scheu-Reisz, Helene, novelist and translator. Miles Franklin had come into contact with her when Franklin was working in London at the National Housing and Town Planning Council.

Scott, Rose, 1847–1925, pioneer Australian feminist who befriended Miles Franklin following the publication of *My Brilliant Career*, 1901. Miles Franklin contributed a chapter on Scott to *The Peaceful Army: A Memorial to the Pioneer Women of Australia, 1788–1938*, published in 1938.

Scott, Thelma, born 1913, actor. Worked almost exclusively in Sydney radio, 1935–51.

S.H. Prior Memorial Prize for literature was awarded from 1935 to 1946. It was instituted by the *Bulletin* in memory of its editor, 1915–33, Samuel Henry Prior. Miles Franklin won the prize in 1936 for *All That Swagger* and again in 1939 for a biography of Joseph Furphy.

Simpson, Helen de Guerry, 1897–1940, expatriate Australian writer. *Boomerang* was published in 1932 and won the James Tait Black Memorial Prize. *The Woman on the Beast* was published in 1933. It consisted of three novellas.

Singleton, Mabel, 1877–1965, businesswoman, companion to Mary Fullerton in London, 1922–46.

Spence, Catherine Helen, 1825–1910, pioneer feminist and social reformer, writer. Her best known book is *Clara Morison*, 1854.

Stamp, Olive Jessie, née Marsh, died 1941, wife of Josiah Charles Stamp, statistician and administrator.

Stead, Christina, 1902–1983, writer. Her books include *The Salzburg Tales*, 1934, *Seven Poor Men of Sydney*, 1934, *House of All Nations*, 1938, *The Man Who Loved Children*, 1940, *For Love Alone*, 1944, and *Letty Fox: Her Luck*, 1946. Patrick White Award, 1974.

Stephen, Alfred Consett, 1857–1939. He married Sir Francis Suttor's daughter, Kate.

Stephens, Alfred George, 1865–1933, journalist and literary critic, first editor of the *Bulletin*'s famous 'Red Page' from 1896 to 1906. He expanded book publishing by the *Bulletin* and was responsible for the publication of Joseph Furphy's *Such Is life*, 1903, much admired by Miles Franklin.

Stephensen, Percy Reginald, 1901–1965, known as 'Inky' Stephensen, publisher, author, nationalist and supporter of Australian writing. Involved in a number of short-lived publishing ventures on his return to Australia from England in 1932. In 1936 his influential book *The Foundations of Culture in Australia* was published. He formed the Australia-First movement in October 1941. It was a right-wing nationalist movement opposed to Australia's involvement in the Second World War. Stephensen was interned without trial in March 1942 for the duration of the war. He was the ghost-writer for almost 70 of Frank Clune's books. He married Winifred Venus Lockyer.

Stewart, J.I.M., Edinburgh-born Professor of English, University of Adelaide, 1935–45. Wrote under the pen-name Michael Innes. Made a famous disparaging comment about the lack of Australian literature.

Stivens, Dallas George (Dal), 1911–1997, writer. Published a volume of short stories in London, *The Tramp and Other Stories*, 1936. He went on to publish further volumes of short stories and novels including *A Horse of Air*, 1970, which won the Miles Franklin Award.

Suttor, Sir Francis Bathurst, 1839–1915. From 1875 served in either the Legislative Assembly or Legislative Council of New South Wales and held several ministerial positions. He was president of the Legislative Council, 1903–15.

Swales, Bert, married May Fogden, a neighbour of Miles Franklin, in 1940.

Tennant, Kylie, 1912–1988, writer. Best known for *Tiburon*, 1935, which won the S.H. Prior Memorial Prize; *The Battlers*, 1941, which also won the S.H. Prior Memorial Prize and the Gold Medal of the Australian Literature Society; *Ride On Stranger*, 1943; *Tell Morning This*, 1967, and a biography of H.V. Evatt, 1970. Married C. Rodd, 1932.

Tennyson, Hallam, 1852–1928, son of the poet, Governor-General of Australia, 1902–03.

Thomas, Wilfred, born 1904, broadcaster. President, Independent Film Group.

Thring, G. Herbert, secretary, Society of Authors, UK.

Thwaites, Frederick Joseph, 1908–1979, popular writer who at the height of his fame was probably Australia's bestselling author. He wrote over 30 novels beginning with *The Broken Melody*, 1930. Some of his novels were published by the Harcourt Press named after his wife, Jessica Harcourt, an actor. Ken G. Hall made a film of *The Broken Melody* in 1938.

Tildesley, Evelyn Mary, 1882–1976, founder, honorary secretary and director, British Drama League, 1937–67. MBE, 1950.

Timms, Edward Vivian, 1895–1960, prolific writer of popular historical romances.

Trendall, Arthur Dale, 1909–1995, Professor of Greek and of Archaeology, University of Sydney from 1939.

Trist, Margaret, 1914–1986, writer. Published three novels and two collections of short stories. Only one book, the short story collection *In the Sun*, 1943, had been published at this time.

Turner, Walter James, 1884–1946, writer, left Australia as a young man and spent the rest of his life in England. Published poetry, plays and fiction.

Vernon, Ivy, Miles Franklin's cousin, employed by Miles Franklin for domestic duties.

Watt, Harry, English film-maker, responsible for *The Overlanders*, 1946, starring Chips Rafferty, and *Eureka Stockade*, 1949.

White, Sir Harold Leslie, 1905–1992, at this time Assistant Librarian, Commonwealth National Library, Canberra. National Librarian, 1960–70. Knighted, 1970.

Whittle, Neroli, writer and actor. Edited and contributed to *Ten Minute Stories*, 1941. Involved with Australian Playwrights Theatre in the latter 1940s. Staged Franklin's 'No Family', 1946, and organised readings of her 'Release', 1947.

Whyte, William Farmer, 1879–1958, editor of Sydney *Daily Telegraph*, 1921–28. Later ran his own Federal News Service.

Wilson, Dolly, a family friend.

Published works by
MILES FRANKLIN

My Brilliant Career. Edinburgh, Blackwood, 1901.

Some Everyday Folk and Dawn. Edinburgh, Blackwood, 1909.

The Net of Circumstance [under pseudonym, Mr and Mrs Ogniblat L'Artsau]. London, Mills & Boon, 1915.

Up the Country: A Tale of the Early Australian Squattocracy [under pseudonym, Brent of Bin Bin]. Edinburgh, Blackwood, 1928.

Ten Creeks Run: A Tale of the Horse and Cattle Stations of the Upper Murrumbidgee [under pseudonym, Brent of Bin Bin]. Edinburgh, Blackwood, 1930.

Old Blastus of Bandicoot: Opuscule on a Pioneer Tufted with Ragged Rhymes. London, Cecil Palmer, 1931.

Back to Bool Bool: A Ramiparous Novel with Several Prominent Characters and a Hantle of Others Disposed as the Atolls of Oceania's Archipelagoes [under pseudonym, Brent of Bin Bin]. Edinburgh, Blackwood, 1931.

Bring the Monkey: A Light Novel. Sydney, Endeavour Press, 1933.

All That Swagger. Sydney, The Bulletin, 1936.

'No Family', in Moore, W. & Moore, T.I. (eds), *Best Australian One-Act Plays*. Sydney, Angus & Robertson, 1937.

Pioneers on Parade [with Dymphna Cusack]. Sydney, Angus & Robertson, 1939.

Joseph Furphy: The Legend of a Man and his Book [in association with Kate Baker]. Sydney, Angus & Robertson, 1944.

My Career Goes Bung: Purporting to be the Autobiography of Sybylla Penelope Melvyn. Melbourne, Georgian House, 1946.

Sydney Royal: Divertissement. Sydney, Shakespeare Head, 1947.

Prelude to Waking: A Novel in the First Person and Parentheses [under pseudonym, Brent of Bin Bin]. Sydney, Angus & Robertson, 1950.

Cockatoos: A Story of Youth and Exodists [under pseudonym, Brent of Bin Bin]. Sydney, Angus & Robertson, 1954.

Gentlemen at Gyang Gyang: A Tale of the Jumbuck Pads on the Summer Runs [under pseudonym, Brent of Bin Bin]. Sydney, Angus & Robertson, 1956.

Laughter, Not for a Cage: Notes on Australian Writing, with Biographical Emphasis on the Struggles, Function, and Achievements of the Novel in Three Half-centuries. Sydney, Angus & Robertson, 1956.

Childhood at Brindabella: My First Ten Years. Sydney, Angus & Robertson, 1963.

On Dearborn Street. St Lucia, University of Queensland Press, 1981.

SOURCES

Location of diary extracts within the Miles Franklin papers, Mitchell Library, State
Library of New South Wales (Ref: ML MSS 364):

18 November 1932	ML MSS 364/2/25
24 November 1932	ML MSS 364/2/25
21 December 1932	ML MSS 364/2/25
30 December 1932	ML MSS 364/2/25
1 January 1933	ML MSS 364/2/26
2 January 1933	ML MSS 364/2/26
31 January 1933	ML MSS 364/2/26
10 February 1933	ML MSS 364/2/26
11 March 1933	ML MSS 364/2/26
12 March 1933	ML MSS 364/2/26
16 March 1933	ML MSS 364/2/26
19 March 1933	ML MS 364/2/26
5 May 1933	ML MSS 364/2/26
12 June 1933	ML MSS 364/2/26
28 June 1933	ML MSS 364/2/26
30 August 1933	ML MSS 364/2/26
28 October 1933	ML MSS 364/2/26
23 November 1933	ML MSS 364/2/26
21 December 1933	ML MSS 364/2/26
21 March 1934	ML MSS 364/2/27
15 August 1934	ML MSS 364/2/27
11 September 1934	ML MSS 364/2/27
11 October 1934	ML MSS 364/2/27 & 364/3/1 pp1–2
24 October 1934	ML MSS 364/2/27
20 November 1934	ML MSS 364/2/27
29 November 1934	ML MSS 364/2/27
1934	ML MSS 364/3/2 pp61–67
January 1935	ML MSS 364/3/3 pp103–106
c. February 1935	ML MSS 364/3/1 pp15–17
15 March 1935	ML MSS 364/2/28
8–13 April 1935	ML MSS 364/3/1 p20
27 April 1935	ML MSS 364/2/28

19 July 1935	ML MSS 364/2/28
20 July 1935	ML MSS 364/3/1 p20a
31 August 1935	ML MSS 364/3/4 p194
1 September 1935	ML MSS 364/3/4 p194
9 September 1935	ML MSS 364/3/4 p198
30 October 1935	ML MSS 364/2/28
2 November 1935	ML MSS 364/3/5 p209
14 November 1935	ML MSS 364/2/28
24 November 1935	ML MSS 364/2/28
26 November 1935	ML MSS 364/2/28
20 December 1935	ML MSS 364/4/1 pp7–8
December 1935?	M MSS 364/4/1 pp9–11
1935	ML MSS 364/3/3 pp126–128 & pp113–114 & 364/3/4 p175 & pp178–182
1 January 1936	ML MSS 364/2/29
8 January 1936	ML MSS 364/4/1 p19
9 January 1936	ML MSS 364/4/1 pp30–31
12 January 1936	ML MSS 364/4/1 pp37–39
20 January 1936	ML MSS 364/4/1 p54
26 January 1936	ML MSS 364/4/1 pp56–60
January 1936	ML MSS 364/4/1 p36 & pp15–16 & 364/4/1 pp25–26
6 February 1936	ML MSS 364/4/1 p72
11 February 1936	ML MSS 364/3/5 pp215
13 February 1936	ML MSS 364/4/1 pp75–76
8 April 1936	ML MSS 364/2/29
18 June 1936	ML MSS 364/3/5 pp230–231
28 June 1936	ML MSS 364/4/1 pp78-93
1 July 1936	ML MSS 364/2/29
15 July 1936	ML MSS 364/2/29
20 August 1936	ML MSS 364/2/29
August 1936	ML MSS 364/4/2 pp2–9 & 364/3/5 pp237–240
c. August 1936	ML MSS 364/3/5 pp240–247
29 November 1936	ML MSS 364/2/29
4 December 1936	ML MSS 364/2/29
c. 1936	ML MSS 364/3/1 p33
12 January 1937	ML MSS 364/4/2 pp11–19
14 February 1937	ML MSS 364/2/29
2 March 1937	ML MSS 364/4/2 pp28–31
22 April 1937	ML MSS 364/2/30
26 April 1937	ML MSS 364/4/2 pp38–45
8–28 June 1937	ML MSS 364/4/3
19 July 1937	ML MSS 364/2/30
23 July 1937	ML MSS 364/2/20
28 October 1937	ML MSS 364/2/20
8 November 1937	ML MSS 364/3/7 p329

23 November 1937	ML MSS 364/4/1 pp93–94 & 364/4/2 pp59–62
29 November 1937	ML MSS 364/4/2 pp65–67
1937	ML MSS 364/3/5 p249 & 364/3/7 p324
9 January 1938	ML MSS 364/3/6 pp289-290
12 January 1938	ML MSS 364/2/31
22 January 1938	ML MSS 364/4/2 pp73–74
28 January 1938	ML MSS 364/4/2 pp75–77
2 February 1938	ML MSS 364/4/2 pp86–87
3 February 1938	ML MSS 364/4/2 pp88–91
4 February 1938	ML MSS 364/4/2 pp92–96
17 February 1938	ML MSS 364/4/2 pp103–104
25 February 1938	ML MSS 364/4/2 pp105–106
28 February 1938	ML MSS 364/4/4 pp9–12
30 March 1938	ML MSS 364/3/9 pp428–430
3 April 1938	ML MSS 364/3/9 p 430 & 4/4 p23
8 April 1938	ML MSS 364/4/4 p27
30 April 1938	ML MSS 364/4/4 pp35–38
29 May 1938	ML MSS 364/4/4 pp39–40
15 June 1938	ML MSS 364/2/31
7 July 1938	ML MSS 364/2/31
26 August 1938	ML MSS 364/2/31
3 September 1938	ML MSS 364/3/31
27 September 1938	ML MSS 364/3/31
30 November 1938	ML MSS 364/2/31
6 February 1939	ML MSS 364/2/32
13 February 1939	ML MSS 364/2/32
14 March 1939	ML MSS 364/2/32
21 March 1939	ML MSS 364/2/32
18 April 1939	ML MSS 364/2/32
9 May 1939	ML MSS 364/2/32
13 June 1939	ML MSS 364/4/4 pp43a–45a
27 June 1939	ML MSS 364/2/32
17 August 1939	ML MSS 364/2/32
3 September 1939	ML MSS 364/2/32 & 364/3/12 pp576–577
4 November 1939	ML MSS 364/2/32
24 November 1939	ML MSS 364/2/32
25 December 1939	ML MSS 364/2/32
30 December 1939	ML MSS 364/2/32
31 December 1939	ML MSS 364/2/32
1 January 1940	ML MSS 364/2/33
28 January 1940	ML MSS 364/2/33
24 April 1940	ML MSS 364/2/33
5 May 1940	ML MSS 364/2/33
7 May 1940	ML MSS 364/2/33
18 May 1940	ML MSS 364/2/33

24 September 1940	ML MSS 364/2/33
3 October 1940	ML MSS 364/2/33
20 November 1940	ML MSS 364/2/33
25 November 1940	ML MSS 364/2/33
November 1940	ML MSS 364/4/1 p94
12 December 1940	ML MSS 364/2/33
1 January 1941	ML MSS 364/2/34
16 January 1941	ML MSS 364/2/34
24 February 1941	ML MSS 364/2/34
9 April 1941	ML MSS 364/4/1 p78a
19 July 1941	ML MSS 364/2/34
10 August 1941	ML MSS 364/2/34
21 September 1941	ML MSS 364/2/34
20 November 1941	ML MSS 364/2/34
27 March 1942	ML MSS 364/2/35
3 May 1942	ML MSS 364/4/4 pp46–54
24 May 1942	ML MSS 364/2/35
30 June 1942	ML MSS 364/2/35
28 August 1942	ML MSS 364/4/4 pp55–58
5 September 1942	ML MSS 364/2/35
11 October 1942	ML MSS 364/3/8 pp372–373
28 October 1942	ML MSS 364/4/4 pp59–62
14 November 1942	ML MSS 364/3/8 pp370–371
1942	ML MSS 364/3/8 p369
6 September 1943	ML MSS 364/4/1 p98–99
6 and 7 October 1943	ML MSS 364/3/1/ pp34–35
24 November 1943	ML MSS 364/4/4 pp74–75
5 December 1943	ML MSS 364/4/1 pp99–100
1943	ML MSS 364/3/8 pp374–379
February 1944	ML MSS 364/3/8 pp379–382
9 August 1944	ML MSS 364/3/37
2 September 1944	ML MSS 364/2/37
c.1944	ML MSS 364/3/8 pp392–393
22 April 1945	ML MSS 364/3/9 pp439–445
7 August 1945	ML MSS 364/3/13 pp651–652
c. August 1945	ML MSS 364/3/10 pp461–464
7 October 1945	ML MSS 364/3/8 p395
5 March 1946	ML MSS 364/3/10 pp464–466
c. August 1946	ML MSS 364/3/10 p469
3 October 1946	ML MSS 364/3/11 pp500–504
23 November 1946	ML MSS 364/3/12 pp540–546
18 Dec 1946 / 10 Jan 1947	ML MSS 364/3/11 pp504–516
21 January 1947	ML MSS 364/3/12 pp548–551
30 January 1947	ML MSS 364/3/11 p522
4 February 1947	ML MSS 364/3/11 pp526–528

25 February 1947	ML MSS 364/3/12
March 1948	ML MSS 364/4/5 p17 & pp31–47 & pp107–109
12 March 1948	ML MSS 364/4/5 pp57–59
c. April 1948	ML MSS 364/3/13 pp627–628
1948	ML MSS 364/4/5 pp131–141
c. 1948	ML MSS 364/3/12 pp580–587 & 364/3/1 p45 & 364/3/14 pp727–731 & 364/3/14 pp749–751 & 364/3/12 pp578–580 & 364/3/13 pp 603–604 & 364/3/13 pp612–622
April 1949	ML MSS 364/4/6 pp1–25
12 June 1949	ML MSS 364/2/42
13 June 1949	ML MSS 364/2/42
25 June 1949	ML MSS 364/2/42
17 July 1949	ML MSS 364/ 2/42
7 August 1949	ML MSS 364/2/42
September 1949	ML MSS 364/4/5 pp171–197
25 September 1949	ML MSS 364/4/5 pp197–201
27 September 1949	ML MSS 364/4/5 p201
c. October 1949	ML MSS 364/3/13 pp641–650
31 January 1950	ML MSS 364/2/43
5 April 1950	ML MSS 364/2/43
3 September 1950	ML MSS 364/2/43
24 September 1943	ML MSS 364/2/43
13 May 1951	ML MSS 364/2/44
10 June 1951	ML MSS 364/2/44
13 June 1951	ML MSS 364/2/44
1 July 1951	ML MSS 364/2/44
22 July 1951	ML MSS 364/2/44
12 September 1951	ML MSS 364/2/44
8 October 1951	ML MSS 364/2/44
5 May 1952	ML MSS 364/2/45
16 August 1952	ML MSS 364/2/45
1 November 1952	ML MSS 364/2/45
20 January 1953	ML MSS 364/2/46
31 March 1953	ML MSS 364/4/6 pp67–77
24 April 1953	ML MSS 364/2/46
25 April 1953	ML MSS 364/2/46
10 May 1953	ML MSS 364/2/46
7 June 1953	ML MSS 364/2/46
17 June 1953	ML MSS 364/2/46
15 September 1953	MLMSS 364/2/46
1 January 1954	ML MSS 364/2/46

INDEX

MF = Miles Franklin. A page reference with *n* attached indicates a footnote.

mother's death   116, 117
as nurse xi
painted by Dobell   180–9
pseudonyms xix, xxi–xxii, 48–9
on public speaking   252–6
radio broadcasts   20, 22
refuses OBE   xxviii, 70–3
regrets limited life of single
   women   248–9
returns to Australia   xxi, xxiv, 3,
   11, 111
as secretary xx
social life   xxvii–xxviii, 165–7,
   178–80, 256
struggles to write   3, 21, 40–1,
   106, 119, 256, 258
support for Australian literature
   12–13, 15–17, 109, 111, 112–14,
   140–1
talks of dying   xviii, xxv, 94, 121,
   126, 133
as tutor   x
unhappy   xx, xxi, xxii–xxiii, 89,
   105, 106–7, 256
views on sex   226–8
war work   xix–xx, 71, 169
wins SH Prior prize   45, 46–50
on writing   35–6, 115–16, 157,
   196, 259
Franklin, Susannah (MF's mother)
   vii–viii, xxiv, xxv, 3, 28, 31, 44, 45,
   91, 128
   birthday 21, 21n, 130
   and books   219–20
   death   116, 127, 135
   effect on MF   4, 5, 6, 28, 40, 51,
      59, 111, 115
   lacks sympathy   35, 94
   opinion of MF's broadcasts   22

seamstress   167–8
senility   5–6, 7, 17, 19, 32, 46, 67,
   115
Freud, Sigmund   229, 230
Frog He Would A-Wooing Go, A   34, 35
Frolich, Paul   165–6, 167
Fullerton, Emily   100, 107, 157
Fullerton, Mary   xx, xxv, xxvi, 89,
   92n, 130, 141, 144n, 157
Furphy, Joseph   xiii–xiv, 111,
   117–18, 124, 145, 273

Gallery, The (Burns)   224–6
Galvin, EM   253
Ganmain   75, 77
Garbo, Greta   60
Garnsey, Arthur H   178
Garran, Sir Robert   72, 273
Gentlemen at Gyang Gyang (MF)   xxix,
   256
Gibson, Mrs   3, 19–20
Gibson, Willie   3, 59
Giles, Kenneth   178, 208
Gillespie, Mary Anne (Mae)   18,
   21, 28, 46, 115, 127, 130, 171
Gilman, Charlotte P   90, 226, 230
Gilmore, Dame Mary   xxviii, 46,
   103, 134, 144
   fame   65–7, 139–40
   family details   67n
   MF visits her   92
   MF's opinion of   47, 63n, 65, 70,
      112
   MF's views of her dameship   72,
      95
   talks of Queen Mary and Irish
      school books   192–3
Give Battle   131
Glaspell, Susan   226

Moore, Peace 47, 95, 111, 112, 189–90, 191
Moore, Tom Inglis 39, 47, 95, 111, 112, 113, 122, 123, 126, 189–90, 191, 192
Morgan, Mrs 3, 117, 118, 135, 256, 258, 263
Morice, Lucy Spence 88, 220
Morley, Robert 252
Morrisby, Camden 157, 163–4, 201–2, 203, 204
Moss, Alice 100
Mudie, Ian 145n
Mudie, Renee 240
Murray River 80
Mutch, Thomas D 50, 98, 130, 147, 263–4
Mutiny of the Bounty (Nordhoff/Hall) 133, 133n
My Brilliant Career (MF) vii, x–xiii, xiv, xxviii, 45, 220
   Havelock Ellis' opinion xii
   Lawson's opinion xi
My Career Goes Bung (MF) xxix, 211n

Napier, Elliott 114, 115
National Housing and Town Planning Council xx, 36n, 86
National Women's Trade Union League xv–xvi, xviii, xix
Neilson, John Shaw 95
Nestor, Agnes 253
Net of Circumstance, The (MF) xix
New South Wales
   sesquicentenary 97, 99n
   women's suffrage 136–7
Newcastle Morning Herald xxix
Newcomes, The (Thackeray) 170

No Escape (Ercole) 109
Norris, Ethel Nerly 89

O'Casey, Sean 221–3
Odet, Clifford 45, 93
O'Dowd, Bernard 65n
Ogilvie-Gordon, Dame Maria 102
Ogniblat L'Artsau, Mr and Mrs xix
O'Harris, Pixie 181, 259
Old Blastus of Bandicoot (MF) xxiv, xxviii, 49n, 150, 199
O'Neill, Josephine 208
Oodnadatta 84–5
Orchid, The 217
O'Sullivan family 5
Outback Marriage, An (Paterson) 146–7

Pageant (Lancaster) 54, 92, 109
Palmer, Nettie 139, 140
Palmer, Vance 24–5, 55–6, 62, 67, 88, 95, 109, 192, 259
Pankhurst, Adela 6, 280
Pansies (Lawrence) 7n
Park, Rosina 193
Park, Ruth 190n, 192, 193
Parker, Catherine Langloh 215, 216
Parkinson, Mr (Actors' Equity) 158, 161, 162
Paterson, AB (Banjo) xiii, 12, 65n, 146–7, 215, 216, 217, 218
Pea Pickers, The (Langley) 144–5
Peaceful Army, The (ed. Eldershaw) 99n, 106
Penton, Brian 12, 62, 64, 108, 109, 188
Penton, Mrs 62